SO-AIV-716

Postcolonial Imagination
and Feminist Theology

REGIS COLLEGE LIBRARY
100 Wellesley Street West
Toronto, Ontario
Canada M5S 2Z5

Postcolonial Imagination and Feminist Theology

Kwok Pui-lan

REGIS COLLEGE LIBRARY
100 Wellesley Street West
Toronto, Ontario
Canada M5S 2Z5

WESTMINSTER
JOHN KNOX PRESS
LOUISVILLE · KENTUCKY

BT
83.55
K865
2005

© 2005 Kwok Pui-lan

All rights reserved. No part of this book may be reproduced or transmitted in any form or by any means, electronic or mechanical, including photocopying, recording, or by any information storage or retrieval system, without permission in writing from the publisher. For information, address Westminster John Knox Press, 100 Witherspoon Street, Louisville, Kentucky 40202-1396.

Scripture quotations from the New Revised Standard Version of the Bible are copyright © 1989 by the Division of Christian Education of the National Council of the Churches of Christ in the U.S.A. and are used by permission.

Scripture quotations from the Revised Standard Version of the Bible are copyright © 1946, 1952, 1971, and 1973 by the Division of Christian Education of the National Council of the Churches of Christ in the U.S.A. and are used by permission.

Book design by Sharon Adams
Cover design by Eric Walljasper, Minneapolis, MN
Cover art: Ruth and Naomi, *by Prof. Dr. He Qi, Nanjing Theological Seminary, www.heqiarts.com*

First edition
Published by Westminster John Knox Press
Louisville, Kentucky

This book is printed on acid-free paper that meets the American National Standards Institute Z39.48 standard. ⊛

PRINTED IN THE UNITED STATES OF AMERICA

06 07 08 09 10 11 12 13 14 — 10 9 8 7 6 5 4 3 2

Library of Congress Cataloging-in-Publication Data

Kwok, Pui-lan.
    Postcolonial imagination and feminist theology / Kwok Pui-lan.
        p. cm.
    Includes bibliographical references and index.
    ISBN-13: 978-0-664-22883-5 (alk. paper)
    ISBN-10: 0-664-22883-6 (alk. paper)
    1. Feminist theology.   2. Postcolonialism.   I. Title.

    BT83.55.K86 2005
    230'.082—dc22   2004048930

In loving memory of my mother,
Cheung Mei-fong

Contents

Acknowledgments

This book was conceived and written within a matrix of personal and professional relationships that have evolved over many years. I would like to thank the following for their invitations to present or contribute the papers that formed the basis of this collection of essays: Mary Elizabeth Moore, Charlotte Methuen, Philip L. Wickeri, Devadasan Premnath, Fernando F. Segovia, Robert Fowler, William T. Cavanaugh, Peter Scott, Dale Martin, Patrick Cheng, Joerg Rieger, Francisco Lozada Jr., Margaret A. Farley, and Serene Jones. I am grateful for the insightful conversations I have had with colleagues of the New Testament Studies and Postcolonial Studies Consultation of the Society of Biblical Literature: Laura E. Donaldson, R. S. Sugirtharajah, Fernando F. Segovia, Richard A. Horsley, and Stephen D. Moore. While I was in the final stage of putting the book together, I benefited from the discussions on globalization and theology of the Workgroup for Constructive Christian Theology. I am indebted to Anne Primavesi and Richard King, whose works I greatly admire, for reading parts of the manuscripts and offering tremendously helpful constructive criticism and suggestions.

Some of the ideas in the book were first tried out in various venues, and I want to thank my hosts and audiences in these institutions: Candler School of Theology, Emory University; Eden Theological Seminary; Garrett-Evangelical Theological Seminary; the Divinity School, Vanderbilt University; Webster University; Perkins School of Theology, Southern Methodist University; University of the Incarnate Word, and Yale University. I have also benefited from the helpful responses and questions from colleagues in the American Academy of Religion, Society of Biblical Literature, and European Society of Women in Theological Research. Three chapters in this book are based on essays originally written for Festschrifts to honor friends and colleagues whom

I have had the privilege of learning from and working with for many years—D. Preman Niles, Letty M. Russell, and Elisabeth Schüssler Fiorenza.

In the course of writing this book, my research assistants Sarah Clark, Anna Greenwood, Gretchen Grimshaw, and Sarah Braik offered invaluable support, edited earlier drafts, checked the footnotes, and made suggestions for putting materials together. Thomas Eoyang not only edited many of the essays in their original form and encouraged me to publish the collection, he also worked on the final manuscript with meticulous care, patience, and efficiency. I am very grateful for the many hours he has devoted to make my writing more precise, idiomatic, and readable. Needless to say, I am solely responsible for the mistakes that remain.

I would like to thank my editor, Jon Berquist, at Westminster John Knox Press, a biblical scholar who has engaged postcolonial theory in his scholarship, for his enthusiasm about this project from the beginning. He has shepherded the book through its various stages of production with professionalism and attention. His colleague Daniel Braden guided me through the production process, and copyeditor Esther Kolb has done a superb job. I am also grateful to the colleagues and students of the Episcopal Divinity School who have listened to me discuss the issues in the book, especially Christopher Duraisingh, Carter Heyward, Joan Martin, Lawrence Wills, and Gale A. Yee. The Theological Writing Fund of the Episcopal Divinity School has provided support for this work, and I am very appreciative of the encouragement of Academic Dean Joanna Dewey.

Many chapters of this volume appeared in other settings and have been included here with revisions, and several with significant expansions. I am grateful for permission to reproduce materials from the following:

"Historical, Dialogical, and Diasporic Imagination in Feminist Studies of Religion," in *The End of Liberation? Liberation in the End! Feminist Theory, Feminist Theology, and Their Political Implications*, Yearbook of European Society of Women in Theological Research, no. 10, ed. Charlotte Methuen and Angela Berlis (Dudley, Mass.: Peeters, 2002), 57–80.

"The Sources and Resources of Feminist Theologies: A Post-Colonial Perspective," in *Sources and Resources of Feminist Theology*, Yearbook of European Society of Women in Theological Research, no. 5, ed. Elisabeth Hartlieb and Charlotte Methuen (Kampen, the Netherlands: Kok Pharos, 1997), 5–23. Parts of it also appeared in Kwok Pui-lan, *Introducing Asian Feminist Theology* (Sheffield: Sheffield Academic Press, 2000), 42–46. Reprinted by permission of the Continuum International Publishing Group.

"Postcolonialism, Feminism, and Biblical Interpretation," in *Scripture, Community and Mission: A Festschrift in Honor of D. Preman Niles*, ed. Philip L. Wickeri (Hong Kong: Christian Conference of Asia, 2003), 269–84. Reprinted by permission of the Council of World Mission.

Kwok Pui-lan, "Response," *Journal of Feminist Studies in Religion* 20, no. 1 (2004): 99–106.

"Finding a Home for Ruth: Gender, Sexuality, and the Politics of Otherness," in *New Paradigms for Bible Study: The Bible in the Third Millennium*, ed. Robert M. Fowler, Edith Blumhofer, and Fernando F. Segovia (New York: T. and T. Clark International, 2004), 135–54. Reprinted by permission of the Continuum International Publishing Group.

"Feminist Theology, Southern," in *The Blackwell Companion to Political Theology*, ed. Peter Scott and William T. Cavanaugh (Oxford: Blackwell, 2004), 194–209.

"Engendering Christ," in *Toward a New Heaven and a New Earth: Essays in Honor of Elisabeth Schüssler Fiorenza*, ed. Fernando F. Segovia (Maryknoll, N.Y.: Orbis Books, 2003), 300–313.

"Mending of Creation: Women, Nature, and Eschatological Hope," in *Liberating Eschatology: Essays in Honor of Letty M. Russell*, ed. Margaret A. Farley and Serene Jones (Louisville, Ky.: Westminster John Knox Press, 1999), 144–55.

Introduction

I was rewriting some of the essays in this volume when I heard the sad news that Edward Said had passed away, after a long illness, in New York on September 26, 2003. The only time I met Said was when he came to Brandeis University several years ago to read from his memoir *Out of Place*.[1] He told the audience that he had written the book for his children so that they might have a glimpse of the world in which he had grown up, a world that had disappeared and existed only in historical memory. He was battling leukemia while writing the memoir and did not expect to live to see it in print. After the lecture I stood in the rain outside the lecture hall, pondering the similarities of Said's experience growing up as a Palestinian in Jerusalem and Cairo and my own childhood years in Hong Kong. We had grown up on different continents, but we had lived under British colonial rule and attended the Anglican Church at a young age.

After the death of the French philosopher Michel Foucault, Said commended "the startling yet sustained force and influence of his thought," hailing Foucault as "a central figure in the most noteworthy flowering of oppositional intellectual life in the twentieth-century West."[2] The same accolades can be lavished on Said, who was one of the most articulate and consequential critics of colonialism and imperialism among the American intelligentsia. Since the publication of *Orientalism* in 1978, Said was widely credited as a groundbreaker in postcolonial criticism, and his works have been judiciously studied and dissected by admirers and critics alike.[3] In Edward

1. Edward W. Said, *Out of Place: A Memoir* (New York: Knopf, 1999).
2. Edward W. Said, *Reflections on Exile and Other Essays* (Cambridge, Mass.: Harvard University Press, 2000), 187.
3. Edward W. Said, *Orientalism* (New York: Vintage, 1979). Page references are given in parentheses in the text below.

Said, we find a preeminent literary critic, an erudite scholar with breadth and depth, a music commentator, a classically trained pianist, as well as a political activist and arguably the most eloquent spokesperson on the plight of the Palestinians.

Although postcolonial studies has made its impact in many academic disciplines and fields of inquiry, the meaning of the term "postcolonial" continues to be vigorously debated. Some critics have warned that the term may be applied to many peoples, nations, and territories across space and time, and hence runs the danger of glossing over vast differences if the geographical and historical particularities of individual cases are overlooked.[4] Others have misgivings about the prefix "post" in the temporal sense and wonder if we have really entered the postcolonial age. Said himself has cautioned that it might be premature to speak of postcolonialism, since colonialism is not over and has simply been superseded by neocolonialism.[5] In the midst of this unsettling debate, Rey Chow's distinction of the various shapes of meaning of "post" provides some clarity to the discussion. A fellow critic from Hong Kong, Chow argues that the prefix connotes "having gone through," "after," and "a notion of time which is not linear but constant, marked by events that may be technically finished but that can only be fully understood with the consideration of the devastation they left behind."[6] For many postcolonial critics, "postcolonial" denotes not merely a temporal period or a political transition of power, but also a reading strategy and discursive practice that seek to unmask colonial epistemological frameworks, unravel Eurocentric logics, and interrogate stereotypical cultural representations. Indeed, the temporal and political dimensions of the term "postcolonial" and its discursive and critical aspects must be held together in productive tension because the colonization process that it criticizes is both social and political as well as cultural and discursive.

In this book, "postcolonial imagination" refers to a desire, a determination, and a process of disengagement from the whole colonial syndrome, which

4. See the criticisms by Anne McClintock, "The Angel of Progress: Pitfalls of the Term 'Postcolonialism,'" *Social Text* 31 and 32 (1992): 84–98; and Ella Shohat, "Notes on the 'Post-colonial,'" *Social Text* 31 and 32 (1992): 99–113; and the response by Stuart Hall, "When Was the 'Post-colonial'? Thinking at the Limit," in *The Post-colonial Question: Common Skies, Divided Horizons*, ed. Iain Chambers and Lidia Curti (London: Routledge, 1996), 242–60.

5. Edward Said, "In Conversation with Neeladri Bhattacharya, Suvir Kaul, and Ania Loomba," in *Relocating Postcolonialism*, ed. David Theo Goldberg and Ato Quayson (Oxford: Blackwell, 2002), 2. Said agreed with some of the criticisms of postcolonial studies expressed in Arif Dirik, "The Postcolonial Aura: Third World Criticism in the Age of Global Capitalism," *Critical Inquiry* 20 (1994): 328–56.

6. Rey Chow, "Between Colonizers: Hong Kong's Postcolonial Self-Writing in the 1990s," *Diaspora* 2 (1992): 152.

takes many forms and guises.[7] The colonial process, as Stuart Hall has pointed out, is doubly inscribed, affecting both the metropolis and the colonies, and the decolonization process also restructures both, though in different ways.[8] Hence, this book is interested not only in analyzing colonial discourse or in deconstructing Western dominant regimes of knowledge, but also in examining the interdependence of the cultural terrain traversed by both the colonizers and the colonized, as well as how the colonial systems of knowledge cast their impact, long after the colonizers are gone. Having gone through a lengthy period of colonial education, I am interested in exploring the steps necessary for a postcolonial intellectual to dislodge herself from habitual ways of thinking, established forms of inquiry, and the reward system vigilantly guarded by the neoliberal academy. By documenting my critical engagement with postcolonial thought, I hope to create a little more space to imagine that an alternative world and a different system of knowing are possible.

Said's *Orientalism* has opened such a space for many readers, for it talks back to the Western authorities by demystifying their cultural representations of the Orient in the colonial period. Following Foucault, Said demonstrates that power and knowledge are intimately related, for the knowledge and representations of the Orient would not be made possible without the financial and institutional support of the colonial regimes. And once this so-called scholarly and objective knowledge was produced, it in turn served the colonial government by providing information about "the natives" and by inculcating a belief that colonialism was necessary and beneficial for these people. *Orientalism* implicates many disciplines that emerged in the academy in the modern period, as well as literature, travelogue, and other popular writings, genres that are often considered above the fray of political contention. The book initiated colonial discourse studies by taking stock of the myths, mind-set, scholarship, and institutional structures that have sustained Western hegemony, and by showing the formidable impact the Orientalist system of ideas has had on academies, books, congresses, and media, as well as defense departments and foreign-service agencies. Just as Said had to "inventory the traces" upon him as the Oriental subject (25), postcolonial intellectuals need to be vigilant about the deep-seated layers of colonialist patterns of thinking in the archaeological excavation of their minds.

Said's work issues a clarion call to Christian theologians and scholars in Christianity because it was the Christian "West" that had constructed and promulgated the negative images of the "Orient" described in the book. He has

7. Ania Loomba, *Colonialism/Postcolonialism: The New Cultural Idiom* (London: Routledge, 1999), 19.
8. Hall, "When Was the 'Post-colonial'?" 246–47.

made this very explicit when condemning the unrelenting Eurocentrism that lay at the heart of European culture during the many decades of imperial expansion: "This accumulated experiences, territories, peoples, histories; it studied them, classified them, verified them, and above all, it subordinated them to the culture and indeed the very idea of white Christian Europe."[9] While reading Said's scathing critique, I kept thinking of how the fields of biblical studies, religion, and theology have contributed to the narratives of empire, and how the great theologians I have admired were influenced or tainted by the colonialist ethos and mentality. For someone like me who has studied Christian theology and read the works of Schleiermacher, Barth, and Tillich since the age of nineteen, there are many questions to be asked and a lot of unlearning to do.

Because Said has focused on British, French, and to a certain extent American scholarship, he has left out the influential and meticulous German Orientalist tradition, which cast a long shadow on the fields of biblical studies, comparative religion, and theology. Said admits that the book does not do justice to the strong impulse toward the study of the Orient in the eighteenth century, when the revolutionary changes in biblical studies took place (17). Even so, *Orientalism* has become a productive and enabling text for biblical scholars to interrogate the assumptions of their discipline and its collusions with colonialism. For while Said elucidates the history of Western anti-Semitism in its Islamic branch (28), his method of inquiry can be extended to include the other branch—the religious practices and culture of the Jewish people. His book discusses in detail how the French philologist Ernest Renan had created the "Semitic languages" in his philological laboratory and concluded that they were less developed than and inferior to the so-called Indo-European languages (132–48). What is not mentioned is that Renan also wrote *La Vie de Jésus* (1863), an influential text in the nineteenth-century quest for the historical Jesus, in which Renan attempted to recast Jesus in his own French bourgeois culture.[10] Elsewhere in the book, Said's sharp criticism of historicism and his sustained exposition of Orientalist structures in historical scholarship also have a direct bearing on the historical criticism of the Bible developed in the last two hundred years.

Following Said's lead, several scholars have documented how the study of the Bible has been influenced by and participated in the European Orientalist

---

9. Edward W. Said, "Yeats and Decolonization," in *Nationalism, Colonialism, and Literature*, ed. Terry Eagleton, Fredric Jameson, and Edward W. Said (Minneapolis: University of Minnesota Press, 1990), 72.

10. Ernest Renan, *The Life of Jesus* (New York: Peter Eckler Publishing Co., 1925).

discourse. James Pasto, for example, extends the Saidian inquiry to investigate how nationalist sentiment among German scholars conditioned their reconstruction of Jewish history. He shows that the works of W. M. L. de Wette (1780–1849) and Julius Wellhausen (1844–1918) have constructed a degenerating Judaism to be superseded and replaced by Christianity.[11] Such an interpretation, Pasto argues, facilitated the development of a common German identity, by fabricating a "Hebrew past that had been completed by Jesus and restored by Luther. This 'Hebraic' past thus gave Germans a past that was Biblical, Christian, Protestant and German in one single genealogy."[12] Another key contribution is by biblical scholar Keith Whitelam, who raises the question central to Said's work: How and why is there a silence or an eclipse of the history and experiences of Palestinians in scholarship? Whitelam charges that biblical scholars have invented an "ancient Israel" by focusing on the so-called emergence of Israel and the founding of an Israelite state. In order to move toward a more complete history of ancient Palestine, scholars need to be free from the constraints of biblical studies and from the biases of Western Orientalist scholarship.[13] In the field of New Testament studies, Shawn Kelley has examined in detail how European race theory and ideological assumptions about the relationship among culture, language, and people have infected European and American biblical scholarship, especially through the influences of G. W. F. Hegel and Martin Heidegger.[14] These critical interrogations of the formation of the discipline of biblical studies, together with the growing postcolonial studies of the Bible from the Third World, have created a lively and critical discourse in biblical scholarship.

In religious studies, scholars such as Donald Lopez Jr. and Richard King have borrowed insights from postcolonial criticism to raise fundamental questions about the constitution of religion as a field of study and the complicity of Western scholars with colonialism.[15] Although I cannot avoid using the term

11. James Pasto, "Islam's 'Strange Secret Sharer': Orientalism, Judaism, and the Jewish Question," *Comparative Studies in Society and History* 40 (1998): 437–74.

12. James Pasto, "When the End Is the Beginning? or, When the Biblical Past Is the Political Present: Some Thoughts on Ancient Israel, 'Post-Exilic Judaism,' and the Politics of Biblical Scholarship," *Scandinavian Journal of the Old Testament* 12, no. 2 (1998): 172.

13. Keith W. Whitelam, *The Invention of Ancient Israel: The Silencing of Palestinian History* (London: Routledge, 1996), 7–8.

14. Shawn Kelley, *Racializing Jesus: Race, Ideology, and the Formation of Modern Biblical Scholarship* (New York: Routledge, 2002).

15. Donald S. Lopez Jr., *Curators of the Buddha: The Study of Buddhism under Colonialism* (Chicago: University of Chicago Press, 1995); Richard King, *Orientalism and Religion: Postcolonial Theory, India and the "Mythic East"* (London: Routledge, 1999).

"religion" in the book, I will use "religious tradition" or "wisdom tradition" when referring to non-Western traditions.[16] Lopez and King elucidate how Western studies of "Buddhism" and "Hinduism" have homogenized these traditions and presented very skewed and self-serving views of them by playing to the spiritual fantasies of Westerners and by adopting a Christianized model as a point of reference. They question the use of universalistic and essentialized paradigms in the comparative studies of religion, the construction of India as the "mythic East," the misappropriation of other people's spiritual resources, and the privileging of textual studies over the vernacular. In addition, scholars in Islam challenge the Western stereotypes of the Muslim culture and practices and the portrayal of Muslim women as pitiful victims behind the veil.[17] In South Africa, David Chidester exposes the racist ideology and social Darwinism in the anthropological study of religion, as well as the biases of imperialistic comparative study of religion at the metropolitan centers.[18]

While biblical and religious scholars have deployed postcolonial theory to scrutinize their respective disciplines, theologians, with a few exceptions,[19] have scarcely paid any attention to this burgeoning field, though many are interested in the related field of postmodern studies. This oversight is unwarranted, given the lengthy history of theology's relation with empire building, especially in the modern period. The rise of modern theology has been attributed to the pioneering work of Friedrich Schleiermacher, and the development of modern theology took place in the cultural and social space defined by the Enlightenment on the one hand and political expansion of Europe on the other. In 1815 Western powers held approximately 35 percent of the earth's surface; by 1914 Europe controlled a total of roughly 85 percent of the earth as colonies, protectorates, dependencies, and commonwealths (41). Today, the United States has superseded the former empires to become the world's sole superpower, with

---

16. Walter Mignolo uses the term "gnosis," which encompasses all those wisdom traditions and knowledge subalternized by Western colonialism; see *Local Histories/Global Designs: Coloniality, Subaltern Knowledges, and Border Thinking* (Princeton, N.J.: Princeton University Press, 2000), 9–12. But "gnosis" can easily be confused with Gnosticism, a tradition considered heresy in early Christianity.

17. Leila Ahmed, *Women and Gender in Islam: Historical Roots of a Modern Debate* (New Haven, Conn.: Yale University Press, 1992); Meyda Yeğenoğlu, *Colonial Fantasies: Towards a Feminist Reading of Orientalism* (Cambridge: Cambridge University Press, 1998); Talad Asad, *Genealogies of Religion: Discipline and Reasons of Power in Christianity and Islam* (Baltimore: Johns Hopkins University Press, 1993).

18. David Chidester, *Savage Systems: Colonialism and Comparative Religion in Southern Africa* (Charlottesville: University Press of Virginia, 1996).

19. See Catherine Keller, Michael Nausner, and Mayra Rivera, eds., *Postcolonial Theologies: Divinity and Empire*, forthcoming from Chalice Press. The work is not published in time to be included in the discussions in this book.

President George W. Bush invoking unabashedly biblical images and Christian rhetoric to justify his global "war against terrorism." In the midst of the ascendancy of American imperialism, the lack of self-reflexivity among theologians may be taken as an indicator of the degree to which theological institutions and scholarship have been enmeshed in the neoliberal economy and right-leaning politics. Even progressive theologians in the United States—feminist, liberationist, and racial minorities among them—who have championed the use of critical categories such as gender, class, and race in their works, have not sufficiently addressed theology's collusion with colonialism in their theoretical frameworks. This book intends to make a small contribution to facilitate this engagement, which is long overdue.

GENDER, COLONIALISM, AND CHRISTIANITY

Some of the intellectual projects that make the crucial connection between religion and colonialism have left out the gender dimension; others that investigate the relationship between gender and colonialism have not taken note of the role of religion in sustaining colonial ideologies. In *Postcolonialism, Feminism, and Religious Discourse*, Laura Donaldson and I argued that gender, religion, and colonialism interplay in intricate and myriad ways, and scholars have to examine these triadic elements together.[20] In her generous review of the book, Grace Jantzen calls for a more detailed analysis of the roots of ideology of colonization in Western traditions, especially Christianity, and the ways this ideology links to modernity and continues to mutate in postmodernity.[21] This critical work, as Jantzen has noted, has barely begun and requires the collaborative effort of many scholars with expertise in the theological, cultural, social, and institutional dimensions of Christianity in different historical epochs. In what follows I outline some of my thoughts on the subject, while pointing to emerging lines of inquiry I find particularly helpful, in hopes of stimulating critical thinking on this crucial subject.

Since the Bible occupies a preeminent position in the Christian tradition, the interrogation of the ideology of colonization in Christianity as well as its decolonizing potential must begin with a radical reappraisal of the biblical heritage. The Bible is a repository of the writings and traditions of the Hebrew

20. Laura E. Donaldson and Kwok Pui-lan, eds., *Postcolonialism, Feminism, and Religious Discourse* (New York: Routledge, 2002).
21. Grace M. Jantzen, review of *Postcolonialism, Feminism, and Religious Discourse*, ed. Laura E. Donaldson and Kwok Pui-lan, *Journal of American Academy of Religion* 71, no. 4 (2003): 944.

people, who had been for centuries under the political yoke of the powerful Babylonian, Assyrian, Persian, Greek, and Roman Empires. If we pay attention to what Said has called the "worldliness of the text,"[22] we would see that litera-ture, history, and politics are inseparably linked in the biblical tradition. Just as with literature produced by the colonized peoples, the Bible does not speak in a single or monolithic voice, but is highly diverse and pluralistic: some texts show the indelible marks of imperialist ideology, while others challenge the dominant power and have liberating possibilities. Examining the early stages of the formation of the canon of the Hebrew Bible under the Persian Empire, Jon Berquist argues that the canon in one sense is a colonial text, authorized and brought into being because of imperialist ideology. But at the same time, it was produced by the social group of colonial administrators and canonizers, wedged between empire and colony, and had postcolonial potential embedded in the texts. Berquist remarks: "The canon is part of a mediation between colonizer and colonized, but it is a troubled mediation, not a smooth dialectic synthesis."[23]

The circumstances surrounding the formation of the New Testament under the shadow of the Roman Empire in the early centuries of the Common Era were no less complicated.[24] The canon became necessary in the politics of truth to demarcate orthodoxy and heresy, and to consolidate power by the church hierarchy. As it turned out, the written canon had effectively left out many of the voices of women, and one notable example was the exclusion of the Gospel of Mary, a second-century text in which Mary of Magdala received special teaching from Jesus and became a leader among the disciples. Karen King has argued that the marginalization of women in the formation of Christianity was produced in part "by the process of canonization as part and parcel of the theological development of 'orthodoxy' that condemned every early Christian theology that was supportive of women's leadership as heresy. Canon and 'orthodoxy' were devised in part to exclude women from positions of leadership and authority."[25]

Given this complex history of what counted as Holy Scripture, the Bible cannot be naively seen as a religious text reflecting the faith of the Hebrew people and early Christians. Instead, it must also be seen as a political text writ-

---

22. Edward W. Said, *The World, the Text, and the Critic* (Cambridge, Mass.: Harvard University Press, 1983), 39.

23. Jon L. Berquist, "Postcolonialism and Imperial Motives for Canonization," *Semeia* 75 (1996): 31.

24. Helmut Koester, *History and Literature of Early Christianity*, vol. 2 (Berlin: Walter de Gruyter, 1987), 5–12.

25. Karen King, "Canonization and Marginalization: Mary of Magdala," in *Women's Sacred Scriptures*, ed. Kwok Pui-lan and Elisabeth Schüssler Fiorenza, Concilium 1998, no. 3 (Maryknoll, N.Y.: Orbis Books, 1998), 35.

ten, collected, and redacted by male colonial elites in their attempts to rewrite and reconcile with history and to reconceptualize both individual and collective identities under the shadow of the empires. A postcolonial feminist interpretation of the Bible needs to investigate the deployment of gender in the narration of identity, the negotiation of power differentials between the colonizers and the colonized, and the reinforcement of patriarchal control over spheres where these elites could exercise control. Two exciting books that have come out in recent years demonstrate the complex and multiaxial reading strategies such an interpretation requires. Using a vigorous ideological criticism that integrates gender, class, race, and colonialism, Gale Yee's *Poor Banished Children of Eve* examines the portrayal of wicked women in the Hebrew Bible and demonstrates how women serve as conduits in the power play between men. Musa Dube's *Postcolonial Feminist Interpretation of the Bible* elucidates the intricate relationship between patriarchy and imperialism in her intertextual reading of the Bible with ancient and modern imperializing texts, and sharply critiques the lack of attention to colonialism in the works of contemporary critics.[26] I will discuss these works in more detail in chapter 3.

The early church was a crucial period in terms of the development of social and religious institutions of the church, the delineation of orthodoxy from heresy, and the change of the church's relationship to the state, especially after the conversion of Constantine. From a persecuted religious sect, Christianity gradually evolved to become the state's religious tradition in the fourth century, and in the process excluded other groups who might have had legitimate claims to being Christian. It also accommodated to the Greco-Roman religiocultural ethos and institutional structures, and appropriated as well the rhetoric of the empire in Christian discourse. As Christianity became more and more institutionalized, women were marginalized from religious leadership and teaching positions, and new relationships among gender, sexuality, and power had to be negotiated. Elisabeth Schüssler Fiorenza has argued that the early house churches, modeled after the voluntary religious associations, allowed women the opportunities to be founders, prophetic leaders, and teachers. But this model of the church, which she has called the discipleship of equals, was replaced by the patriarchicalization of church and ministry, as authority became vested in the local offices of the deacons and bishops in the second century.[27] The Christian missionary movement, which at its beginning

26. Gale A. Yee, *Poor Banished Children of Eve: Woman as Evil in the Hebrew Bible* (Minneapolis: Fortress Press, 2003); Musa W. Dube, *Postcolonial Feminist Interpretation of the Bible* (St. Louis: Chalice Press, 2000).

27. Elisabeth Schüssler Fiorenza, *In Memory of Her: A Feminist Theological Reconstruction of Christian Origins*, 10th ann. ed. (New York: Crossroad, 1984), 285–315.

represented an alternative vision and social structure in the Greco-Roman society, adapted to the Greco-Roman patriarchal household structure and Roman bureaucracy. The episcopacy became the center of unity of patristic Christianity, as women's authority as official prophets and teachers of the church was eliminated and repressed. The ascendancy of the Roman papacy in the fourth century also placed the center of the church at the capital of the state.

Under the imperial patronage of Constantine and subsequent emperors, Christianity had both the material resources and the institutional power to fashion itself, both discursively and institutionally, as an "orthodox" and "catholic" church to the exclusion of other Christian groups. This pattern of exclusion, first begun *within* the Christian tradition, continued when Christianity encountered other religious traditions of the world.[28] Through the new mechanisms of council and creed, and excommunication and exile, the Christian church sought to maintain its symbolic unity and to marginalize ambiguous and polarized differences.[29] According to Averil Cameron, the influence of Christianity was largely due to the triumph of hegemonic discourse, as Christian men "talked and wrote themselves into a position where they spoke and wrote the rhetoric of empire."[30] She notes that comparisons between Christ the king and the earthly ruler were extremely common in fourth-century Christian literature. Christian writers also adopted the common language of ruler theory—available to Christians and pagans alike since Plato—such as "the imagery of the ruler as good shepherd, God as the father of all, man made in the image of God, [and] the magnanimity of the good ruler."[31] The appropriation of these themes and vocabulary for contemporary situations allowed Christian writers to dip into the cultural reservoir to fashion a Christianized political discourse that colluded with imperial power to shore up their influence and to attract larger audiences.

Imperial patronage also cast a long-lasting influence on the formulation of church doctrines, as evident at the Council of Nicaea, convened by Emperor Constantine to settle the divisive Trinitarian debates and Arian controversy. While the New Testament contains diverse images and metaphors for Jesus, and Jesus was widely portrayed as the personification of Wisdom in the second and third centuries, the Nicene Creed unequivocally stated that Jesus was

---

28. For a nonlinear construction of Christianity and for "exclusivism" within Christianity, I benefit from Richard King's comments on an earlier draft of this introduction.

29. Virginia Burrus, *"Begotten, Not Made": Conceiving Manhood in Late Antiquity* (Stanford, Calif.: Stanford University Press, 2000), 34.

30. Averil Cameron, *Christianity and the Rhetoric of Empire: The Development of Christian Discourse* (Berkeley: University of California Press, 1991), 14.

31. Ibid., 132.

the Son of God, begotten, not made. Feminist philosopher Mary Daly has chastised the androcentric metaphors of the father and son in her classic study *Beyond God the Father*.[32] But Virginia Burrus has ingeniously used the Trinitarian doctrine as a site not so much to find out truths about God, but to trace the cultural shift in the conception of masculinity in late antiquity. While the masculinity of the elites was determined by their roles as civic leader and familial patriarch in an earlier period, the increasingly rigid and imperial bureaucracy necessitated a new formulation of manhood and virility. Burrus notes: "When the confession of the full and equal divinity of the Father, Son, and Spirit became for the first time the *sine qua non* of doctrinal orthodoxy, masculinity (I argue) was conceived anew, in terms that heightened the claims of patriarchal authority while also cutting manhood loose from its traditional fleshy and familial moorings."[33] Replacing the classical ideals of civic manhood with their Christian ascetic model of masculinity, the Christian writers imagine themselves as holy men or spiritual fathers, fighting for truth for God and exemplifying the Christian model of living. Just as "the Son attains full divinity in theological discourse, men begin to groom for godliness" by resisting their carnality and focusing on the transcendental words: the Scripture, the creed, commentary, and other liturgical texts.[34]

Such a hypertranscendental masculinity, as Burrus calls it, led to two interesting consequences. First, in order to differentiate itself from a women-identified carnal order, this ascetic masculinity incorporated in itself what was traditionally marked as "feminine," such as virginal modesty, disengagement from the public, reluctance to compete, maternal profundity, and nurturance. Of special importance, as we can see from the Nicene Creed, was the incorporation of the feminized virility of the wounded hero, martyrdom, victimization, and salvific suffering.[35] Second, the female gender was identified as the embodiment of carnality, sex, and evil by the early church fathers, while virginity was upheld as a virtue for young girls and women. Women were told to follow the example of the Virgin Mary, so that they could overcome the penalties of sexuality and marriage associated with the sin of Eve to become worthy brides of Christ.[36]

With the rise of Islam and Arab expansion in the seventh and eighth centuries, Christendom encountered a strong competitor and a mighty political foe. As Tomaž Mastnak has pointed out, while pagans and "barbarians" had always lived among the Christians and wars waged against them were common before

32. Mary Daly, *Beyond God the Father: Toward a Philosophy of Women's Liberation* (Boston: Beacon Press, 1973).
33. Burrus, *"Begotten, Not Made,"* 3.
34. Ibid., 5.
35. Ibid., 6.
36. Cameron, *Christianity and the Rhetoric of Empire*, 171–80.

the Crusades, something new in the medieval period happened when the Latin West forged a common bond and created a common enemy: "the construction of the Muslims as the normative enemies of Christianity and Christendom."[37] Seeing the Muslims as infidels and the enemies of God, the Christian church deemed it necessary to draw a clearer boundary between those who were inside and those outside the Christian fold. Official pronouncements of the church during the Middle Ages were unequivocal in reaffirming that outside the church and its sacrament there was no salvation. Such exclusivistic claims and negative attitudes toward other religious traditions affected the church's outlook toward other peoples for centuries to come.[38]

Even before the Crusades, the church had gradually changed its attitudes toward the use of arms, violence, and waging war, with far-reaching consequences. Although the church has prohibited the clerics from using arms, it was not uncommon for bishops to take part in wars, and in the Carolingian period, bishops and abbots were expected to lead the ecclesiastical contingents on imperial military campaigns. Pope Gregory VII expected the princes to use arms for the service of the church, and he believed that the pope could claim authority over the sword. The church also devised innovative liturgies to promote the growth of a warrior-saints cult through the blessing of banners and the consecration of weapons. Moreover, because of the promise of absolution through appropriate penance, the soldiers, fighting under the direction of the church, could be freed from the sins of using arms.

So when Pope Urban II authorized the First Crusade in 1095, the church saw fighting the Muslim infidels to gain back control of the Holy Land as a holy war and the Christian kings and militia as soldiers of Christ. Urban II urged Christians to stop their fratricidal wars and to march into a just war against the pagans, while promising remission of sins for those who fought against the infidels. As the Crusades became a demonstration of the power of the papal monarch, a radical shift in ecclesiastical attitudes toward war and the military profession occurred. From an institution that was supposed to promote God's peace, the church could now enlist the help of military services, and it became meritorious to use arms at the command of the church. The very idea of papal monarchy was intimately tied to the formation of the crusade idea, especially during a time when the papacy and the empire competed with each other for supremacy within Christendom.[39] At the same time, the cate-

37. Tomaž Mastnak, *Crusading Peace: Christendom, the Muslim World, and the Western Political Order* (Berkeley: University of California Press, 2002), 96.

38. Paul F. Knitter, *No Other Name? A Critical Survey of Christian Attitudes toward the World Religions* (Maryknoll, N.Y.: Orbis Books, 1990), 121–23.

39. Mastnak, *Crusading Peace*, 14–54, 137.

gorization of the crusade as a penitential war, the participation in which would satisfy the demand of God for the forgiveness of sins, found its expression in the atonement theory articulated by Anselm. Anselm formulated his satisfaction theory in *Cur Deus Homo* during the Crusades, and as Anthony Bartlett observes: "The idea of Christ laying down his life for God's honor [was] the theological sophistication of a thought that was coalescing at that very moment in the preparation of the First Crusade."[40]

The Crusades were accompanied by reform movements within the church and the realignment of gender roles in the household and the larger society. Gregory VII's reform movement in the eleventh century had already adopted a more stringent attitude toward clerical marriage. During the Crusades, the physical journey to recover the Holy Land was tied to the spiritual journey to reform in order to prepare for the eternal journey from earth to heaven. The First Lateran Council (1139) declared that any marriage of the ordained was invalid and any sexual relations of the priests were seen as sinful fornication. Rosemary Radford Ruether notes how such attitudes affected the outlook of the society of the higher Middle Ages: "The celibate male clergy, both secular and regular, was sharply distinguished from the married laity. Their celibacy made priests innately superior to married laypeople, whose sexual relations were tarred by the suspicion of sin."[41] In seeing this as a part of the process of controlling male desire and policing male sexual expression, especially among the clergy, Mark Jordan has argued that the medieval church had invented the term "sodomy," and condemned it as a vice against nature.[42] He also noted that the pagan cultures were seen as sodomitic, and sodomy was considered a military vice as it supposedly affected male prowess.[43]

Gender roles during the later Middle Ages and the early modern period shifted, as there was a greater differentiation of political and economic activities apart from the work in the household. This was the time of state formation, as in early modern England and France, and the further development of urban life. Before the cities grew, women in the families of landed nobilities took part in administrating the economic and financial affairs of the state, while women servants, slaves, and girls engaged in such productive labor as the weaving of cloth. As working relations changed, women were excluded from the

40. Anthony W. Bartlett, *Cross Purposes: The Violent Grammar of Christian Atonement* (Harrisburg, Pa.: Trinity Press International, 2001), 103–4.

41. Rosemary Radford Ruether, *Christianity and the Making of the Modern Family* (Boston: Beacon Press, 2000), 58.

42. Mark D. Jordan, *The Invention of Sodomy in Christian Theology* (Chicago: University of Chicago Press, 1997).

43. Mark D. Jordan, *The Silence of Sodom: Homosexuality in Modern Catholicism* (Chicago: University of Chicago Press, 2000), 63, 118.

more specialized and skilled productive work. Politically, they were considered unfit to hold political office because they were irrational and therefore incompetent. Thus, women were relegated to the low-paid and unpaid work of feeding, washing, and taking care of the children, the poor, and the sick.[44]

The "discovery" of the New World in the fifteenth century dramatically changed the worldview of Europe as Christians encountered peoples whose cultures and ways of life were radically different from their own. Since the Renaissance Christians believed that human beings were all descendants of the same family tree, they had to account for the differences between themselves and the Indians portrayed as exotic in travelogues and discovery reports. At first, some even doubted whether these indigenous peoples were human beings. Once the consensus was reached that they were human beings with souls, they were cast as imperfect or incomplete beings. Extrapolating the medieval paradigm, European Christians saw the indigenous peoples as infidels to be incorporated and cajoled into the Christian community. It was revealing that in Columbus's journal, the intruders were not described as Spaniards or Europeans, but as Christians, and the Indians were portrayed not as savages, but as people available for conversion: "They would easily be made Christians, for it appeared to me that they had no creed."[45] As people whom Columbus also described as having no clothes, the Indians symbolized alterity, the Other at the periphery of the "civilized" European world. The eclipse and the violent submission of the Other, Enrique Dussel has argued, were essential to the constitution of the myth of modernity. In his compelling book *The Invention of the Americas*, Dussel says: "The experience not only of discovery, but especially of conquest, is *essential* to the construction of the modern ego, not only as a subjectivity, but as subjectivity that takes itself to be the center or end of history."[46]

From the beginning, the "discovery" and the submission of the indigenous peoples in America were replete with sexual overtones. In 1492, Columbus wrote home from the Caribbean saying that the earth was not round, but shaped like a woman's breast, with a protuberance on its summit in the unmistakable shape of a nipple. Anne McClintock has called Columbus's breast fantasy a genre of "porno-tropics" that draws on "a long tradition of male travel as an erotics of ravishment."[47] In Jan van der Straet's famous portrayal of the "discovery" of

---

44. Ruether, *Christianity and the Making of the Modern Family*, 60–66.

45. *The Journal of Christopher Columbus*, trans. Cecil Jane (New York: Bonanza Books, 1989), 24, as quoted in Nicholas Thomas, *Colonialism's Culture: Anthropology, Travel and Government* (Cambridge: Polity Press, 1994), 73.

46. Enrique Dussel, *The Invention of the Americas: Eclipse of "the Other" and the Myth of Modernity*, trans. Michael D. Barber (New York: Continuum, 1995), 25. Emphasis his.

47. Anne McClintock, *Imperial Leather: Race, Gender and Sexuality in the Colonial Contest* (New York: Routledge, 1995), 22.

America, the encounter was depicted as an eroticized encounter between a man and a woman, with America symbolized by a voluptuous woman, lying naked on a hammock in an erotically inviting position.[48] Such depiction and fantasy, Enrique Dussel argues, masks the fact that the modern ego of the conquistador is also a phallic ego and conceals the erotic violence in the colonization of indigenous women's sexuality.[49]

Andrea Smith, a member of the Cherokee Nation, elaborates on the relationship among Christian imperialism, colonialism, and sexual violence.[50] Citing the works of Native scholars, she contends that the Native peoples are often likened to the Canaanites in the Bible, in the sense that they are the descendants of unsavory sexual relationships and they personify sexual perversity. Indeed, "the evil, barbarity, and licentiousness of the colonized Other are what make possible the goodness, civility, and propriety of the European self."[51] Since Native bodies are considered "dirty" and "unclean," the raping and violation of them do not count. In the racialized colonial discourse, white women symbolize purity and virtue, while "Native women as bearers of a counter-imperial order pose a supreme threat to the imperial order. Symbolic and literal control over their bodies is important in the war against Native people."[52] The colonization of Native women's bodies takes many brutal forms, including rape, sexual mutilation, and murder, which continue today. Christian boarding schools, in particular, were breeding grounds of physical and sexual abuse. Native boys and girls were forcibly taken away from their homes to be educated in these white institutions. Christianity was supposed to save Native women from their exploitative traditional practices, but in fact the arrival of Christianity made them more vulnerable. Thus, Smith insists that the struggle for sovereignty of Native peoples cannot be separated from the struggle against sexual violence.

As Native women were subjected to these unspeakable crimes, the control of women's bodies and sexuality intensified in Europe during the period of the witch hunt. Accused as heretics and witches, many women were tortured or burned at the stake in public for allegedly having sex with the devil and serving Satan. Although some of the witches were quite young, the majority of

---

48. Ibid., 25–26.

49. Dussel, *The Invention of the Americas*, 46.

50. Andrea Smith, "Sexual Violence and American Indian Genocide," in *Remembering Conquest: Feminist/Womanist Perspectives on Religion, Colonization, and Sexual Violence*, ed. Nantawan Boonprasat Lewis and Marie M. Fortune (New York: Haworth Pastoral Press, 1999), 31–52.

51. Michael Hardt and Antonio Negri, *Empire* (Cambridge, Mass.: Harvard University Press, 2000), 127.

52. Smith, "Sexual Violence and American Indian Genocide," 36.

them were poor, older single women, unattractive, and without the protection of men. As healers, midwives, and diviners of their local communities, these women competed with the priests in exercising some forms of healing and pastoral roles. They practiced folk magic and witchcraft, which typically included incantations, the use of herbs, and the repeating of charms. Some of the women brought before the Inquisitors belonged to small covens dedicated to the goddesses of Old Europe. The estimates of the number of women killed during the witch hunts vary a great deal, from one hundred thousand to several million. The public display of the power of the influential men and clergy to punish women in sexually sadistic ways was a form of disciplining women and a teaching tool.

The persecution of the Other within Europe—the heretics, the witches, and the Jews—was linked with early European expansion and its colonial impulse. Maria Mies connects the witch hunt with the rise of science and modern economy and colonialism. She writes: "The counterpart of the slave raids in Africa was the witch hunt in Europe."[53] Similarly, Anne Llewellyn Barstow observes: "The witch hunts took place at the same time as colonial expansion and the Atlantic slave trade, and they were made possible by some of the same ecclesiastical policies and legal changes."[54] She makes the connection between the emerging racism of the epoch and the widespread and large-scale persecution of European women as witches:

> Witches and Indians were ill fated in sharing a number of characteristics in the eyes of European men: both were thought to worship "demons" and to be cannibalistic and should therefore have a war of extermination fought against them—in the name of Christianity. Both were condescended to as children, yet were feared. Both stood for the Other, for all that Western men believed they were not.[55]

The age of the Enlightenment upheld that men were the measure of all things because of their rational faculty and the ability to control their own destiny and nature through progress in history and advance in science. But the great irony of modernity was that the Enlightenment ideas of equality, liberty, and fraternity applied only to some and not to all human beings. The revolutionary movements in Europe and the enfranchisement of European propertied men did not stop the expansion of slavery and colonialism in the same period. If we examine the thoughts of some of the influential thinkers, we can see that philosophers such as Locke, Hume, and Kant harbored strong racial

53. Maria Mies, *Patriarchy and Accumulation on a World Scale: Women in the International Division of Labour* (London: Zed Books, 1986), 69.

54. Anne Llewellyn Barstow, *Witchcraze: A New History of the European Witch Hunts* (San Francisco: Pandora, 1994), 12.

55. Ibid., 163.

biases and prejudices.[56] They created categories of people based on racial and cultural groupings: the "exotic," "oriental," "the East," and the more specific ones like "Negro," "Indian," and "Jews." These people were deemed as either not fully human or exotic and primitive souls, needing the tutelage of the Man of Reason. Enlightenment thinkers saw that it was the responsibility of the West to bring the benefits of their scientific mind-set and Western civilization to the colonized, to enhance the latter's freedom.

The distinction of peoples in an earlier period, marked primarily by their religious difference, was replaced by racial and ethnic origins, and the different groupings of people were placed in a developmental time frame. In *Time and the Other*, Johannes Fabian writes: "Enlightenment thought marks a break with an essentially medieval, Christian (or Judeo-Christian) vision of Time. That break was from a conception of time/space in terms of a history of salvation to one that ultimately resulted in the secularization of Time as natural history."[57] While the pagans and the infidels were candidates for salvation and could be brought into the Christian fold, the savages and the primitives, by contrast, were not yet ready for civilization. As race was seen as determined by biology, the differences between the white people and their counterparts were considered unchangeable and unbridgeable.

As colonial desire and imperialistic violence were masked and reconstituted in a blatant reversal as "civilizing mission," the Christian church played important roles through the sending of missionaries, establishing churches and schools, and propagating ideas of cleanliness and hygiene. Christianization and Westernization became almost a synonymous process in the colonial period. The submission of women and the practices of *sati*, foot binding, polygamy, veiling, and arranged marriages, were considered symptomatic of the inferiority of native cultures, when compared to the Victorian ideals of womanhood. "Saving brown women from brown men,"[58] as coined by Gayatri Chakravorty Spivak, called for and justified colonial and missionary intervention. As such, colonized women faced the unenviable alternatives of being victims of patriarchal practices or objects of Western compassion.[59]

Because of the difficulties in reaching women due to the segregation of the sexes in some societies, Christian missions sent missionary wives and single

56. David Theo Goldberg, *Racist Culture: Philosophy and the Politics of Meaning* (Oxford: Blackwell, 1999), 14–40.

57. Johannes Fabian, *Time and the Other: How Anthropology Makes Its Object* (New York: Columbia University Press, 1983), 26.

58. Gayatri Chakravorty Spivak, "Can the Subaltern Speak?" in *Marxism and the Interpretation of Culture*, ed. Cary Nelson and Lawrence Grossberg (Urbana: University of Illinois Press, 1988), 296–97.

59. Uma Narayan, *Dislocating Cultures: Identities, Traditions, and Third-World Feminism* (New York: Routledge, 1993), 57–58.

women to labor in the field. Although with good intentions to save the souls of "heathen" women, these women missionaries participated in "colonialist feminism" both discursively and institutionally, by propagating the impression that native women were illiterate, oppressed, and waiting for the white women to bring light to them.[60] Judging from the magnitude of women's participation in mission and the amount of money raised to support such activities, the women's missionary movement must be regarded as the largest women's movement in the nineteenth and early twentieth centuries. As industrialization and urbanization increased the separation of the public and private realms, and women's roles were curtailed by the cult of female domesticity, the missionary movement provided an outlet for women, especially for the graduates of the newly founded women's colleges and seminaries. Once in the mission fields, these women, because of their race and Christian affiliation, enjoyed freedom and status not accorded them back home. On the other hand, they were also charged to reproduce domesticity in a strange land and to be guardians of Western morality and religious piety. As Ann Laura Stoler has said: "White women needed to be maintained at elevated standards of living, in insulated social spaces cushioned with the cultural artifacts of 'being European.'"[61] Caught in the politically charged colonial space defined by race and class, these white women were not natural allies of native women. To protect their identity and to minimize the danger of native women's usurping their superior position, it was advantageous not to stress commonality of gender, but to exaggerate racial and class distinctions.

In the late 1960s, when the second wave of the feminist movement emerged and feminist theologians challenged patriarchy of the church and society, they did not pay sufficient attention to how white women had colluded in colonialism and slavery. Thus, some feminist theologians, like the rest of the feminist scholars, reproduced some of the colonialist assumptions in religious discourse. In her much-quoted article "Under Western Eyes: Feminist Scholarship and Colonial Discourses," Chandra Talpade Mohanty details how feminist scholars homogenize non-Western women, while maintaining the superior position of Western women above the rest.[62] This replicated the colonial ideology, as Musa

---

60. Kwok Pui-lan, "Unbinding Our Feet: Saving Brown Women and Feminist Religious Discourse," in Donaldson and Kwok, *Postcolonialism, Feminism, and Religious Discourse*, 64–69.

61. Ann Laura Stoler, "Carnal Knowledge and Imperial Power: Gender, Race, and Morality in Colonial Asia," in *Gender at the Crossroads of Knowledge: Feminist Anthropology in the Postmodern Era*, ed. Micaela di Leonardo (Berkeley: University of California Press, 1991), 65.

62. Originally published in 1986, this essay is collected in Chandra Talpade Mohanty, *Feminism without Borders: Decolonizing Theory, Practicing Solidarity* (Durham, N.C.: Duke University Press, 2003), 17–42.

Dube says, by "portraying the West as the center of all cultural good, a center with a supposedly redemptive impulse, while it relegates all other cultures to the project of civilizing, Christianizing, assimilating, and developing."[63]

As modernity mutated into postmodernity in the West, neocolonialism took a new form in the globalization of markets and capital. Fredric Jameson has suggested that postmodernity is the cultural logic of a new stage of capitalist accumulation and commodification that accompanies the formation of the world market.[64] In their book *Empire*, Michael Hardt and Antonio Negri explain that the new emerging empire does not depend on the traditional notion of the state as bounded space, but on building a globalized and decentralized network of international financial institutions, mass media and communication systems, and multinational corporations with flexible labor and capital.[65] Even war has changed its character, in that during the Gulf War the United States assumed leadership position to manage international justice, "not as a function of its own national motives but in the name of global right."[66] The assertion of American hegemony necessitates a whole new set of negotiations of international rights and networks to channel mediations and conflict resolutions.

Within such an expansive imperial project, space is always open and there is no more outside. While postmodern theorists and some postcolonial writers as well are preoccupied with difference and with challenging the reductionist binary constructions of class, race, and gender, Hardt and Negri argue that such articulations do not challenge imperial rule, because the empire wants to do away with boundaries and appropriate difference as a marketing tool. In fact, postmodernity arrived on the scene because of the rupture in the tradition of modern sovereignty, and it played right into the hands of the new globalized power.[67] The analyses of Hardt and Negri on the emerging new empire building and its cultural politics have direct implications for our theological discussion today. First, it impacts on the current debate on postmodernity and liberation theology. Liberation theology, borrowing social analytical tools from Marxism, has been criticized as outdated and as having failed to provide adequate analysis of new structures of economic power of our time. It has been pointed out that liberation theology, at least in its Latin American form, shares much of modernist thinking, including the belief in

63. Musa W. Dube, "Postcoloniality, Feminist Spaces, and Religion," in Donaldson and Kwok, *Postcolonialism, Feminism, and Religious Discourse*, 104.

64. Fredric Jameson, *Postmodernism, or, The Cultural Logic of Late Capitalism* (Durham, N.C.: Duke University Press, 1991).

65. Hardt and Negri, *Empire*, 166–67.

66. Ibid., 180.

67. Ibid., 142.

humanism, the use of grand narratives, and the projection of a teleological utopia. Some have questioned whether "liberation" and "the preferential option for the poor" are still relevant in our post-Marxist world. But for others such as Mark Lewis Taylor, the postmodern celebration of play and difference and the carnivalesque forms of resistance borders on a kind of fetishization when it masks unequal and oppressive economic, social, and political relations.[68] The challenge will be how the option for the margin will engage postmodernity in new ways and generate new insights for theological, social, political, and economic thinking.

The second issue is closely related to the first, and concerns the future of feminist theology as a global resistance movement and the solidarity of women across racial, economic, and religious differences. In the past three decades, feminist theology has become a multivocal and multireligious movement, as different groups of women began to articulate their theology and new voices are being heard. In critiquing the essentializing tendency of the early feminist Christian writers, much emphasis has been placed on the politics of identity and difference. With the proliferation of these various theological projects, some with new names, such as womanist and *mujerista*, are there common objectives and goals for the feminist project? Added to this confusion is that some have already argued that feminism is passé, and should be replaced by "postfeminism." A younger generation of savvy women have called themselves third wave, and seek "to use desire and pleasure as well as anger to fuel struggles for justice."[69] Does feminism have a future in the new century? What are the achievements of feminist theology, and what shapes might it take in the cultural space defined by the global market?

ABOUT THIS VOLUME

This book contains essays written in the last several years, when I have tried to rethink feminist theology from a postcolonial perspective. Many of the essays were published elsewhere, but have been updated and expanded, reflecting how my thoughts have deepened during the intervening years as new resources have been published and new questions broached. By means of this book I hope to explore a postcolonial feminist hermeneutics of interpreting

68. Mark Lewis Taylor, "Subalternity and Advocacy as *Kairos* for Theology," in *Opting for the Margins: Postmodernity and Liberation in Christian Theology*, ed. Joerg Rieger (New York: Oxford University Press, 2003), 27.

69. Leslie Heywood and Jennifer Drake, "Introduction," in *Third Wave Agenda: Being Feminist, Doing Feminism*, ed. Leslie Heywood and Jennifer Drake (Minneapolis: University of Minnesota Press, 1997), 4.

the Bible and theological texts, as well as to rethink and reformulate some of the guiding questions that had shaped much of the debates in feminist theology since the 1970s. An important characteristic of the book is that I have intentionally brought together feminist theological discourses from different geographical regions and cultural contexts because women's experiences, as I have shown above, overlap and intersect in a way that demands an intercultural approach. I believe that feminist theology is "not only multicultural, rooted in multiple communities and cultural contexts, but is also intercultural because these different cultures are not isolated but intertwined with one another as a result of colonialism, slavery, and cultural hegemony of the West. By intercultural, I mean the interaction and juxtaposition, as well as tension and resistance when two or more cultures are brought together sometimes organically and sometimes through violent means in the modern period."[70] This intercultural approach allows us to theorize identity, experience, agency, and justice through a cross-cultural lens.

For example, in the United States the experiences of white and black women have been and are inseparably linked and mutually constituted because of the ignoble legacy of slavery and racism. When we turn to Europe, the leisure lives of European middle-class ladies and the Victorian cult of female domesticity could not have been sustained without the exploitation of the lower classes and colonized men and women. Thus, the histories of the white mistresses and the slave women and the experiences of the female colonizers and the colonized women must be considered together and read contrapuntally as one intertwined and overlapping process.[71] Since slavery and racism in America were inseparable from colonial expansion, the struggles of black women and other minority women in the United States must not be taken as separate from the struggles of women in the Third World. In fact, as Gayatri Chakravorty Spivak has observed, "In the struggle against *internal* colonization, it is the African-American who is *post*colonial in the United States."[72] Among the womanist theologians, Traci West has explored how the concept of colonization is relevant for the analysis of Afro-American internalization of Euro-American racism and the psychosocial condition of black people. Though she has reservations about certain postcolonial theories, she points to the link between colonization

70. Kwok Pui-lan, "Feminist Theology as Intercultural Discourse," in *The Cambridge Companion to Feminist Theology*, ed. Susan Frank Parsons (Cambridge: Cambridge University Press, 2002), 24–25.

71. For "contrapuntal reading," see Edward W. Said, *Culture and Imperialism* (New York: Knopf, 1994), 18.

72. Gayatri Chakravorty Spivak, "Teaching for the Times," in *Dangerous Liaisons: Gender, Nation, and Postcolonial Perspectives*, ed. Anne McClintock, Aamir Mufti, and Ella Shohat (Minneapolis: University of Minnesota Press, 1997), 478.

and Euro-American racism as particularly pertinent to probe the conditions for black Americans and rape and subjection of black women.[73] Although the struggles of Native or indigenous women are different from that of women in the Third World, Andrea Smith finds using an anticolonial framework helpful in her feminist analysis and in the work for environmental justice.[74]

This book is divided into two sections. Part 1, "Postcolonial Imagination and Feminist Interpretation," attempts to clarify the meaning and processes of postcolonial imagination and apply the insights to the feminist interpretation of the sources of theology, especially the Bible. Drawing from my intellectual history, chapter 1 proposes three distinct and yet overlapping modes of postcolonial imagination: historical, dialogical, and diasporic. It discusses what is involved in stepping outside the worldview created by a theological tradition steeped in Eurocentrism to reencounter one's own history and culture and hence discover one's self and identity anew. It upholds neither a nostalgic nor a romanticized notion of one's heritage, but argues for a critical appropriation such that the past is constantly open to new interpretations. The chapter sets the context for the whole book and makes a critical contribution to unpacking the process of "decolonizing of the mind." It illustrates the complexities of identity formation of a postcolonial feminist theologian and how the experiences of the colonized, the exiled, the immigrant, and the diasporic raise new questions for and broaden the horizon of feminist theology.

Traditionally, the sources of theology include the Scripture, tradition, reason, and experience. Feminist theology has emphasized women's experience as a significant source for theology, because male theologians have often presumed that their experience is universal and generic for all. In the last two decades, women of color and those adopting a poststructuralist stance have questioned the essentialization of white women's experience and the tendency to see patriarchy as everywhere the same. Feminist theologians of different stripes have debated vigorously on how women's experience, given its diversity and historical character, can be used as a foundation for feminist theology. At the same time, the use of Scripture, tradition, and reason in theology is no less contentious.

Chapter 2 uses postcolonial theory to scrutinize these traditional categories—experience, Scripture, tradition, and reason—from a multicultural and global perspective, showing that they have historically privileged the white

73. Traci C. West, "Spirit-Colonizing Violations: Racism, Sexual Violence and Black American Women," in Lewis and Fortune, *Remembering Conquest*, 21.
74. Andrea Smith, "Ecofeminism through an Anticolonial Framework," in *Ecofeminism: Women, Culture, Nature*, ed. Karen J. Warren (Bloomington: Indiana University Press, 1997), 21–37.

Eurocentric tradition. The challenge of the white feminists is not radical enough if they only wish to replace and step into the subject position of white men, without being conscious of their complicity in the colonizing project. The chapter also includes the contributions of Third World women and racial minority women in opening up these traditional categories to expand Christianity into a multicultural and pluricentric tradition.

Chapter 3 focuses on the connection between postcolonial studies and feminist biblical interpretation. After outlining the history of the introduction of postcolonial theory to biblical studies, I discuss the issues that postcolonial biblical critics, such as Gale Yee and Musa Dube, have brought to the interpretive task. Then I proceed to analyze how postcolonial studies can open new avenues to examine gender in early Christianity, by using examples from both the Gospels and the Pauline epistles as illustrations. I argue that only by attending to how gender, class, and race functioned in the Roman Empire in interlocking ways can we fully understand these New Testament texts. I also suggest that postcolonial feminist criticism needs to work with Jewish feminists to debunk deep-seated anti-Judaism in the Christian tradition, which dehumanizes Jewish people and sustains colonial ideology.

Chapter 4 uses the story of Ruth as a case study to illustrate how gender, sexuality, and the politics of otherness intersect in feminist biblical interpretation across a broad spectrum of authors. The book of Ruth has all the ingredients of a postcolonial drama: immigration, interethnic relations, the use of female sexuality for survival, and male genealogy with implications for the national narrative. As one of the two books in the Bible with a female protagonist, the book of Ruth has attracted widespread attention among feminist scholars in both America and the Third World. The chapter uses "home" and its discontent, discussed with passion and rigor in immigrant and diasporic literature, as a heuristic key for reading this intricate tale. By juxtaposing Regina Schwartz's iconoclastic interpretation of monotheism and violence with Laura Donaldson's decolonizing reading, I reflect on the relationship among home, female sexuality, and identity formation and conclude with reflections on how biblical scholars have created a "home" in their discipline.

"Postcolonial Feminist Theological Vision" is the eponymously titled part 2 of the book, with chapter 5 serving as an introduction to this section. In this chapter, I attempt to answer the questions: What is postcolonial feminist theology? Who is to do it? How to do it? For whom is it done? I apply postcolonial theory to a critical scrutiny of feminist theology and queer theology, and suggest that we need to resignify gender, requeer sexuality, and redo theology. Postcolonial feminist theology needs to resignify gender, moving from a liberal humanist position and a poststructuralist emphasis on difference to a transnational approach that foregrounds relation of female subjects in globalization. It also needs to requeer sexuality, through tracing the genealogy of sexual discourses in the wider nexus of race, class, and religious difference in the colonial process. The chapter concludes with suggestions for redoing theology, including a critical appropriation and interpretation of the theological tradition, and different approaches to conceptualizing the scope, themes, and organization of postcolonial feminist theology.

Feminist theology from the Third World, whether using an explicitly postcolonial framework or not, deals with the intersection of national independence, cultural politics, and social transformation. Chapter 6 highlights the contributions of women from the Third World to political theology, and points to the difference of their approaches from those of women from the First World. Since women in the South have been largely marginalized from national politics, they have to redefine and enlarge the scope of politics and the parameters of political theology. This chapter discusses their analyses of the sociopolitical situations of the South, critique of both patriarchy and colonialism, radical reappropriation of the symbols of Jesus and Mary, and emerging insights in ecofeminism. In contrast to their male counterparts, women theologians from the Third World are wary of a too optimistic liberation rhetoric, and they have a more pragmatic assessment about the church's role in social and political change.

In chapter 7, "Engendering Christ," I revisit Rosemary Radford Ruether's famous question "Can a male savior save women?" which has defined the parameters of feminist discussion of gender and Christ for over two decades. After Mary Daly's chastisement of the irredeemable androcentrism of Christian symbolism and the pope's reiteration in the 1970s that women could not be priests because they did not represent Christ, Ruether's question had its historical relevance and potency. But when we look outside of white America and Europe, we discern an interesting phenomenon, in that women in the Third World and in racial minority communities have not been preoccupied with the maleness of Christ as an issue. It is important to bear in mind that some of them have come from cultures that do not construct gender in a fixed and binary way, and they have moved beyond Ruether's question and proceeded to destabilize the gender of Christ and experiment with a dazzling array of new images—from Jesus as the Feminine Shakti to the Bi/Christ! In the process, they have collectively turned the blue-eyed, middle-class, and sexually restrained Aryan Christ—a projection of white men in their own images— upside down.

Religion is a critical category in the Western imagination of the cultures and peoples of the world. Chapter 8 enters into conversations with scholars in religious studies who have engaged postcolonial theory to scrutinize the development of the concept of religion in the comparative study of religion and theology. Tracing the development to Schleiermacher, the chapter argues that the discussion of religion was a central theme in modern Western theology, as theologians tried to define Christian identity and Christianity's relationship to other wisdom traditions and cultures of the world. While most liberal theologians currently want to get on the bandwagon of a "pluralistic theology of religions," I argue that we have to go beyond the comfort zone of pluralism to articulate a postcolonial theology of religious difference. In this critical task, feminist theologians must see gender as a constitutive factor in the intrareligious and interreligous network of relations.

In the final chapter, I discuss women, nature, and hope, paying special attention to the writings of Third World women and indigenous women. I articulate how women and nature have been exploited in the three waves of globalization: colonialism, development, and green imperialism. Using this as a critical context, I evaluate the discussion of the relation between women and nature in feminist religious discourse and demonstrate that the connection cannot be seen in a simple and essentialized way. I articulate the hope of women who have experienced the history of colonialism, conquest, and enslavement. Without romanticizing their cultures and heritages, they hope for the regeneration of human spirit and renewal of creation for the survival of themselves and their communities. They issue a charge to people who live in affluent societies to work in solidarity for protecting the earth and for justice for all.

As I conclude this introduction, I celebrate the opportunities I have had to discuss the ideas in this book with colleagues in different parts of the world. I am aware that the search for emancipatory knowledge and wisdom is not an individual and personal endeavor, but must be done in community. As a former student of mine, Alan Hesse, said, learning takes place in a matrix of relationships. I recognize the privilege I have as a middle-class professor teaching at an American divinity school, with access to library resources and books that my Third World colleagues can only dream of. Yet I experience the daily challenges of a woman of color who must transgress constricted boundaries and negotiate new possibilities for daring to think and act differently. The book illustrates a rite of passage from one who identified herself primarily as an Asian feminist theologian in the past to one who increasingly embraces her diasporic existence. Although the book is very much based on my work in the academy, it is also informed by two grassroots groups I have had the privilege to work with for over a decade. The first is the Pacific, Asian, and North American Asian Women in Theology and Ministry, which I cofounded twenty years ago and presently serve as faculty adviser. The other is the Asian Task Force against Domestic Violence in Boston, a group that provides shelter and advocacy for

Asian women, particularly new immigrants. These commitments have kept my feet on the ground, while my ideas roam the seventh heaven. The Chinese have a saying that one gives out bricks in the hope to receive jade in return. I hope that the bricks I offer in this book will assist others in laying new foundations for our collective praxis for freedom.

PART 1

Postcolonial Imagination and Feminist Interpretation

1

Postcolonial Imagination

Historical, Dialogical, and Diasporic

What postcolonialism signifies is that the future is open and the past unstable and constantly changing.

R. S. Sugirtharajah[1]

I had to change my intellectual and aesthetic beliefs about the world and about what I was doing in it, and I had to keep on changing them as the world changed—and I changed in it—forever.

Nancy Mairs[2]

I have been reflecting on my long intellectual journey to "struggle to know." Why is knowing a struggle? It is a struggle because you have to spend years learning what others told you is important to know, before you acquire the credentials and qualifications to say something about yourself. It is a struggle because you have to affirm first that you have something important to say and that your experience counts. As Leila Ahmed, a professor in women's studies in religion, reminisces about her graduate training at Cambridge University:

> Many of us from the Third World arrived having lived through political upheavals that traumatically affected our lives—for this quite simply has been the legacy of imperialism for most of our countries. But it was not those histories that we had lived that were at the center of our studies, nor was it the perspectives arising from those histories

---

1. R. S. Sugirtharajah, *Postcolonial Reconfigurations* (St. Louis: Chalice Press, 2003), 8.
2. Nancy Mairs, *Voice Lessons: On Becoming a (Woman) Writer* (Boston: Beacon Press, 1994), 21.

that defined the intellectual agenda and preoccupations of our academic environment.[3]

Women's articulation of their experiences of colonization is so new; these
women have been much represented, but until fairly recently have not been
allowed the opportunities to represent themselves. Even if they have "spoken,"
their speech acts are expressed not only in words but also in forms (storytelling,
songs, poems, dances, and quilting, etc.) that the academic and cultural estab-
lishments either could not understand or deemed insignificant. These knowledges have been ruled out as nondata: too fragmented, or insufficiently
documented for serious inquiry.

How do we come to know what we know? How do postcolonial intellectuals begin the process of decolonization of the mind and the soul? What are the
steps we need to take and what kind of mind-set will steer us away from Eurocentrism, on the one hand, and a nostalgic romanticizing of one's heritage or
tradition, on the other? In this chapter, I attempt to trace the itinerary of how
the mind "imagines," for without the power of imagination we cannot envision a different past, present, and future. Without interrogating the mind's
"I/eye," we are left without alternative perspectives to see reality and to chart
where we may be going. For what we cannot imagine, we cannot live into and
struggle for.

What is imagination? How does the postcolonial's mind work? I have written that to imagine means to discern that something is not fitting, to search
for new images, and to arrive at new patterns of meaning and interpretation.[4]
But I have become aware that the process of imagining is more complex, especially when we do not want to construe the imagining subject as the "transcendental I" within the liberal project, who has the power to shape the world
and to conjure meanings. In other words, I have attached more importance to
the cracks, the fissures, and the openings, which refuse to be shaped into any
framework, and which are often consigned to the periphery. These disparate
elements that staunchly refuse to follow the set pattern, the established episteme, the overall design that the mind so powerfully wants to shape, interest
me because they have the potential to point to another path, to signal radically
new possibilities.

As I reflect on my own thinking process as an Asian postcolonial feminist
theologian, I discern three critical movements, which are not linear but over-

3. Leila Ahmed, *A Border Passage: from Cairo to America—a Woman's Journey* (New
York: Farrar, Straus and Giroux, 1999), 211.
4. Kwok Pui-lan, "Discovering the Bible in the Non-Biblical World," *Semeia* 47
(1989): 25–42, reprinted in idem, *Discovering the Bible in the Non-Biblical World* (Maryknoll, N.Y.: Orbis Books, 1995), 8–19, here 13.

lapped and interwoven in intricate ways. They are more like motifs in a sonata, sometimes recurrent, sometimes disjointed, with one motif dominating at one moment, and another resurfacing at another point. I would like to reflect on these three movements—historical, dialogical, and diasporic imagination—to indicate how my mind has changed or remained the same.

HISTORICAL IMAGINATION

> History is best figured not as an accurate record or transcript of the
> past but as a perspectival discourse that seeks to articulate a living
> memory for the present and the future.
>
> *Elisabeth Schüssler Fiorenza*[5]

How do you trace where you have come from? How do women create a heritage of our own? When women's history emerged on the scene, feminist scholars argued that one could not simply add women and stir, but had to question the so-called historical data, periodization, historiography, and in fact, the whole writing of history, as if women counted. The project is to accord or restore to women the status of a "historical subject." But how do we track the scent of women who were multiply marginalized, shuttled between tradition and modernity, and mostly illiterate, and who therefore left no trail that could be easily detected? Hispanic journalist Richard Rodriguez uses the metaphor "hunger of memory" to describe this passionate and relentless quest for one's own historical and cultural past.[6]

Why did Chinese women, who were mostly poor and illiterate, become Christians when Protestant missions began to spread inland in China in the 1860s? Since most of them had adhered to Chinese folk religious practices, what did they find in Christianity that would have been appealing to them? What would it be like for them to worship with men in the Christian churches, when social propriety at the time prescribed the segregation of the sexes? Did they enjoy reading the Bible and singing hymns? What kind of roles did these Chinese Christian women play in the church and society when China was semicolonized?

I wish they had left behind books, diaries, documentaries, interviews, poetry, or their own interpretation of the events. Since these materials are either nonexistent or not readily available, I spent much time collecting and

5. Elisabeth Schüssler Fiorenza, *In Memory of Her: A Feminist Theological Reconstruction of Christian Origins*, 10th ann. ed. (New York: Crossroad, 1994), xxii.
6. Richard Rodriguez, *Hunger of Memory: The Education of Richard Rodriguez* (Boston: David E. Godine Publisher, 1981).

piecing their stories from information scattered in church yearbooks, college bulletins, pamphlets, obituaries, missionary reports, and religious journals. The process is much like "quilt-making," as Schüssler Fiorenza has described: "The quilt-maker carefully stitches material fragments and pieces into an overall design that gives meaning to the individual scraps of material."[7]

The writing of history in China has always been embroiled in political power. Since the establishment of the People's Republic of China in 1949, there has been a massive attempt to rewrite Chinese history, following the Marxist-Leninist-Maoist party line. Until the liberalization of Chinese policies in the late 1970s, the Christian missionary movement was seen as the "running dog of imperialism." Churches were closed during the Cultural Revolution (1966–1976), and Christians were scorned, harassed, put in prison, sent to the countryside, and looked at with suspicion. It would have been taboo to mention the contributions of the Christian churches and the life and ministry of Chinese Christians. In recent years, a more balanced assessment of Christianity's roles in modern Chinese history began to emerge, when historians are no longer coerced to adhere to the Marxist interpretation.

On the other hand, Western missionaries have written voluminous memoirs, histories, reports, letters, and books on their contributions to what they have called the "uplifting" of China. Some of these missionaries subsequently became "China experts" in higher education in Europe and the United States, and have interpreted Chinese history according to a "Western impact and Chinese response" model.[8] Such a model looks at world history as an extension of Western history and overemphasizes the influences of Western powers on the cultures and histories of other peoples. The historical agency of the Chinese people was downplayed, as they became not the actors but the acted upon in the unfolding historical drama of Western expansion and colonization.

Since the 1970s, some male Chinese scholars have challenged the Marxist reductionist method, the missionary approach, and the "Western impact" model by recovering the history of Chinese Christians. They have, however, focused exclusively on the lives and thoughts of male Christians, as if women were not an integral part of the encounter between China and Christianity. To write a history of Christianity in China as if women matter requires a different historical imagination and what Foucault has termed the "insurrection of subjugated knowledge." In my first book, *Chinese Women and Christianity*,

---

7. Schüssler Fiorenza, *In Memory of Her*, xxii.
8. For an analysis of such a model, see Paul A. Cohen, *Discovering History in China: American Historical Writing on the Recent Chinese Past* (New York: Columbia University Press, 1984).

1860–1927, I painstakingly reconstructed Chinese women as actors, writers, and social reformers in the unfolding drama of the Christian movement at the turn of the twentieth century.[9] As I look back at my work, I wish I had had more exchanges with non-Western scholars who were probing the houses of memory of their foremothers, for I have learned much from Evelyn Brooks Higginbotham's work on the women's movement in the Black Baptist Church and Leila Ahmed's book on women and gender in Islam.[10] I would also have benefited from the scholarship by historians and anthropologists who investigated the relationship among race, gender, and imperial power.[11] While I focused on the Chinese archives, Chung Hyun Kyung documented the emergence of Asian feminist theology as a grassroots movement and provided information on the historical context and social organizations that formed the backbone for the movement.[12] Similarly, women scholars from other Third World contexts have also recounted the histories and struggles of Christian women against patriarchy and other forms of oppression in their societies.

In the United States, there has also emerged a significant body of work reconstructing the history and lived experiences of racial minority women. The accomplishments of the womanist scholars are especially impressive. For example, Delores Williams has used the figure of Hagar as a heuristic key to recover the struggle for survival and quality of life of African American women.[13] The works of Zora Neale Hurston, Anna Julia Cooper, and Ida B. Wells-Barnett have been given their due attention by Katie Geneva Cannon, Karen Baker-Fletcher, and Emilie Townes, respectively.[14] Joan Martin has

9. Kwok Pui-lan, *Chinese Women and Christianity, 1860–1927* (Atlanta: Scholars Press, 1992).

10. Evelyn Brooks Higginbotham, *Righteous Discontent: The Women's Movement in the Black Baptist Church, 1880–1920* (Cambridge, Mass.: Harvard University Press, 1993); Leila Ahmed, *Women and Gender in Islam: Historical Roots of a Modern Debate* (New Haven, Conn.: Yale University Press, 1992).

11. For example, Lata Mani, *Contentious Traditions: The Debate on Sati in Colonial India* (Berkeley: University of California Press, 1998); Kumkum Sangari and Sudesh Vaid, eds., *Recasting Women: Essays in Colonial History* (New Dehli: Kali Press, 1989); Anne McClintock, *Imperial Leather: Race, Gender and Sexuality in the Colonial Contest* (New York: Routledge, 1995); Ann Laura Stoler, *Carnal Knowledge and Imperial Power: Race and the Intimate in Colonial Rule* (Berkeley: University of California Press, 2002).

12. Chung Hyun Kyung, *Struggle to Be the Sun Again: Introducing Asian Women's Theology* (Maryknoll, N.Y.: Orbis Books, 1990).

13. Delores S. Williams, *Sisters in the Wilderness: The Challenge of Womanist God-Talk* (Maryknoll, N.Y.: Orbis Books, 1993).

14. Katie Geneva Cannon, *Black Womanist Ethics* (Atlanta: Scholars Press, 1988); Karen Baker-Fletcher, *A Singing Something: Womanist Reflections on Anna Julia Cooper* (New York: Crossroad, 1994); and Emilie M. Townes, *Womanist Justice, Womanist Hope* (Atlanta: Scholars Press, 1993).

deployed slave narratives as resources to uncover the work ethic of enslaved women.[15] Evelyn Brooks Higginbotham and Cheryl Townsend Gilkes have recovered the roles and leadership of black women in the black churches from historical and sociological points of view.[16]

With such a body of knowledge before us, it is time to look back and to clarify some of the issues that have arisen in the ensuing discussions of our works. The first issue concerns what kind of subjectivity we have accorded those women who have historically not been granted subject status. For example, black ethicist Victor Anderson has charged that womanist scholars have essentialized blackness as if it consisted only of suffering, endurance, and survival of life. He further argues that they have followed the masculine construction of the black heroic genius, and stress black women's capacities for survival even against unprecedented oppression.[17] But as Stephanie Y. Mitchem has retorted, the womanists have presented much more multiple and variegated descriptions of suffering, without collapsing all forms of oppression together as equal and homogeneous.[18] Furthermore, as Elisabeth Schüssler Fiorenza has persistently argued, historical writings are rhetorical, serving particular political functions, and are not to be construed as "objective" or "value-neutral."[19] The emphasis on the historical and moral agency of black women is necessary, as Katie Geneva Cannon argues, because the white racist culture reinforces the stereotypes of the inferiority of the black race and promulgates negative images of black women.[20] Like the black women writers they have studied, womanist theologians and ethicists keep in mind the need for self-affirmation and assertion by the black community, to which their works are accountable. To recover black foremothers as strong, resourceful, and enduring is to rewrite a tradition to live by, and to celebrate black women's audacity of creating a way out of no way. Perhaps, when the womanist tradition is more nuanced and developed, and when the social conditions inflicted by white racism improve, we will be able to see black women assuming more varied subject positions in religious discourse.

15. Joan M. Martin, *More than Chains and Toils: A Christian Work Ethic of Enslaved Women* (Louisville, Ky.: Westminster John Knox Press, 2000).

16. Higginbotham, *Righteous Discontent*; Cheryl Townsend Gilkes, *If It Wasn't for the Women . . . : Black Women's Experience and Womanist Culture in Church and Community* (Maryknoll, N.Y.: Orbis Books, 2001).

17. Victor Anderson, *Beyond Ontological Blackness: An Essay on African Religious and Cultural Criticism* (New York: Continuum, 1995), 104–17.

18. Stephanie Y. Mitchem, "Womanist and (Unfinished) Constructions of Salvation," *Journal of Feminist Studies in Religion* 17, no. 1 (2001): 93–94.

19. Elisabeth Schüssler Fiorenza, *Rhetoric and Ethic: The Politics of Biblical Studies* (Minneapolis: Fortress Press, 1999).

20. Cannon, *Black Womanist Ethics*, 6.

In the postcolonial Asian context, Wong Wai Ching has argued that Asian women theologians have a tendency to present Asian women either as victims of multiple oppression or as national heroines fighting courageously for freedom and emancipation. Since Asian women have been constructed as "the poor woman," Asian feminist theology tends to follow the similar plot of revolving around the themes of suffering and liberation. As such, Asian feminist theologians have oversimplified women's multiple experiences, diverse interests, and social locations. They have also inadvertently supported the nationalist politics and agendas of Asian male theologians, and as a result, their feminist theology shares the assumptions and rhetoric of their male counterparts, such as the recovery of Asian identities, the commitment to sociopolitical transformation, and the prioritization of practice over Western academic theory.[21]

I find that Wong tends to oversimplify the ideas of the individual Asian feminist theologians she cites and the development of Asian feminist theology in general. The works of Chung Hyun Kyung, Mary John Mananzan, and myself have presented a much more multiple and diverse portrayal of Asian women than the binary constructs of "victim" and "heroine." The social analysis of Korean feminists, who survived through Japanese colonialism and who currently live in a divided country in one of the most highly militarized zones in the world, is very different from that of Indian feminists struggling against abject poverty, the caste system, dowry, and the mobilization of Hinduism as a national ideology. While these feminists are concerned about the multiple oppression of women, their interpretations of why women suffer are culturally and historically specific. While the struggle for independence provided the historical backdrop for Asian women to enter the public arena, Asian feminist theologians are keenly aware of the patriarchal biases of the national male elite both during independence struggles and in the subsequent fight for democracy. Asian feminist theologians do not blindly follow the lead of the male theologians, nor do they willingly participate in and support their epistemological framework.[22]

Since both Anderson and Wong rely on elements of postmodern thought to critique the construction of an "essentialized" subject in womanist and Asian feminist discourse, it may be worthwhile to reexamine whether the postmodern critique of subjectivity is appropriate and helpful in these contexts. While

---

21. Wong Wai Ching, "Negotiating for a Postcolonial Identity: Theology of 'the Poor Woman' in Asia," *Journal of Feminist Studies in Religion* 16, no. 2 (2000): 5–23.

22. See also my review of Wong's book *The Poor Woman: A Critical Analysis of Asian Theology and Contemporary Chinese Fiction by Women*, in *Quest: An Interdisciplinary Journal for Asian Christian Scholars* 1, no. 1 (2002): 94–104.

postmodern thought may be instrumental in deconstructing the notion of modern "man" as the transcendental unified subject, its application to other contexts where the enslaved and the colonized have never been allowed to assume subject status must be carefully interrogated.[23] Furthermore, it is necessary to distinguish between a Western habit of "essentializing" and "homogenizing" human experience and the self (as most clearly seen in the colonial enterprise) and the womanist and Asian cultural constructions of the self, which are rooted in and understood through the communal experience. When Delores Williams uses the literary figure of Hagar, she is not interested in the individualist protagonist of the narrative, nor does she try to "essentialize" Hagar's experience to speak for all black women. Rather, she explores how the ancient story may serve as a historical prototype to lift up salient aspects of black women's collective experience (such as the predicament of motherhood, the character of surrogacy, the problem of ethnicity, and the significance of the wilderness experience) and as a model to write black women's history.[24]

Similarly, Chung Hyun Kyung has used the stories of comfort women, who were conscripted and lured to serve as sexual slaves for Japanese soldiers during the Second World War, as a root story for Korean feminist theology.[25] Again, she does not intend to "universalize" the experiences of these two hundred thousand comfort women to speak for all Korean women, who belong to different social classes and backgrounds. Nevertheless, she finds these stories to be powerful heuristic models to expose the interlocking oppression of sexism, militarism, colonialism, and sexual violence.

One may wonder why these theologians dwell on the memories of Hagar and the comfort women and do not move on. But as Thomas Laqueur has elo-

---

23. Patricia Hill Collins, "What's Going On? Black Feminist Thought and the Politics of Postmodernism," in idem, *Fighting Words: Black Women and the Search for Justice* (Minneapolis: University of Minnesota Press, 1998), 124–54.

24. My reading of Delores Williams's work is different from that of Serene Jones. From a poststructuralist perspective, Jones finds that Williams has a tendency to treat the meaning of a text in an "overly static" and unambiguous way, and the social reality she draws from it is too fixed and monolithic. See Jones, "Women's Experience between a Rock and a Hard Place: Feminist, Womanist, and *Mujerista* Theologies in North America," in *Horizons in Feminist Theology: Identity, Tradition, and Norms*, ed. Rebecca S. Chopp and Sheila Greeve Davaney (Minneapolis: Fortress Press, 1997), 43–44. I read Williams in the oral tradition of the black people, in which stories are teased out for their multiple meanings to address the needs of the audiences, and there are numerous possibilities of retelling and reinterpretation. The themes Williams lifts up from the Hagar story are suggestive and not definitive or exhaustive.

25. Chung Hyun Kyung, "Your Comfort vs. My Death," in *Women Resisting Violence: Spirituality for Life*, ed. Mary John Mananzan et al. (Maryknoll, N.Y.: Orbis Books, 1996), 129–40.

The historical imagination aims to release the past so that the present is livable

quently written, "It is precisely by remembering in public that the past can become past—and that memory becomes survivable by entering into history."[26] The historical imagination aims not only to reconstitute the past, but also to release the past so that the present is livable. The fact that Hagar and the comfort women are not erased from historical memory is a powerful testimony to the fact that an alternative vision of "social temporality"[27] is possible. Hagar, the Egyptian slave woman, was erased for the most part from the Hebrew Scriptures, while the comfort women were covered up as a national shame by Korean politicians and historians. But these women complicate history, for they insist that slave girls and prostitutes exist in the same temporality with the master, the mistress, the military, and the powerful. These figures disrupt national history, mock the identity formation of a people, challenge sexual normativity, and resist any forms of erasure. Like the haunted ghost in Toni Morrison's *Beloved*,[28] they come back again and again to demand that their stories be remembered. They stubbornly refuse to accept that history is written only by the winners.

Memory is a powerful tool in resisting institutionally sanctioned forgetfulness. Too often, the memory of multiply oppressed women is inscribed on the body, on one's most private self, on one's sexuality. We have yet to find a language to speak in public how the body in such circumstances remembers and passes on knowledge from generation to generation. While French feminist theorists have debunked the law of the father, explored the possibility of women's writing, and urged women to seek their own *jouissance*, many Third World women regard such high-level theory as Eurocentric and a luxury. The body, in an enslaved and colonial context, speaks a language of hunger, beating, and rape, as well as resistance, survival, and healing. It is not that the female subject is so marked with pain that she cannot enjoy pleasure, but rather that the pleasure she seeks lies not so much in asserting her own individualist sexuality or sexual freedom as found in white bourgeois culture, but in the commitment to communal survival and in creating social networks and organizations so that she and her community can be healed and flourish.

From reading the texts of these women theologians, I do not find that they rest their hope on the final *eschaton*, on an unpredictable utopia, or on historical progress. History for them is too full of ambiguities and unpredictable twists and turns to be constructed as linear, progressive, or sprinkled with unchecked optimism. The hope for some of the disenfranchised women may

26. Thomas Laqueur, "The Naming of the Dead," in *London Review of Books* 19, no. 11 (June 5, 1997), 8.

27. See Homi K. Bhabha, *The Location of Culture* (London: Routledge, 1994), 171.

28. Toni Morrison, *Beloved: A Novel* (New York: Knopf, 1987).

be a place to dry their fish on the beach, enough seeds for next spring, or money enough to send their children to school. The future is not a grand finale, a classless society, or even a kingdom of God, but more immediate, concrete, and touchable. It may be the pooling of communal resources, of living better than last year, or of seeing grandchildren grow up healthy and strong. It is a historical imagination of the concrete and not the abstract, a hope that is more practical and therefore not so easily disillusioned, and a trust that is born out of necessity and well-worn wisdom.

DIALOGICAL IMAGINATION

The term *dialogical imagination* describes the process of creative hermeneutics in Asia. It attempts to convey the complexities, the multidimensional linkages, and the different levels of meaning that underlie our present task of relating the Bible to Asia. This task is dialogical, for it involves ongoing conversation among different religious and cultural traditions. . . . Dialogical imagination attempts to bridge the gaps of time and space, to create new horizons, and to connect the disparate elements of our lives into a meaningful whole.

Kwok Pui-lan[29]

When I wrote the article "Discovering the Bible in the Non-Biblical World" (1989), I was interested in how an Asian Christian woman can enter into dialogue with the cultures and religious traditions of the first-century biblical world. I said: "The Chinese characters commonly translated as dialogue mean talking with each other. Such talking implies mutuality, active listening, and openness to what one's partner has to say. Asian Christians are heirs to both the biblical story and to our story as Asian people, and we are concerned to bring the two into dialogue with one another."[30] In a certain sense, my articulation of dialogical imagination was an attempt to work through some of the dilemmas and contradictions of being "Asian" and "Christian." I want to revisit several of my assumptions again to see how my mind has changed in the intervening years.

The primary issue concerns the subject who is doing the "dialogical imagining." The subject I had in mind then was very influenced by the construction of the Western liberal subject, unrestrained by social and historical

29. Kwok, *Discovering the Bible*, 13.
30. Ibid., 12.

location, free to create, to think, to mold consciousness, such that he or she can shape disparate parts into the "whole." I was influenced by Gordon Kaufman's understanding of theology as an imaginative human construction, and his Kantian notion of human consciousness.[31] The power of human imagination also undergirds Gadamer's "fusion of horizons," in which two different historical worlds or horizons can be fruitfully brought together.

As a postcolonial subject who has been thrown into situations not of her choosing and who has to negotiate different cultural worlds constantly, I have to admit that the drive to "imagine the whole"—a unified country, an undefiled nation, an intact cultural tradition—is strong and often irresistible. It is a longing for what one has never possessed and a mourning of a loss one cannot easily name. It may also be a quest for certainty that one knows is not there! While I do not wish to undermine anyone's desire for a meaningful whole, I want to caution against the enormous power of that desire—the lure to shape things into one, unified, seemingly seamless whole. While such a desire may have the positive effect of resisting the fragmented and disjointed experience imposed by colonialism, it may also lead to the danger of reification of the past and the collapse of differences from within.

Although I still think that human creativity can often transcend social and historical circumstances, I did not pay enough attention in that essay to the analysis of the fragmented subjectivity or the multiple fractures of the colonized subject's mind and psyche in the imaginative process. In his response to my work, the late George Soares-Prabhu, a distinguished Indian biblical scholar, wrote:

> Unlike a Hindu reading of the Vedas, or a Buddhist reading of the Pali Canon, an Asian reading of the Bible is never a "natural" reading, taking place spontaneously within a living tradition. It always has to be a deliberate strategy, a forced and somewhat artificial exercise, a reading against the grain, a challenge to church orthodoxy or academic parochialism.[32]

My hope to bring the biblical and Asian traditions together through dialogical imagination may have underestimated the fact that an Asian reads the Bible from a situation of great alienation. And I did not sufficiently problematize how the "Asian story," which is so diverse and complex, could be brought into a mutually illuminating relationship with the equally multifaceted "biblical

---

31. Gordon D. Kaufman, *The Theological Imagination: Constructing the Concept of God* (Philadelphia: Westminster Press, 1981).

32. George M. Soares-Prabhu, "Two Mission Commands: An Interpretation of Matthew 28:16–20 in the Light of a Buddhist Text," *Biblical Interpretation* 2 (1994): 270.

story." Throughout the 1990s, mostly due to my readings in postcolonial theories, I have rethought some of my own assumptions about the relation between "Asia" and "the West"—a process necessitated by the fact that I now live and teach as a racial minority in the United States.

I do not believe that most Asian male or female theologians consciously or unconsciously construct an "essentialized" notion of "Asia" and proceed to write and articulate an "Asian" theology. Many of these theologians have traveled widely in Asia, and any ecumenical Asian gathering, with its diversity of languages and national costumes, would show how any easy generalization of "Asia" is doomed. The naming of theology as "Asian" must therefore be seen as a discursive and political construct, arising out of the particular historical moment of the recovery of political and cultural autonomy in the 1960s. Though Asian theologians might have vastly diverse understandings of what constituted "Asian," the deployment of the term signified a collective consciousness against the theological hegemony of the West and a concomitant affirmation that God's revelation and actions could be discerned through the histories and cultures of Asian peoples. The self-affirmation of Asian peoples as part of the people of God was crucial at the time and a dominant theme in Asian theology.

It is also important to remember that soon after independence, most Asian countries had to fight simultaneously against the legacy of imperialism and the centralization of power by the national bourgeois or the military junta. In denouncing authoritarian governments and military dictatorships, progressive Asian theologians recognized clearly that the culture in any Asian country was not monolithic, but multifaceted and stratified. Thus, C. S. Song urged the use of popular myths, stories, and legends of the common people, and *minjung* theologians in Korea rediscovered shamanism, the mask dance, and political satire as resources for doing theology.[33] Such an approach differed markedly from earlier attempts of indigenization, in which Christianity was brought into dialogue mostly with the elitist cultures of Asia. When Asian feminist theologians entered the scene, they, too, paid special attention to women's popular cultures, for they were wary of the patriarchal biases in the elitist traditions.

The emphasis on the use of Asian resources, by, for instance, the Ecumenical Association of Third World Theologians and the Programme for Theology and Cultures in Asia, was timely and necessary because of the colonial legacy of theological education. Asian students were busy digesting the Tillichs, Bultmanns, and Barths while their compatriots were demonstrating

---

33. See C. S. Song's many books, for example, *Tell Us Our Names: Story Theology from an Asian Perspective* (Maryknoll, N.Y.: Orbis Books, 1984); Commission on Theological Concerns of the Christian Conference of Asia, *Minjung Theology: People as the Subjects of History* (Maryknoll, N.Y.: Orbis Books, 1981).

on the streets or taking turns going to prison for democracy. For, sadly, theological training in Asia at the time continued the process of colonizing Asian
minds, even long after the colonizers had packed up and gone home. For Asian
theologians who were trying to gain their own voices, Asian theology should
have emerged from and responded to Asian realities, rather than reflect someone else's theological puzzles conceived in the faraway Western academy.
These Asian theologians were not interested in creating a distinctive "Asia,"
the essence of which can be found only in the pristine past, undefiled by colonization. Instead, they wanted to establish a dialogue with the living traditions of Asia, especially with people's religiosity, and with emergent issues in
Asian politics and history. They did not construct "Asia" and the "West" or
"Asia" and "Christianity" as binary opposites. The fact that one can construct
"Christianity"—often understood to be a Western tradition—by Asian stories
and idioms subverts the binarism of what is "Asian" and what is "Western."
Asian liberation theology assumes the posture of a "fighting literature"
because it challenges and undermines the power of setting up rigid boundaries
in the attempt to safeguard the cultural purity of Western Christianity.

Having said that, I would argue that in emphasizing the use of Asian myths,
stories, and religious resources (as opposed to Western influences), Asian theologians have not sufficiently theorized how Asian cultures have been transformed by the colonial regimes—be they French, British, Japanese, Spanish,
Portuguese, Dutch, or American. The question of how colonization has
reconstituted or reconfigured Asian cultures has not been discussed with the
intellectual rigor it clearly warrants. Since many Asian countries have gone
through a lengthy period of colonization, how can we conceptualize the complicated process of cultural encounter between the colonizers and the colonized? The many modes of such cultural interaction—parody, mimicry,
hybridity, syncretism, double inscription, contact zone, translation, and transculturation—discussed with profound insights in postcolonial literature,[34]
unfortunately have seldom entered into theological discourse.

Moreover, the impact of global capitalism on cultural formation in general
and on theology in particular has not been clearly articulated, because the
analysis of the religio-cultural dimensions is often separated from the rapidly
changing socioeconomic conditions, especially in the Asia-Pacific region. For
example, some of the grassroots theological movements, such as *minjung* theology, lost their appeal and efficacy both in their own contexts and abroad during the period of economic expansion in the 1980s, when the so-called Asian

34. See, e.g., Stuart Hall, "When Was the 'Post-colonial'? Thinking at the Limit,"
in *The Post-colonial Question: Common Skies, Divided Horizons*, ed. Iain Chambers and
Lidia Curti (London: Routledge, 1996), 251.

miracle began to take place. Today, Taiwan, South Korea, Hong Kong, and Singapore, for instance, can hardly be called "developing" countries or regions. Indeed, some of the Asian cultural traditions have been revived to serve the interests of global capitalism (the Chinese silk changsam comes into vogue in Hollywood), and various religious fundamentalisms have been resuscitated to serve nationalist interests. In East Asia, the unholy alliance of capitalism, patriarchy, and Neo-Confucianism sustains the booming economy by supporting oligarchies of old men and by providing a flexible supply of cheap female labor.

The above analysis does not imply that dialogical imagination as an interpretive strategy is no longer useful in some respects, particularly in its emphasis on dialogue with other religious traditions and interpretation as a creative process,[35] but it does call for a more explicit discussion of its theoretical grounding and a deepened engagement with postcolonial theories and cultural studies. In the face of cultural and religious pluralism, many liberal theologians have also used the model of dialogue or conversation as a mode to engage the Other.[36] In fact, the terms "pluriphonic," "multivocal," "symphony," or "assembly of voices" have popped up frequently in religious and theological discourses as ways to imagine inviting "Others" to the table. But it should be pointed out that in our postcolonial world, all the voices are not equal and some cultures dominate center stage, with the power to push the rest to the periphery. The debate on multiculturalism in the United States has pointed to its inadequacy in dealing with diversity, because it fails to confront the dominant white culture's power to define, appropriate, and assimilate minority cultures, in other words, its power to set the rules of the game. Following Homi Bhabha, I have come to see the limitations of *cultural diversity* when articulated within a liberal paradigm, which treats different cultures as mutually interacting and competing on the same footing in the public square. Such an approach often assumes the stance of cultural relativity, which calls for cultural exchange, the tolerance of diversity, and the management of conflicts through democratic means. Instead, Bhabha uses the term "cultural difference" to underscore that the interaction of cultures in the postcolonial world is always imbued with power

35. I am grateful for Dr. Mrinalini Sebastian's comments at the "Post-colonial Hermeneutics" seminar of the Bossey Ecumenical Institute, 2001. She affirms my emphasis on interreligious dialogue and, as a literary critic, she stresses that the term "imagination" allows for creativity.

36. David Tracy, *Plurality and Ambiguity: Hermeneutics, Religion, Hope* (San Francisco: Harper and Row, 1987), 92–94; Paul F. Knitter, "Toward a Liberation Theology of Religions," in *The Myth of Christian Uniqueness: Toward a Pluralistic Theology of Religions*, ed. John Hick and Paul F. Knitter (Maryknoll, N.Y.: Orbis Books, 1987), 181–90.

and authority. Difference arises not because there are many preconstituted cultures existing side by side, but is manufactured through particular discourses at critical moments when the status quo is questioned:

> Cultural difference is not difficult, if you like, because there are many
> diverse cultures; it is because there is some particular issue about the
> redistribution of goods between cultures, or the funding of cultures,
> or the emergence of minorities or immigrants in a situation of . . .
> resource allocation.[37]

Furthermore, the tension and anxieties elicited by cultural difference are always overlaid and heightened by the issues of race, class, gender, and sexuality.

Dialogical imagination will need to consider the theoretical challenge coming from the studies of the contact zone, which foreground the modes and zones of contact between dominant and subordinate groups, between people with different and multiple identities.[38] The interaction between two cultures with asymmetry of power is often not voluntary and one-dimensional, but is full of tensions, fractures, and resistance. The imposition of the colonizers' language, the institution of the Queen's birthday as a public holiday, and the naming of the street and school as Prince Edward Road and King's College are but a few conspicuous examples. Many Asian people remain hostile to the Christian church because it continues to signify the pain and suffering of the colonial contact. While the creation of a new narrative discourse of Christianity through the use of Asian idioms and stories may be a sincere attempt on the part of Asian theologians, it can be seen as yet another incidence of trying to fit local histories into the global design of Christianity,[39] if it does not self-consciously challenge imperialistic impulses. As such, it would be an ironic example of colonization of the mind—this time, not by the colonizers, but with the full consent and complicity of the formerly colonized.

Dialogical imagination also has to capture the fluidity and contingent character of Asian cultures, which are undergoing rapid and multidimensional changes. We can no more conceive culture as static, offering a secure group boundary and an unambiguous sense of belonging. Many postcolonial theorists and cultural critics have deployed traveling metaphors to denote the transient,

37. Gary A. Olson and Lynn Worsham, "Staging the Politics of Difference: Homi Bhabha's Critical Literacy," in *Race, Rhetoric, and the Postcolonial*, ed. Gary A. Olson and Lynn Worsham (Albany: State University of New York Press, 1999), 16.

38. Mary Louise Pratt, *Imperial Eyes: Travel Writing and Transculturation* (New York: Routledge, 1992).

39. This is from the title of Walter Mignolo's book *Local Histories/Global Designs: Coloniality, Subaltern Knowledges, and Border Thinking* (Princeton, N.J.: Princeton University Press, 2000).

unsettling nature and displacement in late twentieth-century culture. Instead of speaking of the home or the roots, James Clifford proposes the *route* to capture the sense of "traveling-in-dwelling" and "dwelling-in-traveling."[40] Much related to this is the notion of *transition*, which destabilizes a fixed time and space, and resists pinning down by preconceived identities or satisfaction with ready-made answers. Provisional and going in different directions, the notion of transition is radically open to new spaces and questions. In a more religious vein, there is the time-honored notion of *pilgrimage*, conceived as either an outward or upward journey, wherein one leaves the local and the familiar to search for the sacred, the global, or the divine. Whether one finds it or not is not the ultimate question, for in going, one leaves traces for others to follow and to critique. This brings me to the diasporic imagination, which occupies much of my current thinking.

DIASPORIC IMAGINATION

It made the colonies themselves, and even more, large tracts of the "post-colonial" world, always-already "diasporic" in relation to what might be thought of their cultures of origin. The notion that only the multi-cultural cities of the First World are "diasporia-ised" is a fantasy which can only be sustained by those who have never lived in the hybridized spaces of a Third World, so called "colonial," city.
Stuart Hall[41]

Diaspora has increasingly become a global phenomenon because of cultural and economic regrouping after decolonization, forced or voluntary migration, and transnational linkages in an age of global capitalism, communications, and transport. The term "diaspora," with its root in the Jewish experience, has become a traveling concept, appropriated by and extended to a wide range of cultural and geographical contexts: Jewish, Muslim, African, Latin American, Caribbean, Chinese, Japanese, Indian, Russian, Iranian, and so forth. In doing research for this original essay, I was surprised to find that there were almost 950 entries with the keyword "diaspora" in the titles within the Harvard University library system. On the Chinese diaspora alone, publications can be found issuing from the United States, Australia, France, Hong Kong, and Southeast Asia, in several languages. How can we capture and theorize the

---

40. James Clifford, *Routes: Travel and Translation in the Late Twentieth Century* (Cambridge, Mass.: Harvard University Press, 1997), 36.
41. Hall, "When Was the 'Post-colonial'?" 250.

diasporic moment, which has become such a far-reaching global experience at our historical juncture?

William Safran suggests that there are several characteristics of the Jewish diaspora, which include: (1) a collective forced dispersion of a religious and ethnic group from the "center" to two or more "peripheral" places, (2) retaining a collective memory or myth about the original homeland, (3) believing that they are not fully accepted by the host land, (4) regarding their ancestral homeland as their ideal home to be returned to when conditions are appropriate, (5) believing that they should be committed to the maintenance or restoration of the safety or prosperity of their homeland, and (6) continuing identification with that homeland, personally or vicariously.[42] Although Safran wants to create something like an "ideal type" based on the Jewish experience of Babylonian captivity and the Roman exile and their contemporary history after the establishment of the Jewish nation-state, when the return to the homeland becomes a historical possibility, his description does not fit the experiences of all the Jewish people at all times.[43] In particular, Jewish people scattered throughout the world may have constructed their "homeland" differently (and not just in Palestine), and secularized Jews may have an understanding about their communal myth/history quite different from orthodox religious narratives.

Since the 1960s, the term "diaspora" has been more generalized to apply to many contexts besides the classic cases of Jewish, Greek, and Armenian diasporas. Such a development is the result of the migration of formerly colonized peoples to the metropolitan West, the weakening of the nation-state, and the displacement of people because of the massive transnational flows of capital and labor in late capitalism. Today, the term "diaspora" shares a broader semantic domain that includes words like immigrant, expatriate, refugee, migrant worker, exile community, and ethnic and racial minorities.[44] Diasporic discourse is currently appropriated by peoples who may not have experienced forced dispersion, who do not share the longing for a return to the homeland, or who may shuttle between the homeland and the host land in continuous commute. It connotes at once the experience of decentered and yet multiple-centered, displaced and yet constantly relocated, peoples who crisscross many borders. Diasporic discourse has become a fluid and challenging site to raise questions about the construction of the center and the periphery,

42. William Safran, "Diasporas in Modern Societies: Myths of Homeland and Return," *Diaspora* 1 (1991): 83–84.

43. Jon Stratton, "(Dis)placing the Jews: Historicizing the Idea of Diaspora," *Diaspora* 6 (1997): 307.

44. Khachig Tölölian, "The Nation State and Its Others: In Lieu of a Preface," *Diaspora* 1 (1991): 4.

the negotiation of multiple loyalties and identities, the relationship between the "home" and the "world," the political and theoretical implications of border crossing, and the identity of the dislocated diasporized female subject. James Clifford describes the situation of those living in diaspora in this way:

> Diaspora communities, constituted by displacement, are sustained in hybrid historical conjunctures. With varying degrees of urgency, they negotiate and resist the social realities of poverty, violence, policing, racism, and political and economic inequality. They articulate alternate public spheres, interpretive communities where critical alternatives (both traditional and emergent) can be expressed.[45]

In his important book *The Black Atlantic: Modernity and Double Consciousness*, Paul Gilroy attempts to write back the diasporic history of black people in Britain, Europe, and the Caribbean into a history overdetermined by African American narratives. He argues that black culture is multiply centered, diasporic in the Atlantic space, and cannot be narrowly inscribed in an ethnically or racially defined tradition. He opines, "The history of the black Atlantic yields a course of lessons as to the instability and mutability of identities which are always unfinished, always being remade."[46] He is fond of using the images of the ships and sea voyages to imagine the map/history of crossing, migration, exploration, and travel. As his images of travel and movement from place to place may reflect a more masculinist script, I want to propose another trope to signify diasporic imagination. It is the image of the storyteller who selects pieces, fragments, and legends from her cultural and historical memory to weave together tales that are passed from generation to generation. These tales are refashioned and retold in each generation, with new materials added, to face new circumstances and to reinvent the identity of a people.

I want to conjure a female diasporic subject as multiply located, always doubly displaced, and having to negotiate an ambivalent past, while holding on to fragments of memories, cultures, and histories in order to dream of a different future. Such a female subject may not easily find a language with which to speak, as the heroine of Maxine Hong Kingston's classic Chinese American novel *The Woman Warrior* has her tongue clipped. And when she speaks, she has to constantly spin and weave the Chinese stories, legends, and myths into the new fabric of American culture and history.[47] In *The Joy Luck Club*, Amy Tan weaves a complex tapestry of women's memories across generations, with

---

45. Clifford, *Routes*, 261.
46. Paul Gilroy, *The Black Atlantic: Modernity and Double Consciousness* (Cambridge, Mass.: Harvard University Press, 1993), xi.
47. Maxine Hong Kingston, *The Woman Warrior: Memoirs of a Girlhood among Ghosts* (New York: Knopf, 1976).

both continuities and ruptures and elements from here and there—the United States and China.[48] The texture of the tapestry is rich and thick because there are two weavers at the same time—the mother and the daughter. The intergenerational difference of the weavers is clearly shown, as the same story may be knotted and tied differently to the whole piece, one showing the front, the other the reverse side in a quite contrasting manner.

Since the diasporic female subject is multiply located, it would require multiple tactics of intervention to unravel the dominant discourses and to negotiate a different cultural politics. In considering how to apply current theories in the emergent field of Chinese cultural and literary studies, Rey Chow demonstrates how the diasporic mind of "here" and "there" is constantly negotiating, shifting, and changing contexts. While she is skillfully trained in postmodern and poststructuralist theories, she is mindful that the postmodern moment may not have arrived in Third World countries, wherein the myths of modernity are still running strong. While adept in French and Euro-American feminist scholarship, she is keenly aware that much of this work is done in a relatively secure and safe environment, which may not be able to provide tools to weave the complex tales of women crossing borders, constantly shuttled between tradition and modernity.[49] At the same time, she does not let the postcolonial intellectuals in the West off the hook, challenging repeatedly their assumed positions as "authentic" spokespersons or informants of the Third World, when they are less vigilant about their own privileges of class, education, and sometimes gender.[50]

The works of Rey Chow and other theorists in diasporic and borderland discourses have helped me raise new questions and make fresh connections in the feminist study of religion. If religious tradition has been deployed to provide powerful narratives of "home" and "roots" for people, feminists need to interrogate how such narratives of communal identities have been constructed leaving out women and others whose identities have been policed or negated. Judith Plaskow's classic text *Standing Again at Sinai: Judaism from a Feminist Perspective* is important not only as the first book-length work of Jewish feminist theology, but also as a heart-wrenching reminder of how women's participation had been disallowed or discredited at critical moments in the shaping of communal story and memory.[51] Plaskow's work points to the need

48. Amy Tan, *The Joy Luck Club* (New York: Putnam's, 1989).

49. Rey Chow, *Writing Diaspora: Tactics of Intervention in Contemporary Cultural Studies* (Bloomington: Indiana University Press, 1993), 55–72.

50. Ibid., 17.

51. Judith Plaskow, *Standing Again at Sinai: Judaism from a Feminist Perspective* (San Francisco: HarperCollins, 1990).

for women to examine, however painful the process may be, the myth/history that a diasporic people have created and retold for survival and continuity. Bringing questions and ruptures to the "continuous" memory, Plaskow opens new possibilities for renegotiating identity and forms of community. At the same time, one has also to be mindful of the complicit roles women have played in spawning the myths of origin and upholding the rituals and celebrations that put them in a subordinate position, while simultaneously giving shape and meaning to "home" in a less than friendly environment. Laura Levitt writes about her ambivalent search for "home" as a Jew in the feminist discourse and as a female subject in rabbinic discourse. She writes:

> This home was the site of a great many conflicting desires. It was a place of both comfort and terror. The knowledge that home could be both de/ and re/constructed was visceral. . . . From the beginning I was engaged in a process of reconfiguring home on many fronts.[52]

Levitt's experience of finding herself simultaneously situated on the boundaries of different discourses, shifting in and out, is shared by Islamic feminists who must resist multiple axes of patriarchal marginalization at the same time: globalization, Islamization, and local nationalisms. With Islam as a transnational tradition and Mecca as the "home" of Muslims, Islamic feminists have to find their way through the dense web of significations of their national/ transnational, religious, and familial narratives. Miriam Cooke observes that they have to reject the Islamic groups' using women as passive cultural emblems, resist the patronizing "compassion" of Western feminists, and sustain their struggle through imaging an alternative vision of women in Islam. Since these Islamic feminists have to balance "their collective and individual identities while interacting with multiple others," Cooke argues that they have developed a multiple critique: "a multilayered discourse that allows them to engage with and criticize the various individuals, institutions, and systems that limit and oppress them while making sure that they are not caught in their own rhetoric."[53]

The image of having to negotiate with multiple others to develop an oppositional discourse and praxis can also be aptly used to describe a postcolonial feminist interpretation of Christianity. Diasporic imagination has to decenter and decompose the ubiquitous logic and "common sense" that says that the cultural form and norm of Christianity is defined by the West. It resists a pre-

---

52. Laura Levitt, *Jews and Feminism: The Ambivalent Search for Home* (New York: Routledge, 1997), 2.

53. Miriam Cooke, "Multiple Critique: Islamic Feminist Rhetorical Strategies," in *Postcolonialism, Feminism, and Colonial Discourse*, ed. Laura E. Donaldson and Kwok Pui-lan (New York: Routledge, 2002), 151.

determined and prescribed universalism and a colonial mode of thinking, by insisting on reterritorization of the West and by tracing how the so-called center and periphery of Christianity have always been doubly inscribed and mutually constituted. I have argued that Christian feminist theology is an intercultural discourse. For example, the nineteenth-century Western feminists developed their sense of superiority by deploying racial rhetoric and by portraying women in the colonies as waiting for their benevolence and their "gospel of gentility." Reading history cross-culturally, we can see the policing of European and American women's sexuality in the Victorian period occurred at a time when colonial and missionary discourse condemned promiscuity, polygamy, foot binding, and veiling in what has been called "colonialist feminism." A diasporic consciousness, which is located here and there, reads back metropolitan history and regimes of knowledge from multiple vantage points because people in diaspora are "outsiders" from within.[54]

Diasporic imagination recognizes the diversity of diasporas and honors the different histories and memories. The diasporic experiences of being a Chinese in the United States are different from those of a Chinese in Indonesia or in Peru. The Jewish, Armenian, Chinese, Japanese, and Asian Indian diasporic communities in the United States are different not only because of history and religious tradition, but also because of class, race, and ethnicity. As different "outsiders" within, the diasporic communities can learn from others to forge new cultural, religious, and political coalitions. I have been interested in Jewish feminist discourse for some time because I want to learn how Jewish women have reimagined their tradition, which is so much intertwined with Christianity. At the same time, as a Christian theologian, I have to pay attention to the charge of anti-Jewish and anti-Semitic tendencies that surface not only in white feminist theological reconstruction, but may also appear in the work of some Third World feminists.[55] But I have begun to see that apart from the Jewish-Christian axis, there are other axes that I can relate to Jewish women's experiences. In my postcolonial study of Christianity, I have found anti-Semitism, women's subordination, and colonialism as operating in the same episteme of nineteenth-century European religious discourse. The critique of liberalism and colonialism as two sides of the same coin by Laura Levitt has shed further light on the intersection of postcolonial critique, feminism, and religious discourse.[56] The

54. Patricia Hill Collins, "Learning from the Outsider Within Revisited," in idem, *Fighting Words*, 3–10.

55. Amy-Jill Levine, "Lilies of the Field and Wandering Jews: Biblical Scholarship, Women's Roles, and Social Location," in *Transformative Encounters: Jesus and Women Re-viewed*, ed. Ingrid Rosa Kitzberger (Leiden: Brill, 2000), 329–52.

56. Levitt, *Jews and Feminism*, 51–62.

imperial impulse of cleansing the Jews as the Others within Europe had much to do with the universalizing of Western culture and homogenizing the Others from without. The evolutionary understanding of religion in the late nineteenth century, for instance, was premised on Christianity's displacement of Judaism on the one hand and the falsification and misrepresentation of other wisdom traditions on the other.

As a Chinese in diaspora, I also detect a Chinese-Jewish axis that features prominently in my own consciousness. A quite significant number of leading scholars in Chinese studies in the United States are Jewish. My professor at Harvard, who guided me in the study of Chinese culture and listened patiently to my feminist critique, was the late Professor Benjamin Schwartz. A Jewish scholar of great learning, he had once spoken about the Tao of the Chinese in a Jewish synagogue. Some Jewish scholars, such as Vera Schwarcz, have found study of Chinese history to be a fruitful comparison with Jewish cultural memory. As a scholar of China and daughter of holocaust survivors, Schwarcz uncovers the resonance of narratives of Chinese intellectuals recovering from the Cultural Revolution and the halting tales of her parents. Her book *Bridge across Broken Time* seeks to create a bridge between Chinese and Jewish memories.[57] From the other side, the Jewish diasporic discourse and the critique of the narratives of "homeland" offer an invaluable mirror for my critical interrogation of Chinese identity, whether it is founded on the land, a "shared" tradition, or an "imagined community."[58] The Jewish diasporic discourse, in its radical critique of the Zionist ideology and the questioning of the power of the state of Israel, offers profound testimony to the richness and strength of the Jewish tradition, which provides comfort and consolation in times of weakness and prophetic witness in times of power.

A diasporic consciousness finds similarities and differences in both familiar territories and unexpected corners; one catches glimpses of oneself in a fleeting moment or in a fragment in someone else's story. For nearly seven years Indian diasporic writer Bharati Mukherjee could not write anything because of her experience of racism in Canada, and feared she would never write again. She was encouraged when she read Bernard Malamud's stories about Russian and Jewish people in the Lower East Side of Manhattan, and saw that "his characters were hers, his themes hers" and took up her pen again.[59] André

---

57. Vera Schwarcz, *Bridge across Broken Time: Chinese and Jewish Cultural Memory* (New Haven, Conn.: Yale University Press, 1998).

58. Benedict R. Anderson, *Imagined Communities: Reflections on the Origin and Spread of Nationalism*, rev. ed. (New York: Verso, 1991).

59. See the introduction written by Mukherjee's husband, Clark Blaise, in *The Workshop*, ed. Tom Grimes (New York: Hyperion, 1999), 163.

Aciman, a Jewish writer originally from Alexandria who writes about exile, diaspora, and dispossession and who calls himself "a literary pilgrim," may be right when he says:

> We write about our life, not to see it as it was, but to see as we wish others might see it, so we may borrow their gaze and begin to see our life through their eyes, not ours. Only then, would we begin to understand our life story, or to tolerate it and ultimately, perhaps, to find it beautiful.[60]

60. André Aciman, "A Literary Pilgrim Progresses to the Past," in *Writers on Writing: Collected Essays from "The New York Times"* (New York: Henry Holt, 2001), 6–7.

2

Searching for Wisdom

Sources of Postcolonial Feminist Theologies

My beads mark my presence
Beads of wisdom, beads of sweat

Mercy Amba Oduyoye[1]

My mother, of course, didn't know all these ideas, all these theories about the position of women. But she knew all these things in
practice.

Rigoberta Menchú[2]

In the summer of 1992 I met Felipe and Elena Ixcot and their children during
a conference in Stony Point, New York, that commemorated the five centuries
of struggles of Native peoples in the Americas. Felipe and his family were leaders of the weeklong event, during which they graciously shared their creation
myths and stories of their Mayan culture, as well as playing the marimba,
introducing us into the enchanting world of the Mayans. I vividly remember
one afternoon when Elena told us the meanings of the symbols and animals
on the colorfully woven costume she was wearing. Demonstrating how she
wrapped her braid with a colorful piece of cloth, she said she wore the braid
on the left side when the sun rose up and on the right side when the sun went
down. Even though the conquistadors had killed many Mayan people and
burned their books and stolen their artifacts, trying to convince the world that
Mayan civilization was destroyed, the Mayans have managed to keep their her-

1. Mercy Amba Oduyoye, *Daughters of Anowa: African Women and Patriarchy* (Maryknoll, N.Y.: Orbis Books, 1995), vii.
2. Rigoberta Menchú, *I, Rigoberta Menchú: An Indian Woman in Guatemala*, trans.
Ann Wright (London: Verso, 1984), 221.

itage, continue to sing their songs, and pass their wisdom on to their children from generation to generation.

About five hundred years ago, Africans, Asians, people in the Americas, the Caribbean, and Pacific peoples were forced to join the emerging world order with Europe as its center. The genocide of indigenous peoples, the colonial empire building, the imposition of slavery, and the systemic rape and sexual oppression of subjugated women led to the accumulation of wealth and power in the North and poverty and marginalization of people in the South. Since the Second World War, most of the colonies have become independent political entities, but they have been subjected to the continued control of the West through transnational capitalism, the mass media, information technology, international debt, and high-tech military intervention. The rapid transformation in the late 1980s has led to the redrawing of the world map, the reexamining of the legacy of the cold war, and the revisioning of the world order. Political scientist Samuel Huntington has predicted the "new world order" would be a clash of civilizations; his conceptualization of civilization and his forecast were much debated after September 11.[3] Another suggested it will be a struggle between the "Jihad" and the "McWorld"— the "Jihad" referring to religious and tribal fundamentalism and "McWorld" meaning global consumerist capitalism.[4] What will be the prospects of the formerly subjugated and colonized peoples in this "new world order"?

This chapter raises questions concerning the sources and resources of feminist theology from a postcolonial perspective. It scrutinizes the categories that are traditionally understood to be important sources of theology—experience, Scripture, tradition, and reason—and exposes how they have masked or excluded the voices of multiply marginalized women. A postcolonial feminist theology will have to look beyond the confines of Eurocentric tradition and the logic of the "Man of Reason" to be able to articulate the theological visions of those African women who continue to mark their presence with their beads and the Mayan women who persist in wearing their hair according to their tradition as a sign of preserving their culture.

WOMEN'S EXPERIENCE

Since feminist theologians cannot rely on the androcentric interpretation of Scripture and church tradition for truth claims, they have appealed to women's

---

3. Samuel P. Huntington, *The Clash of Civilizations and the Remaking of World Order* (New York: Simon and Schuster, 1996).

4. Benjamin R. Barber, *Jihad vs. McWorld: How Globalism and Tribalism Are Reshaping the World* (New York: Ballantine Books, 1996).

experience as a source and criterion of truth. Women's experience has been invoked to challenge the orthodox notions of revelation and dogma by exposing their historical and constructed character. It has also served as the basis to debunk and demystify the androcentric bias of humanism in liberal theology.[5] As Rosemary Radford Ruether has said: "The uniqueness of feminist theology lies not in its use of the criterion of experience but rather in its use of *women's* experience, which has been almost entirely shut out of theological reflection in the past."[6] But women's experience is the most contested source of feminist theology. First, as Grace Jantzen has pointed out, the concept of experience has deep roots in masculinist Enlightenment thinking, and the appeal to religious experience in the philosophy of religion gained prominence during the nineteenth century, a time of the triumph of imperialism and capitalism.[7] Second, feminist theologians have different opinions on what constitutes women's experience and how experience, given its diverse and changing nature, can be normative in theology. I would like to analyze four issues that have emerged in the discussion of the use of women's experience in feminist theology: the truth claim of theology based on women's experience, the universalizing tendency in feminist discourse, the postmodern challenge to the notion of "subject," and the politics of difference and solidarity among women.

Euro-American feminist theology, emerging in the late 1960s, was influenced by the intellectual climate and feminist theory developed at the time. The early wave of feminist theory, produced by Sherry Ortner, Gayle Rubin, and Nancy Chodorow in the 1970s, did not pay sufficient attention to cultural and historical specificity. These theorists were trying to search for grand theoretical explanations for the social reproduction of gender and women's universal subordinate status. The earlier works of Mary Daly and other white feminist theologians assumed that patriarchy was the common enemy of women, and set out to exorcise Christianity of its androcentric symbols and practices. But as Delores Williams has pointed out, there are substantial differences between white women's and black women's experiences of patriarchy in the United States. While white women are oppressed by patriarchy, they at the same time benefit from the protection and privilege bestowed by the patriarchal white-controlled American institutions. Such protection is not offered to black women.[8] Williams

5. Mary McClintock Fulkerson, *Changing the Subject: Women's Discourses and Feminist Theology* (Minneapolis: Fortress Press, 1994), 51–52.

6. Rosemary Radford Ruether, *Sexism and God-Talk: Toward a Feminist Theology* (Boston: Beacon Press, 1983), 13.

7. Grace M. Jantzen, *Becoming Divine: Toward a Feminist Philosophy of Religion* (Bloomington: Indiana University Press, 1999), 116, 118.

8. Delores S. Williams, "The Color of Feminism; or, Speaking the Black Women's Tongue," *Journal of Religious Thought* 43, no. 1 (1986): 48–49.

further observes that while white feminists give priority to issues such as rape, domestic violence, women's work, inclusive language, the gender of God, and so on, black women focus on the issues of physical survival, economic justice, educational opportunities, political participation, and encountering God as family (masculine and feminine, father, mother, and child).[9]

In the 1980s, the use of women's experience as a foundation or normative claim for feminist theology has been challenged by white women scholars. Sheila Greeve Davaney argued for a historicist understanding of women's existence and pointed to the futility of the search for sure foundations in feminist theology.[10] I do not think that the feminist theologians she critiqued, such as Rosemary Radford Ruether and Elisabeth Schüssler Fiorenza, were looking for ontological or metaphysical foundations for feminist theology, for they too understood women's experience as historically constructed. Davaney is more helpful when she warns against universalizing white women's experience to cover up racial and class privileges, when the appeal to women's experience is to "assert a universal and common essence that somehow defined women as women, and that laid the basis for feminist solidarity as well as providing the content for feminist reflection."[11] Responding to the charge of universalizing white women's experience, Schüssler Fiorenza proposes to shift from patriarchy, based on gender dualism, to kyriarchy (the rule of emperor/master/lord/father/husband over his subordinates), to signal more comprehensive, interlocking, and multiplicative forms of oppression.[12] In a colonial situation, the fact that there is a foreign kyriarchy superimposed on and intersecting with the local one requires a much more complicated analysis than her model has so far laid out. In such a case, the people of the colonizing nation, including the rich and the poor, men and women, dominate and exert control over the colonized people by imposing their systems of power.[13] For instance, once in the colonies, white women enjoyed freedom and power not accorded them at home because of their relatively privileged status.

9. Ibid., 52.

10. Sheila Greeve Davaney, "Problems in Feminist Theory: Historicity and the Search for Sure Foundations," in *Embodied Love: Sensuality and Relationship as Feminist Values*, ed. Paula M. Cooey, Sharon A. Farmer, and Mary Ellen Ross (San Francisco: Harper and Row, 1987), 79–85.

11. Sheila Greeve Davaney, "Continuing the Story, but Departing the Text: A Historicist Interpretation of Feminist Norms in Theology," in *Horizons in Feminist Theology: Identity, Tradition, and Norm*, ed. Rebecca S. Chopp and Sheila Greeve Davaney (Minneapolis: Fortress Press, 1997), 200.

12. Elisabeth Schüssler Fiorenza, *Jesus: Miriam's Child, Sophia's Prophet* (New York: Continuum, 1994), 14.

13. Musa W. Dube, *Postcolonial Feminist Interpretation of the Bible* (St. Louis: Chalice Press, 2000), 36.

Given the fact that women live in different, socially constructed worlds, what are the factors giving rise to a universalized way of thinking about women's experience? In *Inessential Woman*, Elizabeth Spelman traces the philosophical roots of this problem in the Western tradition.[14] Plato and Aristotle, she points out, used the argument that human natures are different to justify the unequal position of different groups in society. To counteract such claims, feminist thinkers such as Simone de Beauvoir and Nancy Chodorow choose not to highlight the differences among women to avoid a hierarchical ranking, and to posit that sexism affects all women alike. Spelman shows that "the notion of a generic 'woman' functions in feminist thought much the way the notion of generic 'man' has functioned in western philosophy: it obscures the heterogeneity of women."[15]

Universalizing, however, is more than the philosophical trap Spelman suggests. It is also rooted in the complex social and material contexts of the expansion of the West and the superimposition of Western cultures onto other peoples. Samuel Huntington has rightly pointed out: "Universalism is the ideology of the West for confrontation with non-Western cultures. . . . The non-Wests see as Western what the West sees as universal."[16] The assumption that the human experience of Western people is the norm for all people is not just an intellectual blind spot, but is heavily influenced by the colonial experience. The appeal to universal human experience and the inability to respect diverse cultures are expressions of a colonizing motive: the incorporation of the Other into one's own culture or perspective.

Just as white women in North America have to investigate how their gendered selves are also racialized, European women have to ask how their construction of gender is affected by their experience of colonizing others. Historian Evelyn Brooks Higginbotham has pointed out that the cult of true womanhood that taught women to be gentle, domestic, and ladylike in nineteenth-century America was not applicable for black women such as Sojourner Truth, who had to plow, plant, and gather into barn. Furthermore, the cult of white womanhood was made possible only with the exploitation of the labor of black women.[17] Borrowing insights from Higginbotham, we have to ask in what ways the accumulation of wealth and the exploitation of women in the colonies affected Victorian conceptions of womanhood. How did the experi-

---

14. Elizabeth V. Spelman, *Inessential Woman: Problems of Exclusion in Feminist Thought* (Boston: Beacon Press, 1988).

15. Ibid., ix.

16. Huntington, *The Clash of Civilizations*, 66.

17. Evelyn Brooks Higginbotham, "African-American Women's History and the Metalanguage of Race," *Signs* 17 (1992): 256–57.

ences of colonialism influence the literary imagination of British women? In the rush to reclaim Jane Eyre as the heroine of a "feminist" novel, why have so many feminists forgotten the imperialist impulse that set the stage for Charlotte Brontë's story?[18]

At a time when women are claiming their historical and theological subjectivity, postmodern and poststructuralist theories challenge the very notion of the "subject." These theoreticians point out that there is no autonomous and transcendent "I" that is not marked by social coding and discursively constituted. The ensuing debate among feminists focuses on whether we can speak of "women," of "subjectivity," and of "agency" and on the implications of these concepts for the struggle against injustice. Feminist theorists who work within a poststructuralist framework emphasize the subject as constructed by discourse. Others who are suspicious that this will lead to "no reality outside the text" argue for women's subjectivity and agency for social change. I will discuss this debate more fully in chapter 5.

In the United States, some of the second-generation feminist theologians use postmodern and poststructuralist frameworks to critique the essentialism of the earlier feminists. Rebecca Chopp, for example, points out that it was the reliance on the theoretical assumptions of modern theory that led the first generation of feminist theologians to universalize their experience and adopt an essentialist viewpoint. She critiques the basic tenets of modern theory, including the belief in a coherent self with essential structure, the importance attached to human reason, and the assumption that language is transparent and without ambiguities.[19] But Chopp's postmodern critique does not interrogate the racial prejudice of many of the influential thinkers who shaped modern consciousness, including Locke, Hume, and Kant. Their racist theories have justified the institution of slavery and the expansion of colonial powers to the ends of the earth.

While the critique of essentialism of first-generation feminist theologians has become commonplace,[20] Beverly Harrison has warned that the use of postmodern and poststructuralist frameworks is not without problems. The first generation of feminist theologians, she retorts, are more involved with the women's liberation movement and the structural changes of the church and society, while some second-generation feminists have been preoccupied with

18. This insight is from Gayatri Chakravorty Spivak, "Three Women's Texts and a Critique of Imperialism," *Critical Inquiry* 12 (1985): 244–47.

19. Rebecca S. Chopp, "Theorizing Feminist Theology," in Chopp and Davaney, *Horizons in Feminist Theology*, 216–17.

20. See, e.g., Chopp and Davaney, *Horizons in Feminist Theology* and the critical conversations about the book in "Roundtable Discussion: From Generation to Generation," *Journal of Feminist Studies in Religion* 15, no. 1 (1999): 102–38.

feminist theory current in the academy. For Harrison, those feminist theologians who are more interested in correct theory than political activism risk losing touch with the rank and file of the women's movement. They will be easily co-opted by the predominantly white neoliberal academy and use language and theory that are too abstract, understandable only by the elites.[21] As I have noted in chapter 1, second-generation black scholars and Asian scholars have also relied on postmodern and poststructuralist theories to critique the alleged essentialism in the construction of "Asianness" and "blackness." I think Harrison's observation may also be applicable, and her warning should be heeded. I do not deny that we need a pluralistic and diverse understanding of *mujerista*, Asian, or black women beyond the stereotypes, but I am keenly aware of the need for strategic deployment of certain generalized representations by a subalternized group at a particular stage of the political struggle, while keeping in mind that these representations are provisional, open to change, and negotiable.[22]

Since feminist theory and theology have shifted from focusing on women's commonalities to theorizing about women's differences, how can we speak of solidarity across differences? Two dominant metaphors have been offered to denote the solidarity of women in feminist theological discourse: "sisterhood" and "women-church." In *Beyond God the Father*, Mary Daly suggests that women who left the patriarchal church can form the "sisterhood of cosmic covenant."[23] The use of "sisterhood" has been criticized because of its familial ideology, its bourgeois individualism, its assumption of the nurturing and reproductive roles of women within the family, and its confining to women with common roots.[24] Furthermore, Daly displayed condescension toward her Third World "sisters" when she can only imagine Indian women as burned-alive immolated subjects, Chinese women as eroticized feet-bound subjects, and African women as geni-

A just question, my hope!

---

21. Beverly Wildung Harrison, "Feminist Thea(o)logies at the Millennium," in *Liberating Eschatology: Essays in Honor of Letty M. Russell*, ed. Margaret A. Farley and Serene Jones (Louisville, Ky.: Westminster John Knox Press, 1999), 156–71.

22. See the multilayered discussion of cultural identities in Stuart Hall, "Cultural Identity and Diaspora," in *Identity: Community, Culture, Difference*, ed. Jonathan Rutherford (London: Lawrence and Wishart, 1990), 222–37. For a discussion of strategic essentialism, see Serene Jones, *Feminist Theory and Christian Theology: Cartographies of Grace* (Minneapolis: Fortress Press, 2000), 42–48.

23. Mary Daly, *Beyond God the Father: Toward a Philosophy of Women's Liberation* (Boston: Beacon Press, 1973), 155.

24. See Elizabeth Fox-Genovese, "The Personal Is Not Political Enough," *Marxist Perspectives* 2 (1979–80): 94–113; and Elisabetta Donini, "Women and a Politics of Diversity: A Perspective of Radical Immanence," in *Ecofeminism and Theology*, ed. Elizabeth Green and Mary Grey, Yearbook of the European Society of Women in Theological Research, no. 2 (Kampen, the Netherlands: Kok Pharos Publishing House, 1994), 65.

tally mutilated subjects.[25] And we have to take note of how the space metaphor is used in "global sisterhood" or "cosmic sisterhood." Daly says that the new sisterhood occupies a new space. At times she refers to this space as abstract and mental, "a province of the mind."[26] At other times, she describes such space in concrete spatial terms: "our space set apart," "it is not static space but constantly moving space," and "its center is on the boundaries of patriarchy's spaces."[27] Daly's spatial imagery suggests there is a common space we can call "ours" and there is a "transparent space" in which we can find each other and ourselves because everything is visible under our gaze.[28] A postcolonial perspective must insist that not all women are included in the pronoun "our," the boundaries of patriarchy's space are not the same, and the transparent space is constructed because of the power difference implicit in the white gaze.

Elisabeth Schüssler Fiorenza has proposed the much-debated image of women-church. Her explanation of "women-church" has been constantly refined in response to critics[29] and she currently prefers to render it as "*ekklesia* of wo/men."[30] *Ekklesia* is a political term denoting an assembly of free citizens to decide their own affairs. Schüssler Fiorenza admits that the translation of the term to "church" does not hold together the double meanings of "democratic assembly" and "church."[31] In response to postmodern challenges, she introduces the term "wo/men" to indicate that "women are not a unitary social group but rather are fragmented and fractured by structures of race, class, religious affiliation, heterosexuality, colonialism, age, and health."[32]

In a postcolonial setting, "ekklesia of wo/men" can only be understood by a few academic elite. "Wo/men" is hardly translatable because other languages may not have similar devices to indicate the "fracture" and "fragmentation." Except in Korea where there is a small women-church in Seoul, the notion of women-church is a nonstarter in Asia because the church is associated not only with patriarchal authority but also with colonial power. Whether as the assembly of self-identified women and supportive men, or as a feminist space

25. Mary Daly, *Gyn/Ecology: The Metaethics of Radical Feminism* (Boston: Beacon Press, 1978).

26. Daly, *Beyond God the Father*, 156.

27. Ibid., 157.

28. Alison Blunt and Gillian Rose, "Introduction: Women's Colonial and Postcolonial Geographies," in *Writing Women and Space: Colonial and Postcolonial Geographies* (New York: Guilford Press, 1994), 6.

29. See Elisabeth Schüssler Fiorenza, *But She Said: Feminist Practices of Biblical Interpretation* (Boston: Beacon Press, 1992), 5–7.

30. Schüssler Fiorenza, *Jesus: Miriam's Child, Sophia's Prophet*, 24–27.

31. Schüssler Fiorenza, *But She Said*, 128.

32. Schüssler Fiorenza, *Jesus: Miriam's Child, Sophia's Prophet*, 24.

or public sphere to articulate a counterhegemonic discourse against kyriarchal power, the concept of women-church has not made explicit the material conditions in which women of such diversity can gather and work together. Why do formerly colonized subjects want to gather with their oppressors or to occupy the same space? How can we guarantee that such women-church is not a false inclusion, a democracy dictated by the interests of the powerful, and a space marked by the interests of the few?

I agree with womanist theologian M. Shawn Copeland when she urges us to go beyond the clichéd rhetoric of solidarity and raise the question of the moral obligation of speech in relation to action.[33] She elaborates:

> Solidarity is a wrenching task: to stand up for justice in the midst of injustice and domination; to take up simplicity in the midst of affluence and comfort; to embrace integrity in the midst of collusion and co-optation; to contest the gravitational pull of domination.[34]

She does not see difference as a problem for solidarity, because she insists "not difference, but indifference, ignorance, egoism, and selfishness are obstacles to solidarity."[35] The plurality of feminist theological discourse will be a threat and a fragmentation if the politics of identity leads to competition and parochialism. This happens when identity is seen as a possession or treated like a commodity to be exchanged and competed for in the market. On the other hand, the multiplicity of theological voices will provide mutual critique and enrichment if we understand that identity is always constructed in relation to others. We cannot understand ourselves without listening to others, especially to those we have oppressed or have the potential to oppress. Such critical engagement is the beginning of solidarity.

SCRIPTURE

For women who choose to remain within the Christian tradition, the Bible is an important source and resource for theology. Using the critical lens of a hermeneutics of suspicion, feminist scholarship has critiqued many traditional claims regarding the Bible. Feminist theologians have challenged the authority of the Bible, the boundary of the canon, and the androcentric bias of the text and the history of interpretation. Seeking to construct feminist models of

33. M. Shawn Copeland, "Toward a Critical Christian Feminist Theology of Solidarity," in *Women and Theology*, ed. Mary Ann Hinsdale and Phyllis H. Kaminski (Maryknoll, N.Y.: Orbis Books, 1995), 18.

34. Ibid., 29–30.

35. Ibid., 24.

interpretation, they have scrutinized the master's tools, created feminist frames of meaning, and developed different norms of interpretation. Reconstructing women's early Christian history, they examined the everyday lives of women, women's religious leadership in church and synagogue, and the marginalization of women in the patriarchalization of the church. Reclaiming the Bible as bread and not stone for women, they proposed new liturgical usage of the Bible, alternative methods of feminist Bible study, and liberating paradigms of teaching biblical studies.[36]

These issues are significant for women in diverse contexts. In the past two decades, feminist scholars from the Third World and from minority communities in the United States have increasingly contributed to the emerging feminist biblical scholarship.[37] From a postcolonial situation, we need to discuss a few issues before the Bible can be used as a resource for feminist theology: the use of the Bible in colonial discourse, the influence of colonialism in the academic study of the Bible, and the development of postcolonial readings of the Bible.

The Bible is an integral part of the colonial discourse. The introduction of the Bible and Christian faith to foreign lands was used to justify the political and military aggression of the West. For example, Hong Kong was ceded to the British in the same unequal treaty of 1842 that granted permission for missionaries to preach in the seaports of China. To teach the Bible and to spread the gospel were seen as the "civilizing mission" of the West, or the "white man's burden." Selective passages from the Bible were emphasized to justify this cause and to show the superiority of Christianity. For example, the Matthean commission of Jesus to go and make disciples of all nations (Matt. 28:19) and the Acts of the Apostles were mobilized in the eighteenth and nineteenth centuries to justify missionary efforts. These texts were dormant and disregarded by Reformation thinkers, but were reinvoked during the evangelical revival, which coincided with the rise of Western imperialism.[38]

Revered as the revealed Word of God, the Bible was seen as a prized possession of the West. The Bible thus served as a signifier that functioned to support Western beliefs in the inferiority and deficiency of "heathen" cultures.

36. For a helpful guide to the breadth of feminist scholarship on the Bible, see Elisabeth Schüssler Fiorenza, ed., *Searching the Scriptures*, vol. 1, *A Feminist Introduction* (New York: Crossroad, 1993).

37. See, e.g., Renita J. Weems, *Battered Love: Marriage, Sex, and Violence in the Hebrew Prophets* (Minneapolis: Fortress Press, 1995); Elsa Tamez, *The Amnesty of Grace: Justification by Faith from a Latin American Perspective*, trans. Sharon H. Ringe (Nashville: Abingdon, 1993); and Kwok Pui-lan, *Discovering the Bible in the Non-Biblical World* (Maryknoll, N.Y.: Orbis Books, 1995).

38. R. S. Sugirtharajah, "The Postcolonial Exploration of Collusion and Construction in Biblical Interpretation," in *The Postcolonial Bible*, ed. R. S. Sugirtharajah (Sheffield: Sheffield Academic Press, 1998), 95.

Furthermore, revelation through the Bible was regarded as special revelation. Insights and wisdom offered by other traditions could at best be classified as general revelation. This biased view reinforced the superiority of Christianity in the evolutionary scheme of "religions." Even the "great" theologians of the twentieth century were not immune from seeing the world from this superiority complex. Although Karl Barth insisted that God judges all "religions," including Christianity, he upheld the Bible as God's special revelation, more important than other revelations. Karl Rahner, in his generosity, would label people of other faiths as "anonymous Christians."[39]

The introduction of the Bible to other cultures was a mixed blessing for women. In order to teach women to read the Bible, Christian missions established girls' schools, catechism classes, and women's Bible study classes. However, the curriculum of these mission girls' schools was meant to instill the cult of true womanhood and to reinforce the domesticity of women.[40] Because of sexual propriety, women missionaries were sent to mission fields to work among women. These women missionaries wrote voluminous amounts of material about their lives in foreign lands in mission pamphlets, local religious news, and memoirs in order to generate support for mission. Such religious literature popularized the idea that "heathen" women were miserable, groping in the dark, waiting for the light to be brought to them. Before the advent of the mass media, this widespread literature shaped the perception of Third World women by European and American women, a legacy that had far-reaching effects in the past and continues to affect us in the present.

While the ethnocentrism of the missionaries working "in the frontiers" has been criticized, the academics studying the Bible in the metropolitan centers of Europe were seen as immune from cultural imperialism. In the past, little reflection has been given to the relationship between the emergence of the historical-critical method and the ascendancy of European power. There are two reasons for this oversight. First, the historical-critical method was seen as a progressive tool to challenge church dogma and the authority of the church in the West. Second, the method was considered by its practitioners as scientific, objective, and value-neutral. Focusing on the bygone eras of Hebrew history and the Greco-Roman world, historical-critical research was not supposed to be clouded by the political interests of its time.

However, if we examine historical criticism from an international frame, a different picture begins to emerge. I can cite as an example the first quest for

---

39. Karl Rahner, "Observations on the Problem of 'Anonymous Christian,'" in *Theological Investigations*, vol. 14 (New York: Seabury, 1976), 280–94.

40. See Kwok Pui-lan, *Chinese Women and Christianity, 1860–1927* (Atlanta: Scholars Press, 1992), 104–6.

the historical Jesus, a paramount concern of historical criticism.[41] Some of the key spokespersons of the first quest were not disinterested scholars. David Friedrich Strauss (1808–74) was an ardent supporter of a strong and unified Germany under the hegemony of Prussia, and defended the Prusso-Austrian war. Ernest Renan (1823–92), who was passionate about French landscape and taste, went to Phoenicia and Syria under the auspices of Napoleon III. His *La Vie de Jésus* reflected his love of French high culture and portrays a Jesus that served bourgeois interests. An interpreter of Bach's organ music, Albert Schweitzer (1875–1965) left behind not only the classic *The Quest of the Historical Jesus*, but also an autobiography detailing his life as a "jungle doctor."[42] Labeling African people as "primitive creatures" without much progress, his autobiography displayed deep-seated cultural superiority.

The expansion of Europe into other parts of the world affected these scholars' conceptualization of both Western civilization and Christianity. The comparative study of myths and "religions" at the time showed that "primitive" people were mythical, superstitious, and idolatrous. To prove that Christianity was superior to other wisdom traditions and could withstand the criticism of science, all the nonsense of virgin birth, miracles, and supernatural happening surrounding Jesus had to be questioned. This can be done only by a "critical" and "scientific" study of the Bible, which would lead to a historical Jesus free from the mythological trappings. The quest of the historical Jesus was far from being value-neutral. The political interests of Europe determined the questions to be asked, the gathering of data, the framework of interpretation, and the final outcome.

The rise of the historical-critical method must be situated with the cultural space and political configurations of its time. As Shawn Kelley has written:

> The nineteenth century was a time of vast social engineering, fueled by the widely held category of race. We should also note that this is the formative period of modern biblical scholarship, when its categories were developed, when seminal theories were proposed and debated, and when methods were developed and institutionalized. Is it possible that biblical scholarship could exist untouched by the ideological context during which it was conceived?[43]

41. Kwok Pui-lan, "Jesus/the Native: Biblical Studies from a Postcolonial Perspective," in *Teaching the Bible: The Discourses and Politics of Biblical Pedagogy*, ed. Fernando F. Segovia and Mary Ann Tolbert (Maryknoll, N.Y.: Orbis Books, 1998), 69–85.

42. Albert Schweitzer, *The Quest of the Historical Jesus* (1906; reprint, New York: Macmillan, 1968), and *Out of My Life and Thought: An Autobiography* (New York: Henry Holt, 1949).

43. Shawn Kelley, *Racializing Jesus: Race, Ideology, and the Formation of Modern Biblical Scholarship* (New York: Routledge, 2002), 25.

Thus, we must begin to question the assumptions about historical consciousness, historicity, and historiography of the so-called scientific historical-critical method. The historical questions raised by this method may be too limiting for people in other contexts. As Renita Weems has said, the negative result of the historical criticism has been "to undermine marginalized reading communities by insisting that their questions and experiences are superfluous to Scripture and their interpretation illegitimate, because of their failure to remain objective."[44] In fact, other cultures have their own assumptions about history and their own historical method. A *Western* historical criticism should not be taken as universally valid, because *Western* notions of historical process are not universally valid. We have to learn from other cultures insights to broaden our historical imagination.[45]

The discussion of postcolonial interpretation of the Bible has gained momentum among Third World scholars and intellectuals within the indigenous and diasporic communities.[46] R. S. Sugirtharajah has said that the postcolonial perspective will have to go beyond mimicry of Western critical method and an Orientalist valorization of ancient precolonial cultures.[47] It has to negotiate a different past, one that is not reified, glorified, or unitary. Employing tools from critical theory and cultural studies, postcolonial criticism exposes the relationship between power and knowledge, challenges both imperialist and nationalist claims, and maintains the posture of a "fighting literature." There are several characteristics of postcolonial criticism: (1) it challenges the totalizing forms of Western interpretation, exposing its co-optation by imperial interests and destabilizing its frame of meaning; (2) it is a counterhegemonic discourse, paying special attention to the hidden and neglected voices in the Bible; (3) it places the Bible within the multifaith context of many Third World situations; (4) it encourages and welcomes contributions from marginalized groups that have not been fully heard: the Dalits, the indigenous peoples, the migrants, people in diaspora and in borderland, and especially women in these communities; and (5) it debates with and draws insights from other hermeneutical frameworks, such as postmodernism.

Postcolonial feminist criticism looks at the Bible from the vantage point of women multiply oppressed because of race, class, conquest, and colonialism.

44. Renita J. Weems, "Reading *Her Way* through the Struggle: African American Women and the Bible," in *Stony the Road We Trod: African American Biblical Interpretation*, ed. Cain Hope Felder (Minneapolis: Fortress Press, 1991), 66.

45. See, e.g., Brian K. Blount, *Cultural Interpretation: Reorienting New Testament Criticism* (Minneapolis: Fortress Press, 1995).

46. A series titled "The Bible and Postcolonialism" has been published by Sheffield Academic Press with R. S. Sugirtharajah as the series editor.

47. See R. S. Sugirtharajah, *Asian Biblical Hermeneutics and Postcolonialism: Contesting the Interpretations* (Maryknoll, N.Y.: Orbis Books, 1998).

Laura Donaldson, a scholar of Cherokee and Scotch-Irish descent, has objected that feminist biblical scholars have often used the single-axis framework of gender in their interpretation, without paying attention simultaneously to other power dynamics at work in the text. She points out that while feminist scholars condemned the extravagance of violence, torture, murder, and dismemberment of the unnamed concubine in Judges 19,[48] they have not equally denounced the slaughtering of the Benjaminites and the burning of their cities in Judges 20. That story of war against the Benjaminites has been used to justify the genocide of the Native Americans and the taking of their land.[49] A postcolonial reading needs to pay attention not only to violence against women, but also to the political conflicts between different peoples, and the ways the stories in Judges help pave the way for the rise of the monarchy in Israel.

Postcolonial feminist criticism also examines how marginalized women in the Bible are rendered invisible, consigned to signify the Other, and denied speech. As we have seen, Delores Williams has used the story of Hagar to develop a womanist hermeneutics, arguing that there is not only the tradition of liberation in the Bible, but also the tradition of the struggle for survival and for quality of life. The Hagar story illustrates the multiple oppression of black women and reveals the tension and hidden scars of their relationship with white women in America. Another story that has been frequently discussed among postcolonial critics is that of the Syrophoenician woman (Mark 7:24–30; Matt. 15:21–28). White feminist critics have moved her from the margin to the center by either reclaiming her as a foremother of gentile Christians or by praising her faith and her wit, which enables her to win the argument over Jesus and broaden Jesus' perspective toward the Gentiles. Postcolonial critics, however, emphasize that she is a woman of other faith and her story is inscribed within the master discourse of the Christian canon and interpreted to justify mission to the Gentiles.[50] In addition, the significance of the daughter possessed by the spirit is highlighted to show how her illness, which is considered taboo, challenges the boundaries of normalcy, health, and order of society.[51]

Postcolonial studies contribute to the feminist study of the Bible in some significant ways, as I will discuss in the next chapter. It questions the presumptions and ideologies behind current paradigms of the study of women and

48. See, e.g., Phyllis Trible, *Texts of Terror: Literary-Feminist Readings of Biblical Narratives* (Philadelphia: Fortress Press, 1984), 65–91.

49. Laura Donaldson's presentation at the annual meeting of the Society of Biblical Literature, Boston, 2000.

50. See Kwok Pui-lan, "Overlapping Communities and Multicultural Hermeneutics," in *A Feminist Companion to Reading the Bible: Approaches, Methods, and Strategies*, ed. Athalya Brenner and Carole Fontaine (Sheffield: Sheffield Academic Press, 1997), 103–18.

51. Laura Donaldson's presentation at the annual meeting of the Society of Biblical Literature, Toronto, 2002.

gender in the Bible and challenges the construction of "feminist issues," the mobilization of data, and the frameworks of analysis. It contests the meaning of women's history by raising new questions and issues. Postcolonial theorists have argued that gender inequalities are essential to the structure of colonial racism and imperial authority. This has important implications for the analysis of the body politic of the early church, a colonized community living under the shadow of the Roman Empire. It also illuminates how the Bible was selectively cited to legitimate imperial authority through the claim that Christianity was superior to other religious traditions because of its treatment of women.

TRADITION

Tradition is an important source of theology for Catholic theologians. Although its influences may not be so pervasive in Protestantism, most Protestant theologians acknowledge it has bearings on their theological reflection. Discussion of tradition is critical in feminist theology because tradition defines the memory of the Christian community. Women have been shut out from shaping the collective memory of the church: they have been excluded from discussions of biblical canon, the debates on the creeds, the deliberation on church pronouncements, and the formulation of church doctrines. In the past several decades, Western feminist theologians have exposed the androcentric bias of Western Christian tradition. In her earlier work, Letty Russell identifies what she has called a "usable past" for women and delineates a liberating tradition within the tradition. Using the method of correlation, Ruether argues that the radical prophetic tradition can be correlated with women's experiences.[52] Schüssler Fiorenza, who is more critical of the biblical heritage, argues that all tradition must be scrutinized through the critical feminist lens, and women have the freedom to choose and reject traditions.[53]

A postcolonial feminist theologian brings another set of questions to tradition that are seldom raised by Western feminist critics. Women who are not of European or Euro-American descent often feel that the Western theological tradition has been taken for granted as the universal tradition for churches around the world. From a postcolonial perspective, the notion of tradition and its boundaries must be reconceptualized and radically expanded. Three issues

52. Letty Russell, *Human Liberation in a Feminist Perspective* (Philadelphia: Westminster Press, 1974); and Rosemary Radford Ruether, "Feminist Interpretation: A Method of Correlation," in *Feminist Interpretation of the Bible*, ed. Letty M. Russell (Philadelphia: Westminster Press, 1985), 111–24.

53. Elisabeth Schüssler Fiorenza, "The Will to Choose or to Reject: Continuing Our Critical Work," in Russell, *Feminist Interpretation of the Bible*, 125–36.

need to be addressed: the move beyond Eurocentrism to multicultural investigations of Christian tradition, the use of resources from cultures historically not shaped by Christianity, and future visions of tradition informed by feminist insights and struggles from the global context.

Eurocentrism means placing Europe at the center of attention, as the focus of the production of knowledge and as the reference point with which to judge human development and civilizations of the world. In *Provincializing Europe*, Dipesh Chakrabarty argues that Europe has constructed its history to put itself as the center of the world and as the model of modernity for all societies to follow. He seeks to displace the highly constructed "Europe" as the center from which all historical imagination gravitates, so that other narratives can be thought and articulated.[54] The need to decenter or provincialize Europe is paramount if we are to develop a vibrant, polycentric, and plurivocal theological imagination. For even though Christianity first emerged from West Asia on the shores of the Mediterranean and has had a long history of the Eastern Orthodox tradition, European history and theology have defined what is usually thought of as the Christian tradition.

In order to reterritorize Europe and to place Christian history in proper perspective, we must develop an international and multicultural understanding of Christian tradition. One of the ways is to examine how Christianity has defined itself through its contacts with Others: Judaism and Hellenistic traditions, the so-called barbarian attack, the rise of the Muslim world, and the encounter with cultures and peoples of the Third World. Since the conversion of Constantine, Christianity has had complex relationships with imperial powers. The rise and fall of empires affected theologians' outlook of the world order and their views about morality and social order. For example, Augustine's formulation of original sin would not have gained acceptance without the changing political situation in the late fourth and early fifth centuries.[55] A multicultural and postcolonial evaluation will help us see in sharp relief how the Christian tradition has been shaped by interactions with other cultures throughout the ages. For example, the work of Jewish feminist theologians, such as Judith Plaskow, has pointed to the troubling anti-Semitic trends in Christian thought, including those of feminists.[56]

Feminist theologians from many parts of the world can participate in this inquiry by posing new questions, revealing Western cultural bias, and con-

54. Dipesh Chakrabarty, *Provincializing Europe: Postcolonial Thought and Historical Difference* (Princeton, N.J.: Princeton University Press, 2000), 45–46.

55. Elaine Pagels, *Adam, Eve, and the Serpent* (New York: Vintage Books, 1989), 98–126.

56. Judith Plaskow, "Anti-Judaism in Feminist Christian Interpretation," in Schüssler Fiorenza, *Searching the Scriptures*, vol. 1, 117–29.

structing new discourse. For example, Elsa Tamez has critically evaluated the central notion of justification by faith from the vantage point of Latin American dehumanizing situations. To interrupt the subjective and individualistic interpretation of justification by faith in liberal Christianity, she accents the justice of God and interprets justification as God's solidarity, in Jesus Christ, with those who are excluded.[57] In her controversial presentation at the Canberra assembly of the World Council of Churches, Chung Hyun Kyung challenged doctrinal purity to argue for a life-affirming, survival-centered understanding of the work of Holy Spirit.[58] These insightful discussions have radically transformed our way of looking at traditional doctrines and enlarged our collective memory.

Besides critiquing Western Christian tradition, feminist theologians from diverse cultures are exploring the use of myths, legends, and other oral and literary resources for theology. In many Third World countries, the white male Christian tradition has been treated as the normative text, while indigenous traditions become the context in the processes of inculturation or contextualization. But from a postcolonial perspective, the primacy of the whole Western tradition is contested, and indigenous resources should be used on an equal footing and interpreted intertextually with Western sources. For example, Mercy Amba Oduyoye of Ghana uses the rich depository of popular wisdom in what she calls "folktalk" in her articulation of the saving power of God.[59] Some Asian feminist theologians also begin to draw insights from a wide array of resources, including Asian philosophy, shamanism, women's literature, and wisdom of women passed from generation to generation.

The use of these indigenous sources has been derogatorily condemned as syncretistic by some Western male theologians.[60] They look at the new theological landscape with alarm and suspicion because the terrain is so unfamiliar to them. They have completely forgotten that Rudolf Bultmann has called Christianity syncretistic, without any negative connotations.[61] In fact, it was the success of Christianity in adapting to its cultural context and its ability to change as circumstances required that made it a viable tradition. In the history of Western Christianity, many cultural elements of the West have been

57. Tamez, *The Amnesty of Grace*, 14.

58. See her controversial address at the World Council of Churches, "Come, Holy Spirit—Renew the Whole Creation," in *Signs of the Spirit: Official Report, Seventh Assembly*, ed. Michael Kinnamon (Geneva: World Council of Churches, 1991), 37–47.

59. Oduyoye, *Daughters of Anowa*.

60. See the discussion in Jeffrey Gros, "Christian Confession in a Pluralistic World," *Christian Century* (June 26–July 3, 1991), 644–46.

61. Rudolf Bultmann, *Primitive Christianity in Its Contemporary Setting* (London: Thames and Hudson, 1956), 177–79.

adopted, including philosophy, art, symbols, and music. Nobody raises an eyebrow and condemns such practices as syncretistic. But when feminist theologians around the world are exploring new expressions of faith, they are labeled as heretic or syncretistic!

The use of indigenous resources, however, does not mean going back to the premodern stage when one's culture and tradition were undefiled by the conquistadors and the colonizers. As Sugirtharajah has noted: "At a time when societies are becoming more multicultural, where traditions, histories, and texts commingle, and interlace, a quest for unalloyed pure native roots could prove to be not only elusive but also dangerous."[62] The exploration of one's cultural resources does imply challenging the hegemony of Europe and Euro-America and a determination to resist the globalized culture of the McWorld. Instead of "postmodern," which is largely based on the experiences of the Western world, Enrique Dussel has coined the term "transmodern" to describe the stage when formerly colonized peoples who have modernity thrust on them can look back and reassess its ambivalent legacy and its collusion with colonialism. At the same time, they would have the space and freedom to evaluate their own heritage and would not be coerced to act and think like the white people. Transmodernity will need to make room for the reason of the Other and, within such a project, "all ought to be welcomed in their alterity, in that otherness which needs to be painstakingly guaranteed at every level."[63] Just as the early church fathers did not need to give up Plato and Aristotle, Christians in the non-Western world would not be required to give up their cultures in order to become Christians. A genuine intercultural dialogue, for Dussel, "endeavors to construct not an abstract universality, but an analogic and concrete world in which all cultures, philosophies, and theologies will make their contribution toward a future, pluralist humanity."[64]

In the twenty-first century, I anticipate an increasing demand from formerly colonized and enslaved peoples to participate in shaping and expanding the Christian tradition. The postcolonial era offers unique opportunities for Christianity to interact with diverse cultures in the world, not as a missionizing force or a conquering ideology. With the shift of demographics of Christians and the majority of the Christians living in the South, Christianity is on the threshold of becoming more multicultural than before, and must open

62. R. S. Sugirtharajah, *Postcolonial Criticism and Biblical Interpretation* (Oxford: Oxford University Press, 2002), 197.

63. Enrique Dussel, *The Invention of the Americas: Eclipse of "the Other" and the Myth of Modernity*, trans. Michael D. Barber (New York: Continuum, 1995), 132. I benefited from conversations with Dussel in June 2003.

64. Ibid.

itself to learn from other traditions. Just as it has interacted in the past with Greek philosophy, scholastic thought, the Enlightenment, and the scientific revolution, Christianity will be brought into dialogue with other cultures in a more sustained way in the future. Christianity may not be the same as before, but it will learn to speak many peoples' tongues. Postcolonial feminist theologians, together with other liberation theologians committed to justice and peace, are at the forefront of this emerging process. They are aware that because of the lack of educational opportunities and access to the media, only a small number of Third World women's voices have been heard. In the future, they hope that creative ways can be found so that minority women in the Third World, indigenous women, migrant women workers, Dalit women, and younger women can contribute to the articulation of global feminist theologies.

REASON

The relation between faith and reason has been controversial in Christian theology. For Anselm, theology is *fides quaerens intellectum*, faith seeking understanding. But there have been continuing debates on whether faith transcends reason and whether God's revelation can be grasped by human's rational faculty or is beyond human's mental capacity. Although theologians may take different positions on these issues, few will go so far as to say that reason is not necessary in theological reflection. Karl Barth and other theologians even called theology a "science," in the German sense of the word, because it has a definite object of knowledge and utilizes a consistent method. In his *Systematic Theology*, Paul Tillich delineates helpfully the three senses in which theology can be considered rational. First, semantic rationality means that theologians should use their terms and language with precision and clarity. Second, logical rationality entails the capacity to make cogent and coherent argument and to avoid contradictions, although theology does make effective use of paradoxes and dialectical tension. Third, methodological rationality refers to the use of a consistent method, the crafting of an orderly presentation, and the construction of a systematic system as the final outcome.[65]

But "reason" is a heavily loaded term for postcolonial feminist theologians, because the "Man of Reason," created by the Enlightenment, has put them in double jeopardy. As women, they were considered emotional and irrational when compared to men, and as the colonized, they were seen as childlike and immature, in need of the tutelage of white people. In her article "Gender

65. Paul Tillich, *Systematic Theology*, vol. 1 (Chicago: University of Chicago Press, 1951), 54–55.

and Knowledge in Modern Western Philosophy," Sarah Coakley traces the development of various constructions of "Man of Reason" from Francis Bacon (1561–1626) to Immanuel Kant (1724–1804).[66] For Bacon, the task of the male scientific mind is to unlock the secret and eventually to gain control over nature, imagined to be feminine. Of critical importance is the much-criticized dualistic formulation of the mind over body by René Descartes (1596–1650). While in principle the exercise of reason is open to men and women, Descartes made it perfectly clear in his correspondence that the arduous demands of his particular form of abstract reasoning would be too rigorous for women to sustain. The formulation of an autonomous, individualist "Man of Reason," shunning sexual love and passion, reached its height in Kant, whose essay "What Is Enlightenment?" (1784) helped to define a historical epoch. Kant implored individuals to enter the public realm of universal reason and morality, and he imagined this autonomous individual as sexless. But he did not carry this through in his political writings, for he was adamant in supporting the bourgeois arrangement of husband ruling the household of his time because he believed in the "natural superiority of the husband over the wife."

If we place the Enlightenment in an international context, we will see that this passionless and autonomous "Man of Reason" created by the philosophers was considered not only fit to rule over women, but also destined to be the master of the world and to remake other peoples in his image. Sexual metaphors have been frequently deployed to describe the unequal relationship between the colonizers and colonized. Both the colonized people and their land have been referred to as feminine. Amerigo Vespucci named the land he "discovered" by the feminine form "Ameriga" or "America." As I have said, in his voyages in search of "the East," Christopher Columbus fantasized that the world was not round, but pear shaped and much like a woman's breast, with a nipple. Laura Donaldson has noted that "breasts possess a colonial history and that the female mammary glands constitute a significant part of imperialism's political anatomy."[67] Another metaphor frequently used to describe the colonized is that of the child, immature, unruly, and uncivilized, whose culture and society lagged far behind of those of Western men. Durkheim, Freud, and Jung have labeled native and indigenous peoples variously as elementary,

66. Sarah Coakley, "Gender and Knowledge in Modern Western Philosophy: The 'Man of Reason' and the 'Feminine' 'Other' in Enlightenment and Romantic Thought," in idem, *Powers and Submissions: Spirituality, Philosophy and Gender* (Oxford: Blackwell, 2002), 89–97.

67. Laura E. Donaldson, "The Breasts of Columbus: A Political Anatomy of Post-colonialism and Feminist Religious Discourse," in *Postcolonialism, Feminism, and Religious Discourse*, ed. Laura E. Donaldson and Kwok Pui-lan (New York: Routledge, 2002), 42.

primitive, dreamlike, or childlike, while missionaries in the field routinely treated native converts as if they were children or pupils. Poor and illiterate "heathen" women, in particular, were seen as objects of Western compassion, waiting to be taught to read and to take care of basic hygiene.

Given the misgivings about the "Man of Reason," should postcolonial feminists rely on reason when doing theology? Some have argued that postcolonial theology should not mimic the forms of Western philosophical debates and their styles of argument or create huge systematic tomes modeled after Barth or Tillich, and instead should be free to experiment with new forms and genres. While we still need more samples to envisage what these experimental forms would look like, I submit that whatever creative forms of doing theology emerge, they would still involve some use of reason, and it is pressing to discuss the style and shape of postcolonial reasoning. For this concerns the fundamental questions of the approaches of feminist epistemologies, the foundation of knowing, and the self-critique of postcolonial reason.

An obvious point to begin is with the deconstruction of the "transcendent I," who stands outside the material world and who derives knowledge and gains control through his mental and rational capacity. Sarah Coakley distinguishes three ways by which feminist epistemologies have called into question the privileged "knower" of mainstream epistemology. First, feminists unmask the political, gendered, and racial specificity of this "knower" and demand that other "knowers" previously excluded be taken into account. Second, some feminists have turned to a "standpoint epistemology," emphasizing that what you see depends on where you stand. Two major strands of standpoint theory have evolved: radical feminists such as Mary Daly argue that women's knowing is ontologically different from men's, and socialist feminists such as Nancy Hartsock stress the socially constructed nature of the knowing subject and partiality of vision. Third, some French feminist theorists have appealed to an intrinsically gendered form of "knowing" that is subversive to male reasoning.[68]

A postcolonial feminist epistemological framework debunks any claims to the innate form of feminine knowing that is superior to or subversive of male knowing and finds embarrassing any romanticizing suggestions that women, by nature, are more caring and loving, or closer to God. The colonizers have been both men and women, and female colonizers, either through their overt support of the colonial regimes, or through their silent complicity, have not

---

68. Sarah Coakley, "Analytic Philosophy of Religion in Feminist Perspective: Some Questions," in *Powers and Submissions*, 103. See also Rebecca Chopp, "Eve's Knowing: Feminist Theology's Resistance to Malestream Epistemological Frameworks," in *Feminist Theologies in Different Contexts*, ed. Elisabeth Schüssler Fiorenza and Mary Shawn Copeland, Concilium 1996, no. 1 (Maryknoll, N.Y.: Orbis Books, 1996), 116–23.

demonstrated themselves to know more about loving and God. Thus, a mere shifting from the male to the female knowing subject is not enough, without being vigilant of the temptation to step into the position of the masculinist knowing subject, who assumes sovereign status in controlling the material world as well as the production of knowledge. A postcolonial knowing subject insists that changing the gender of the subject is not enough, without simultaneously taking into consideration how race, religious affiliation, sexual orientation, age, physical abilities, and colonialism form an intricate web to shape both the identity of knower and her "situated knowledge."

The discussion on postcolonial reason must also debunk the myth that there is an evolutionary development in human thinking which entails an inevitable progress from "mythos" to "logos." Myths have been seen as opposed to, or incompatible with, rationality. The earlier or "primitive" stage of human civilization was called the mythic stage, and mythological consciousness has to be replaced with science and technological reason in the march toward modernization and secularization. Partly because of their mission to save the "lost civilizations" and partly because of their fascination with the Other, Western anthropologists and historians of religions have been obsessed with the myths and legends of indigenous and native peoples. They treated these myths as rich depositories of a human mind that is not dominated by consciousness, reason, and technical proficiency. Mircea Eliade has argued that archaic myths are important for modern people and has described favorably Western people's fascination with Asian religious practices, ancient and prehistoric spiritual values, and shamanistic practices as a way to compensate for the stress and alienation of modern life.[69]

A postcolonial critic is keenly aware that the myths and religiosity of non-Western peoples have been appropriated and commercialized to ease the ills of and provide healing for modern living. She would refuse to create "mighty opposites"[70] and see the world in a dichotomous manner: that myth and reason are diametrically opposite to each other, and that Easterners or indigenous peoples think in mythical or symbolical ways, while Westerners think in scientific and logical ways. Such simplified generalizations not only are reductionistic, they also fail to appreciate that different societies interpret myths in radically different ways, and do not necessarily see them as contrary to reason. In fact, myths often show a form of reasoning that has its own logic, though

69. Mircea Eliade, "Waiting for the Dawn," in *Waiting for the Dawn: Mircea Eliade in Perspective*, ed. David Carrasco and Jane Marie Law (Boulder, Colo.: University Press of Colorado, 1991), 11–16.

70. See Zhang Longxi, *Mighty Opposites: From Dichotomies to Differences in the Comparative Study of China* (Stanford: Stanford University Press, 1998).

different from that of our own. Myths provide a focus for thought, put the mind of the contemporary in touch with that of the forebears and ancestors, validate present practice in the wider picture of time and space, and offer a set of attitudes and ideas for grounding group identity.[71] In the midst of the environmental crisis, many Western thinkers have spoken of the need for the reenchantment of the world and the discovery of the power of ancient myths, such as the Gaia story.[72] It seems to me that in the face of Derrida's persistent challenge of logocentrism in Western philosophy and the postcolonial critique of the studies of myths,[73] a simple dichotomy between mythos and logos is untenable and we have to attend to cultural specificity in terms of modes of thinking and reasoning.

This leads us to the question whether there exists an international division of labor in feminist work, that is, will Third World feminists merely talk about stories of their lives, while First World feminists do theory? Implicit in this question is that "theory" means Western academic feminist theory, with a distinct and strong French accent. We need to recall that during the colonial period, Third World peoples provided raw data and materials for Western "experts" to examine, analyze, and theorize. In our present time, those who are not engaged with high academic theory and discourse are considered naive, unsophisticated, and uninitiated. I do not underestimate the usefulness of theory, be it Marxist, feminist, poststructuralist, or postcolonial, but I am critical of the heavy-handedness of the superimposition of Western theory onto Third World realities. The warnings by Barbara Christian in her essay "The Race for Theory," published eighteen years ago, are still relevant today. As a black literary critic, Christian bemoans the hegemony of Western philosophies and French feminist theories in the academy, and insists that people of color have always theorized, not in the form of Western abstract logic, but often "in narrative forms, in the stories we create, in riddle and proverbs, in the play with language, since dynamic rather than fixed ideas seem more to our liking."[74] She implores us to read black women's literature with an eye to develop a literary theory that is rooted in practice, which is culturally relevant and appropriate. To heed her charge, postcolonial feminists need to take each other's works seriously and establish an alternative community of discourse so that

71. Kenneth McLeish, *Myth: Myths and Legends of the World Explored* (London: Bloomsbury, 1996), v.

72. Anne Primavesi, *Gaia's Gift: Earth, Ourselves and God after Copernicus* (London: Routledge, 2003), 118–21.

73. See especially the critique of Eliade's work in Russell T. McCutcheon, *Manufacturing Religion: The Discourse on Sui Generis Religion and the Politics of Nostalgia* (New York: Oxford University Press, 1997).

74. Barbara Christian, "The Race for Theory," *Cultural Critique* 6 (1987): 52.

we can encourage each other in theory building. Henry Louis Gates Jr. has warned against the uncritical use of Western theory:

> The concern of the Third World critic should properly be to understand the ideological subtext which any critical theory reflects and embodies, and the relation which this subtext bears to the production of meaning. . . . To attempt to appropriate our own discourses by using Western critical theory uncritically is to substitute one mode of neocolonialism for another.[75]

The Third World critic can ill afford to remain insular or parochial, for, as Edward Said has said, ideas and theories, like persons, travel from place to place and such movements are an integral part of academic life and an enabling condition of intellectual activity. But when the traveling theory is applied, it would have to be accommodated to the new situation and assume "a new position in a new time and place."[76] The power dynamics embedded in such traveling theory when it migrates from the West to other parts of the world must be seriously considered and attended to, given the enormous difference of the cultural, social, and economic backgrounds of the First and Third Worlds.

I would like to conclude this chapter by emphasizing the necessity of self-critique of postcolonial intellectuals. The works of postcolonial critics have also been criticized as highly abstract and difficult, paying more attention to Western literary theory and criticism than to political economy. As such, their output is in danger of speaking primarily to the Western audience and engaging more with the concerns of the Western academy than with actual social and political change. In her book *A Critique of Postcolonial Reason*, Gayatri Chakravorty Spivak chastises postcolonial intellectuals as performing the roles of former "native informants," by assuming to speak for and represent the oppressed.[77] She underscores the privileges of these intellectuals and the great gulf that separates them from the subalterns. As someone who is highly skilled in deconstruction theory, feminism, and Marxism, Spivak has turned her attention to translating Bengali writer and activist Mahasweta Devi's stories, and during the last decade has been involved in literacy projects in India. Spivak challenges postcolonial intellectuals to regard our privilege as our loss.

75. Henry Louis Gates Jr., "Editor's Introduction: Writing 'Race' and the Difference It Makes," in *"Race," Writing, and Difference*, ed. Henry Louis Gates Jr. (Chicago: University of Chicago Press, 1996), 15.

76. Edward W. Said, "Traveling Theory," in idem, *The World, the Text, and the Critic* (Cambridge, Mass.: Harvard University Press, 1983), 227.

77. Gayatri Chakravorty Spivak, *A Critique of Postcolonial Reason: Toward a History of the Vanishing Present* (Cambridge, Mass.: Harvard University Press, 1999), ix.

Because of our relatively affluent position and education, we do not have the life experience and perspectives of those less fortunate. Therefore, though with good intention, we may not be able to see the world from the underside of history. Such an honest admission of our privileged location and our limited epistemological vision does not undermine our work, but it does qualify it and reminds us to listen to the voices of those who are less privileged and those whom we have the potential to oppress.

3

Making the Connections

Postcolonial Studies and Feminist Biblical Interpretation

> In their feminist practices of reading and writing, Two-Thirds
> World women call for the decolonization of inherited colonial edu-
> cation systems, languages, literary canon, reading methods, and the
> Christian religion, in order to arrest the colonizing ideology packed
> in the claims of religious conversion, Western civilization, mod-
> ernization, development, democratization, and globalization.
>
> *Musa W. Dube*[1]

Some time ago, when I was reading the writings of women missionaries in a
library archive, I came across a fascinating story about a Chinese woman. A
female missionary reported at the turn of the twentieth century that a Chinese
woman who could barely read used a pin to cut from the Bible verses where
Paul instructed women to be submissive and remain silent in church. I have
long forgotten where I read the story, but it lodged in my mind as a vivid testimony to the fact that Chinese women were not passive recipients of biblical
teachings. Instead of subscribing to Paul's sexist ideology, this woman exercised
the freedom to choose and reject what she thought was harmful for women.

A postcolonial feminist interpretation of the Bible creates a space so that the
reading of this and other women in similar colonial and semicolonial situations
can be remembered in order to enliven our historical and moral imagination.
For this story demonstrates how oppressed women have turned the Bible, a
product introduced by the colonial officials, missionaries, and educators, into

---

1. Musa W. Dube, "Postcoloniality, Feminist Spaces, and Religion," in *Postcolonialism, Feminism, and Religious Discourse,* ed. Laura E. Donaldson and Kwok Pui-lan (New
York: Routledge, 2002), 115.

a site of contestation and resistance for their own emancipation. Continuing this critical task, postcolonial feminist critics not only recover the insights of ordinary women readers but also unmask the myriad ways in which biblical scholars, feminists among them, have been complicit with or oblivious to colonialism and neocolonialism.

POSTCOLONIAL CRITICISM
AND FEMINIST BIBLICAL INTERPRETATION

While postcolonial criticism has been used by literary critics and by those in humanities and social sciences for some time, its use in the field of religious studies and Christian studies is fairly recent. Postcolonial theories were introduced to the field of biblical studies in the 1990s, mainly through the works of critics from the Third World and from racial minorities in the United States. In *Decolonizing Biblical Studies*, Fernando Segovia traces the development of biblical criticism from the early nineteenth century through the end of the twentieth.[2] He argues that until the last quarter of the twentieth century, historical criticism was the reigning paradigm in the discipline. Beginning in the 1970s and continuing to the present, biblical studies experienced the rapid rise of literary criticism and cultural or social criticism. The late 1980s and early 1990s saw the irruption of cultural studies and the resulting competing modes of discourse. He characterizes such a development as a process of "liberation" and "decolonization," in which the universal, objective reader is gradually replaced by the interested, local, and perspectival reader. He notes that the field of biblical studies is no longer the monopoly of white, middle-class men. The addition of Western women, men and women from outside the West, as well as non-Western minorities in the West has resulted in a diversity of method and theory, an expansion of scope of inquiry, and an explosion of interpretive voices.

It is important to stress that postcolonial criticism does not reject the insights of historical criticism, because much of the work of the historical critics contributes to the understanding of the "worldliness" of the text, that is, the material and ideological backgrounds from which the texts emerged and to which the texts responded. The difference is that postcolonial critics pose new questions about the historical and literary contexts and thereby enlarge the moral imagination of the interpretive process. For example, postcolonial critics scrutinize the colonial entanglements in the texts, highlighting the

---

2. Fernando F. Segovia, *Decolonizing Biblical Studies: A View from the Margins* (Maryknoll, N.Y.: Orbis Books, 2000), 121–22.

impact of empire and colonization in shaping the collective memory of the
Jewish people, the literary production and redaction of biblical texts, and the
process of the formation of the canon. The cultural production and literary
imagination of the Hebrew people and early Christians were invariably shaped
by the social and political domination of successive empires: in Assyria, Babylon, Persia, Greece, and Rome. Postcolonial critics in their reconstructive
readings of the text highlight the struggles and resistance in the different colonial contexts, lift up the voices of women and other subalterns, and are sensitive to postcolonial concerns such as hybridity, deterritorialization, and
hyphenated or multiple identities.[3] Thus, postcolonial criticism has the potential to open up the interpretive process, making the Bible a highly relevant and
invaluable resource for our postcolonial situation.

Some may wonder whether postcolonial analysis, developed largely from
the experiences of modern colonialism, can be applicable to ancient situations,
which may not be comparable to modern cases.[4] I would like to point out that
history is interpreted according to the mental apparatus and framework we
have constructed. Since the 1970s, biblical scholars using social scientific
methods, including those with a Marxist bent, have not shied away from
employing "modern" theories to illuminate ancient societies. Postcolonial
theories add a critical dimension by focusing on the empire and colonization,
the center and the periphery, the exiled and the diasporized. For example, in
his comparison of Trito-Isaiah with the postcolonial situation of Hong Kong,
Archie Lee does not argue that imperial/colonial experience is similar across
time and culture, though there may be resemblances.[5] What he seeks to show
is that the problems facing the hybridized Hong Kong people in returning to
China may shed new light on the meaning of return as well as the quarrels and
disputes in the postexilic community. In doing so, he invites us to use a postcolonial imagination to enter into the cultural world of the returnees after the
exile for a better comprehension of the complex and wrenching identity-
formation process.

Besides illuminating ancient texts, postcolonial criticism makes visible the
ways modern readings of the texts collude with colonial interests in the West.
Emerging during the expansion of European powers, the historical-critical
method gathered momentum as imperialism and colonization reached its

3. R. S. Sugirtharajah, *The Bible and the Third World: Precolonial, Colonial and Postcolonial Encounters* (Cambridge: Cambridge University Press, 2001), 251–53.
4. See David Jobling's contribution to *"The Postcolonial Bible*: Four Reviews," *Journal for the Study of the New Testament* 74 (1999): 117–19.
5. Archie C. C. Lee, "Identity, Reading Strategy and Doing Theology" *Biblical Interpretation* 7 (1999): 156–73.

zenith in the late nineteenth century. Shaped by the drive toward rationality and the development of historical consciousness begun in the Enlightenment, the historical-critical method was embedded in the sociocultural ethos of its particular time. Hailed as scientific, academic, and objective, its nineteenth-century practitioners employed Orientalist philology, racial theory, and an evolutionary understanding of "religions."[6] Once the historical-critical method was established as the norm for studying the Bible, it excluded the validity of other contextual readings and devalued the contributions of nonacademic interpretations.

In addition to scrutinizing biblical interpretive practices in the West, postcolonial studies also provide a useful framework to assess the history of biblical interpretation in the Third World. In the last three decades, biblical scholars and theologians from the Third World and from indigenous and Dalit communities have presented a wide array of biblical criticism using insights from oral hermeneutics, literary theory, reader-response criticism, and other indigenous methods. R. S. Sugirtharajah has provided a useful comparative framework to organize the growing data of biblical interpretations coming from Asia, Africa, and Latin America to discern their different hermeneutical interests, and to compare and contrast the many approaches.[7] Based primarily on biblical interpretation and commentaries from the South Asian context, Sugirtharajah proposes four different approaches to Asian hermeneutics, which he argues can also be found in other parts of the Third World. The Orientalist mode invokes the golden age of Indian civilization, based on Sanskrit and Brahmanical texts. Contrary to this, the anglicists try to replace the indigenous texts with Western learning, so that the colonized can be assimilated to the culture of the colonizers. The nativist mode challenges both Western theories and the elitist Orientalist approach by reviving the vernacular tradition and the use of popular resources. Sugirtharajah espouses the postcolonial approach, which he thinks can best analyze the colonial trappings in biblical texts; offer alternative readings that address nationalism, identity, ethnicity, and subaltern and feminist concerns; as well as interrogate both colonial and metropolitan interpretations.

Although the works of postcolonial male critics may include some discussion of women's scholarship, gender remains a marginal issue in their overall analysis. Postcolonial feminist critics have stressed the intricate relationship

---

6. Kwok Pui-lan, "Jesus/The Native: Biblical Studies from a Postcolonial Perspective," in *Teaching the Bible: The Discourses and Politics of Biblical Pedagogy*, ed. Fernando F. Segovia and Mary Ann Tolbert (Maryknoll, N.Y.: Orbis Books, 1998), 69–85.

7. Sugirtharajah, *The Bible and the Third World*; and R. S. Sugirtharajah, *Asian Biblical Hermeneutics and Postcolonialism: Contesting the Interpretations* (Maryknoll, N.Y.: Orbis Books, 1998).

between colonialism and patriarchy such that the analysis of one without the other is incomplete. Those male postcolonial critics who leave out gender run the risk of overlooking that colonialism involves the contest of male power and that patriarchal ideology is constantly reshaped and reformulated in the colonial process. On the other hand, those feminist critics who isolate gender from the larger economic and colonial context court the danger of providing a skewed interpretation that tends to reflect the interests of the socially and economically privileged. The exploration of the interstices of different forms of oppression under the shadow of the empire constitutes the exciting postcolonial feminist project. As Asian American biblical scholar Gale Yee has said, "I have become convinced in my feminist investigations of the Bible over the years that the study of gender must include race, class, and colonial status as categories of analysis."[8]

Feminist scholars interested in postcolonial criticism adopt different approaches of interpretation, from ideological criticism to literary-rhetorical method, but they share some common concerns. First, they want to investigate how the symbolization of women and the deployment of gender in the text relate to class interests, modes of production, concentration of state power, and colonial domination. In *Poor Banished Children of Eve*, Gale Yee uses a sophisticated ideological criticism to reveal how the "wicked women" in the Hebrew Bible function as "sexual metaphors" and "symbolic alibis" for the contests of male elites who wield political, economic, and social power. For instance, in Ezekiel 23, two sexually insatiable sisters were used to symbolize the two rival kingdoms, personified as Oholah (Samaria) and Oholibah (Jerusalem), in love with the foreign nations of Egypt, Assyria, and Babylon. Yee argues that the violent pornographic story must be situated in the context of colonial relation between Israel and Judah and the foreign powers, which led eventually to the conquest and exile of the elites.[9] The story was seen through the lens of a colonized male of the priestly elite during the final days of the nation and the imminent exile of the upper-class sector. In the text, the woman was used as a trope for the land and the nation, and sexual images became tropes for colonial dominance. Ezekiel subscribes to the patriarchal ideology of gender and depicts Judah and Israel as feminine, the subjugated colonial subjects, while the foreign aggressors are hypermasculine. The foreign Others were racialized and sexualized, with far superior male prowess and virility than that of the emasculated Judean leadership. For Yee, Ezekiel 23 was an attempt of the prophet to deal with the personal and collective trauma of colonization, conquest, and exile of

---

8. Gale A. Yee, *Poor Banished Children of Eve: Women as Evil in the Hebrew Bible* (Minneapolis: Fortress Press, 2003), 4.
9. Ibid., 111–34.

the Judean royal and priestly aristocracy, of which he was a part. Her multiaxial interpretation demonstrates why focusing on gender and sexuality alone, as some feminist interpreters have done, fails to grasp the polyvalent signification of the sexual metaphors. She writes: "The pornography of these texts should be coded not simply as another form of patriarchal violence, but as colonial ethnic conflict framed as a sexualized encounter."[10]

Second, postcolonial feminist critics pay special attention to the biblical women in the contact zone and present reconstructive readings as counternarrative. A contact zone is the space of colonial encounters where people of different geographical and historical backgrounds are brought into contact with each other, usually shaped by inequality and conflictual relations.[11] One such figure is the prostitute Rahab in Joshua 2 during the siege of Jericho. In the story, Rahab was rewarded for having protected the spies sent by Joshua, and as a Canaanite Other, she crossed over to live in Israel and was elevated to high status as the ancestress of David and Jesus (Matt. 1:5). Laura Donaldson reads the Rahab story not from the Jewish but from the Canaanite perspective, and situates it within the cultural and historical predicament of Native women during conquest. Rahab's story reminds her of the co-optation and exploitation of Native women's sexuality as an integral part of the white colonial myths and ideology.[12] The story of Rahab illustrates the double colonization of women: their bodies are open to taking by foreign men, and their land is possessed. Musa Dube of Botswana uses the story as a springboard for her postcolonial feminist method and calls it "Rahab's reading prism." She says Rahab's reading prism highlights "the historical fact of colonizing and decolonizing communities inhabiting the feminist space of liberation practices."[13] Dube argues that those feminist readers who belong to the colonizing community will need to adopt a decolonizing stance, while doubly colonized women will have to privilege imperial oppression over a patriarchal one. A decolonizing reading would need to present a counternarrative by lifting up the memory of the many "Rahabs" who have risen up against the colonizers and subverted the master's genre. Such a reading will cultivate new postcolonial spaces for spinning new narratives that speak of equality and freedom.

10. Ibid., 111.

11. Mary Louise Pratt, *Imperial Eyes: Travel Writing and Transculturation* (London: Routledge, 1992), 6.

12. Laura E. Donaldson, "The Sign of Orpah: Reading Ruth through Native Eyes," in *Vernacular Hermeneutics*, ed. R. S. Sugirtharajah (Sheffield: Sheffield Academic Press, 1999), 29–32.

13. Musa W. Dube, *Postcolonial Feminist Interpretation of the Bible* (St. Louis: Chalice Press, 2000), 122.

Third, postcolonial feminist critics scrutinize metropolitan interpretations, including those offered by both male and feminist scholars, to see if their readings support the colonizing ideology by glossing over the imperial context and agenda, or contribute to decolonizing the imperializing texts for the sake of liberation. Using the story of the Syrophoenician woman in Matthew 15:21–28 as a case study, Dube shows that white male scholars have not paid attention to how the divine claims of salvation history, Davidic kingship, and universal mission can be used as colonizing ideology. Moreover, they have shown no effort to investigate the relation among gender, mission, and empire. In short, their gender, race, and class privilege accounts for their lack of interest in problematizing the power relations inscribed in the text.[14] Although white feminist scholars have focused on gender as a major category of analysis, their works in general do not consider the imperial context of Matthew and how the different local groups were vying for the favor of the empire. They have also failed to question the ideology of mission in the text and continue to assume that biblical traditions are universally valid for all cultures. Thus, even with the good intention of reclaiming the Gentile woman as a foremother within the history of early Christianity, their reconstructive project does not deconstruct the power relation embedded in the mission passages. From her analyses of the works of male and female metropolitan interpreters, Dube concludes that, by and large, they have bracketed imperialism and thus subscribed to it. Moreover, her scrutiny of white feminist interpretations has shown that "the patriarchal category of analysis does not necessarily translate into imperial criticism."[15]

Fourth, in order to subvert the dominant Western patriarchal interpretations, postcolonial feminist critics, especially those in Africa, emphasize the roles and contributions of ordinary readers. As Dube explains, ordinary readers are not just nonacademic readers—they include most Third World readers, who are outside the accepted academic traditions of the biblical interpretation and who are relegated to the periphery of the global economic structures. The inclusion of ordinary readers is meant to enlarge the interpretive community and to stress that these readers possess the "suppressed knowledges" that academic elites often dismiss. When Dube and her colleagues went to visit women in the African Independent Churches, they did not assume that as academically trained women they had the knowledge to teach the women. They went not just to *read with* the nonacademic women, but also to *read from* them, believing that these women offer strategies of interpretation born from their struggles

14. Ibid., 168–69.
15. Ibid., 184.

with imperialism and sexism.[16] They find that these ordinary women readers are not preoccupied with a textual approach, but adopt communal and participatory modes of interpretation, through the use of songs, dramatized narration, and interpretation through repetition. As members of the professional guild, the academically trained women often find that they are not equipped to understand these lively oral modes of engaging the Bible, and have to retool and relearn from this experience.[17]

Finally, postcolonial feminist critics pay increasing attention to what Mary Ann Tolbert has called the politics and poetics of location. By politics of location, Tolbert means the complexity of one's social background, such as gender, race, and sexual orientation, as well as one's national and institutional context and economic and educational status, which determine who speaks and who is likely to listen. By poetics of location, she says, "Any interpretation of a text, especially a text as traditionally powerful as the Bible, must be assessed not only on whatever its literary or historical merits may be but also on its theological and ethical impact on the integrity and dignity of God's creation."[18] White women who participate in postcolonial interpretation are aware of their multiple identities as both oppressors and oppressed. For instance, Sharon Ringe has articulated how white feminists and others with power with the ambivalent status as both colonized and colonizers have to work to mitigate the practices of colonial authority and to share the table fellowship with others for greater inclusiveness.[19] Similarly, the African academically trained women are cognizant of the privileges they have over ordinary women readers because of their economic and educational attainment. They are very conscious of the ambivalent efforts of speaking on behalf of them or presenting their views in the academic setting.[20] In the case of Gale Yee, she notes that in American popular culture Asian and Asian American women are depicted as highly eroticized fig-

16. Musa Dube, "Readings of *Semoya*: Batswana Women Interpretations of Matt. 15:21–28," *Semeia* 73 (1996): 111–29; Gloria Kehilve Plaatjie, "Toward a Post-apartheid Black Feminist Reading of the Bible: A Case of Luke 2:36–38," in *Other Ways of Reading: African Women and the Bible*, ed. Musa W. Dube (Atlanta: Society of Biblical Literature, 2001), 114–42.

17. Dube, *Postcolonial Feminist Interpretation of the Bible*, 190–92.

18. Mary Ann Tolbert, "When Resistance Becomes Repression: Mark 13: 9–27 and the Poetics of Location," in *Reading from This Place*, ed. Fernando F. Segovia and Mary Ann Tolbert, vol. 2 (Minneapolis: Fortress Press, 1995), 333.

19. Sharon H. Ringe, "Places at the Table: Feminist and Postcolonial Biblical Interpretation," in *The Postcolonial Bible*, ed. R. S. Sugirtharajah (Sheffield: Sheffield Academic Press, 1998), 136–51.

20. Plaatjie, "Toward a Post-apartheid Black Feminist Reading," 119–20; Beverley G. Haddad, "Constructing Theologies of Survival in the South African Context: The Necessity of a Critical Engagement between Postmodern and Liberation Theology," *Journal of Feminist Studies in Religion* 14, no. 2 (1998): 5–18.

ures as a means to resolve racist anxieties and the fear of foreigners. Such stereotypical cultural representations make her sensitive to the symbolization of women as evil in the Hebrew Bible.[21] Her attention to the use of rhetoric of sexuality in the Bible is much influenced by her Asian American social location.

POSTCOLONIALISM, GENDER, AND EARLY CHRISTIANITY

Postcolonial criticism offers critical insights to examine the intersection among gender, empire, and the formation of Christian communities in the New Testament. Yet, feminist scholars in the past have seldom utilized such insights in their studies of women's position or gender construction in early Christianity because they have not foregrounded the Roman imperial context within which both Jews and Christians lived. One of the reasons is that biblical scholarship in the nineteenth and twentieth centuries has dichotomized the cultural context of Christian origins into Judaism versus Hellenism. A lot of effort has been devoted to determining whether the background of a Christian text could be traceable to its Jewish or Hellenistic sources or influences. When the discussion was framed in such a way, and frequently with an anti-Jewish bias, Roman imperial ideology and politics were largely obscured or deemed insignificant to the interpretive task at hand.[22] Furthermore, as Mary Rose D'Angelo has poignantly observed: "The nineteenth- and twentieth-century imperial cultures in which classical and biblical studies have been done (Germany, England, France, the United States) were deeply and explicitly identified either with the Roman Empire itself (Germany, England, France), or the imperial republic (France and the United States)."[23] Scholars tended to see the empire as either beneficial or neutral because of their social location, and did not question the political context harshly, as liberation theologians have done.

Without ignoring this larger cultural and political context of biblical scholarship, I would argue that there are also specific reasons why the interpretive models constructed by feminist scholars have downplayed the Roman imperial

21. Yee, *Poor Banished Children of Eve*, 159.

22. Mary Rose D'Angelo, "Early Christian Sexual Politics and Roman Imperial Family Values: Rereading Christ and Culture," in *The Papers of the Henry Luce III Fellows in Theology*, ed. Christopher I. Wilkins, vol. 6 (Pittsburgh: Association of Theological Schools, 2003), 24–25. Warren Carter also notes that the study of the Gospel of Matthew has been preoccupied with its Jewish context to the neglect of the influence of the Roman Empire; see Warren Carter, *Matthew and Empire: Initial Explorations* (Harrisburg, Pa.: Trinity Press International, 2001).

23. D'Angelo, "Early Christian Sexual Politics," 30.

context. The historical-reconstructionist model debunks the claims of objectivity made by androcentric historians and sets to reclaim women's history at the center of the development of early Christianity. The focus is on reclaiming women's heritage, especially the stories of the Christian foremothers, who emerged as playing such important roles as apostles, prophets, missionaries, and founders and leaders of house churches. Since the emphasis is on recovering women's significant leadership in the early church, researchers tend to concentrate on women leaders, or the elite women of the church, sometimes to the neglect of women of the lower classes. As Musa Dube has pointed out, the emphasis on patriarchy and the resurrection of women's history might downplay the imperial setting of early Christianity and bracket the imperial prescriptions and constructions of biblical texts. The accent on the early Christian foremothers may lead to overlooking the lives of non-Christian women and to glossing over the power dynamics of mission strategies in biblical narrative.[24]

The second approach investigates women in the social world of the early church and attempts to present a feminist social history of early Christianity. While some scholars have borrowed from the honor and shame model of cultural anthropologists, others have deployed various sociological and theoretical frameworks. Instead of focusing on the female leaders and elite women, this approach yields a wealth of data concerning the ordinary lives of women in the period of the early church, from women's struggle for bread and money, women's work and occupation, to the lives of slave women and widows. Moreover, women's family life, work, income, illness, and resistance are set in the context of Roman imperial society, governed by the marriage institution, legal norms, and economic systems.[25] What I find missing is a nuanced understanding of the diversity of women's social worlds as shaped by local, regional, and submerged histories within the Roman Empire. Postcolonial historiography has increasingly paid attention to the danger of making generalized statements and has aimed to resurrect subaltern histories.[26] Another problem is that while women's oppression is highlighted, there is insufficient discussion of gender as a constitutive factor, intersecting with ethnicity, class, and social status, to uphold not only patriarchy, but also imperial control and authority.

---

24. Dube, *Postcolonial Feminist Interpretation of the Bible*, 28–30.

25. See, e.g., Luise Schottroff, *Lydia's Impatient Sisters: A Feminist Social History of Early Christianity* (Louisville, Ky.: Westminster John Knox Press, 1995).

26. Richard A. Horsley has emphasized the need to foreground local histories; see, e.g., idem, "Subverting Disciplines: The Possibilities and Limitations of Postcolonial Theory for New Testament Studies," in *Toward a New Heaven and a New Earth: Essays in Honor of Elisabeth Schüssler Fiorenza*, ed. Fernando F. Segovia (Maryknoll, N.Y.: Orbis Books, 2003), 93–94. For a discussion of regional differentiation of the Roman family, see Beryl Rawson, "'The Roman Family' in Recent Research: State of the Question," *Biblical Interpretation* 11 (2003): 132.

The third model is the rhetorical model, which sees the text not as a window to historical reality, but as a social and linguistic construct performing particular rhetorical functions to shape action and the ethos of the community. Rhetorical criticism focuses on the persuasive power of the text to motivate the audience to action and its communicative functions in specific historical and political contexts. Instead of accepting the androcentric language and reality construction of biblical texts, rhetorical criticism uncovers and points to women's struggles for participation and power in early Christianity. Its reading strategy does not define patriarchy as men dominating women, but as an interlocking system of oppression because of racism, classism, colonialism, and sexism. Its aim is to create an alternative feminist rhetorical space in which women can participate as equals to men, defined by the logic of radical democracy.[27] Feminist rhetorical criticism of the New Testament has so far focused much of its energy on unmasking the rhetoric of the patriarchal household and the patriarchalization of the early church. More work needs to be done to explore how the imperial rhetoric, cultus, propaganda, and ideology affected the interlocking system of oppression and influenced the rhetoric and proclamation of the early church. We may also need to ask, How can this feminist rhetorical space be an anti-imperial space so that it will welcome Third World women and women who belong to other faiths?

I think these different models of feminist studies of the New Testament can benefit from postcolonial insights into how gender, race, and sexuality interplay in colonial situations. The works of Ann Laura Stoler and Anne McClintock have pointed to the fact that gender inequalities were essential to maintain the structure of colonial racism and imperial authority. Stoler's studies of Southeast Asian colonies elucidate how imperial authority and racial distinctions were fundamentally structured in gender terms. The management of sexual activity of women, reproduction, and intermarriage was fundamental to maintain distinctions between the colonizers and colonized, and to signify imperial power.[28] Anne McClintock's work on colonial discourses in Britain shows that gender was used to mark cultural and racial differences as well as to secure class distinction. Gender is not "simply a question of sexuality but also a question of subdued labor and imperial plunder; race is not just a question of skin color but also a question of labor power, cross-hatched by gender."[29]

---

27. Elisabeth Schüssler Fiorenza, *But She Said: Feminist Practices of Biblical Interpretation* (Boston: Beacon Press, 1992), 40–47, 150–51.

28. Ann Laura Stoler, *Carnal Knowledge and Imperial Power: Race and the Intimate in Colonial Rule* (Berkeley: University of California Press, 2002).

29. Anne McClintock, *Imperial Leather: Race, Gender, and Sexuality in the Colonial Contest* (New York: Routledge, 1995), 5.

Several scholars of early Christianity have applied such a multilayered and interactive approach to the study of gender relations in the complex negotiation of cultural and religious identities within the Palestine Jewish community and the Hellenistic Jewish diaspora under the Roman Empire. For example, Mary Rose D'Angelo has insightfully broadened the debate on Jesus' reference to God as Abba within the context of Roman imperial theology. While feminist scholars have decried the predominant use of patriarchal and parental imagery for God, some liberal theologians tried to downplay such a critique by insisting that Jesus had a special and intimate "abba experience." The argument is largely based on the influential study of Joachim Jeremias, who claims that the word "abba" denoted an intimate relationship with God, which was something new and not found in Judaism.[30] Jewish scholars have contested that claim, arguing that the use of "father" for God could be found in Jewish piety and would have been easily communicable to the Jewish audience. While much discussion has focused on the Jewish context, D'Angelo adds a new dimension by tracing the use of "father" in the Roman imperial context. She points out that the title of father was awarded to Julius Caesar and reflected "an understanding of the empire as a great *familia* in which the emperor functions as a *paterfamilias*."[31] During the reign of Augustus, the consolidation of his empire was reinforced with legal measures aiming at strengthening the patriarchal family. Given the fact that Jesus died at the hands of the Romans, D'Angelo surmises that Jesus' use of "abba" challenges imperial and paternal authority, for the father he refers to is not the Roman imperial father, but the father who rules heaven and earth. Still, she cautions that the use of "father" cannot be said to be nonpatriarchal, as the name still reflects a social system in which privileged males had power over women, children, slaves, and other lesser males.[32]

Richard Horsley's postcolonial reading of the Gospel of Mark also places gender relations in the larger economic-political power relations operative under Roman imperial rule.[33] As a story about Galileans' and Judeans' strug-

30. Joachim Jeremias, *Abba: Studien zur neutestamentlichen Theologies und Zeitgeschichte* (Göttingen: Vandenhoeck and Ruprecht, 1966).

31. Mary Rose D'Angelo, "Abba and 'Father': Imperial Theology and the Jesus Traditions," *Journal of Biblical Literature* 111 (1992): 623.

32. Mary Rose D'Angelo, "Theology in Mark and Q: Abba and 'Father' in Context," *Harvard Theological Review* 85 (1992): 174.

33. Richard A. Horsley, *Hearing the Whole Story: The Politics of Plot in Mark's Gospel* (Louisville, Ky.: Westminster John Knox Press, 2001), 203–29; and a shorter version in idem, "Feminist Scholarship and Postcolonial Criticism: Subverting Imperial Discourse and Reclaiming Submerged Histories," in *Walk in the Ways of Wisdom: Essays in Honor of Elisabeth Schüssler Fiorenza*, ed. Shelly Matthews, Cynthia Briggs Kittredge, and Melanie Johnson-Debaufre (Harrisburg, Pa.: Trinity Press International, 2003), 301–5.

gles in resistance against harsh Roman domination, Mark's Gospel describes women as playing pivotal and instrumental roles in the renewal movement, in sharp contrast to the lack of faith of the disciples. Horsley interestingly does not read the stories of the hemorrhaging woman (Mark 5:25–34) and the twelve-year-old daughter of the assembly leader (Mark 5:35–43) as individuals, but as figures representative of Israel, a people bleeding and virtually dying under Roman exploitation. He takes into account local histories and discusses how Magdala, the region where Mary of Magdala came from, suffered from severe military violence and enslavement under Roman armies, as well as financial hardship imposed on the family by heavy taxation. The conquest of Palestine by the Romans brought acute pressure and instability to village life and the patriarchal family, undermining the authority of many fathers as the head of household. Seen from this larger context, Jesus called the whole village to form a "familial" community based on the Mosaic covenantal commandment to provide the supportive functions that used to be performed by the family. Horsley thinks that it would be anachronistic to say that Mark's Jesus opposed patriarchal marriage and championed an egalitarian social order, but Jesus' covenantal understanding of marriage placed it on a less patriarchal footing when compared to the teachings of the Pharisees.[34] Jesus did not want to abolish the family, and his insistence on marriage as indissoluble (Mark 10:2–9) was not simply an incidence of teaching about sexual ethics, but an argument for the protection of the family as the fundamental socioeconomic unit. Such a provision guaranteed the economic security of women and children against the liberalization of divorce by the Pharisees, which facilitated the consolidation of landholdings of the Herodian and other elite. Reading gender and women's stories in the larger political plot of Mark's Gospel, Horsley presents the different forms of oppression as interlocking and multiplicative.

New Testament scholars have also paid more attention to the imperial culture and ideology in the interpretation of Paul's context and his corpus of writings. In the past, scholars have polarized the Jewish background and the Hellenistic influence in Paul, or bifurcated Paul as either a Jew or a Christian. The dominant interest has been to contrast between "particularistic" or "ethnocentric" Judaism with the "universalism" of Paul, as the apostle who established Gentile Christianity. But Paul's identity was never so clear-cut, and

---

34. For other readings of Jesus and the patriarchal family, see Elisabeth Schüssler Fiorenza, *In Memory of Her: A Feminist Theological Reconstruction of Christian Origins*, 10th ann. ed. (New York: Crossroad, 1994), 140–51; and a contrasting view, John H. Elliot, "Jesus Was Not an Egalitarian: A Critique of an Anachronistic and Idealist Theory," *Biblical Theology Bulletin* 32, no. 3 (2002): 75–91.

in today's postcolonial parlance, his identity must be considered as highly hybridized. Paul did not envisage he was joining a new religious movement, but rather saw it as a development of Israelite traditions, and therefore needed to clarify his position vis-à-vis the Jewish leaders who held to a more traditional way of life. As a Greek-speaking diasporic Jew apparently born in exile, Paul joined a popular movement and moved out to the Gentiles, thus risking alienation from his fellow "Judeans."[35] Paul's debates with the other apostles on circumcision and eating food that had been offered to idols were of critical importance at the time, because circumcision and food served as crucial markers of religious and cultural difference. And at the same time, as Antoinette Clark Wire has observed, Paul as a freeborn and educated Jewish male, with other Greek-speaking city gentry, saw "their independence disintegrate under Roman rule."[36] Paul experienced a loss of status as a result of his joining the Jesus movement. By so doing, he compromised the privileges of his Jewish status as a Pharisee, and the Christian teachings of submission to Christ placed restrictions on his advancement in the Roman Empire.

Paul's political stance toward the state and empire has long been a bone of contention among biblical scholars and theologians. For some, Paul as a Roman citizen was a social conservative, who accepted the status quo and exhorted his followers to be subjects of governing authorities (Rom. 13:1-7). For others, Paul was anti-imperial, and the movement he participated in and the local communities he was building represented an alternative society in opposition to the Roman imperial order. Neil Elliot argues that Paul's remarks of submission were issued out of a particular historical context, and his aim was to safeguard the most vulnerable among the Roman Christians against the anti-Jewish sentiment in Rome.[37] Horsley, using rhetorical criticism to study 1 Corinthians, argues that Paul used terms and language of Greco-Roman rhetoric and Roman imperial ideology to oppose the imperial order.[38] But if we add the gender dimension to scrutinize Paul's anti-imperial stance, the picture emerging is more complicated, for Paul supported the subordination of women to men (1 Cor. 11:2-16; 14:33b-36, though some consider the latter

35. Richard A. Horsley, "Submerged Biblical Histories and Imperial Biblical Studies," in Sugirtharajah, *The Postcolonial Bible*, 162-63.

36. Antoinette Clark Wire, *The Corinthian Women Prophets: A Reconstruction through Paul's Rhetoric* (Minneapolis: Fortress Press, 1990), 70.

37. Neil Elliot, "Romans 13:1-7 in the Context of Imperial Propaganda," in *Paul and Empire: Religion and Power in the Roman Imperial Society*, ed. Richard A. Horsley (Harrisburg, Pa.: Trinity Press International, 1997), 184-204.

38. Richard A. Horsley, "Rhetoric and Empire—And 1 Corinthians," in *Paul and Politics: Ekklesia, Israel, Imperium, Interpretation*, ed. Richard A. Horsley (Harrisburg, Pa.: Trinity Press International, 2000), 91.

as Deutero-Pauline). Some argue there is a "double standard" in Paul, for while he allowed for the transformation of the relationship between Jews and Gentiles and might have advocated resistance to the Roman order, he did not challenge gender roles and sexual relationships. In the study of modern anti-colonial movements, postcolonial feminists have also shown that the struggle against the colonial regime does not automatically lead men to give up their patriarchal privileges, and in many cases they want to reinscribe male-dominated norms to protect their "manhood."

In her analysis of the rhetoric of 1 Corinthians, Cynthia Briggs Kittredge argues that Paul used the language of the Roman patronage system to construct a pattern of linked hierarchical relationship in the Corinthian church. She says: "God's subjection of Christ is the ultimate symbolic legitimization of the father's position between the children and Christ and the husband's position between his wife and God."[39] Thus, she wonders whether Paul had replicated the language of subordination in the patronage system and thereby reinscribed imperial power relations. If Paul reinscribed gender inequality and preached about the submission of wives to their husbands in his letters, he was not alone in doing so. Mary Rose D'Angelo has shown that the authors of Luke-Acts, the Pastorals (Deutero-Pauline), and the *Shepherd of Hermas* had to construct masculinity and gender relations in the context of promulgation of imperial family values during the reigns of Trajan and Hadrian in the late first and early second centuries. In order to maintain the harmony of the Roman order, proper governance of the household was seen to be necessary, which demanded the display of submission of women, children, and slaves. Because of the threat of persecution, these Christian writers wanted to argue that Christians demonstrated exemplary moral character and family life, to avoid denunciation. Thus, Roman family values cast their influence on the formulation of sexual ethics in the early Christian community.[40]

Sheila Briggs examines the rhetoric of Paul from another angle by focusing on his discourses on bondage and freedom.[41] Briggs's study would also complicate the claim of an anti-imperial stance for Paul, since Paul did not condemn the institution of slavery, which upheld the imperial order alongside the emperor cult, the paterfamilias, and the patronage system, and which pervaded

39. Cynthia Briggs Kittredge, "Corinthian Women Prophets and Paul's Argumentation in 1 Corinthians," in Horsley, *Paul and Politics*, 107.

40. Mary Rose D'Angelo, "'Knowing How to Preside over His Own Household': Imperial Masculinity and Christian Asceticism in the Pastorals, *Hermas*, and Luke-Acts," in *New Testament Masculinity*, ed. Stephen D. Moore and Janice Capel Anderson (Atlanta: Society of Biblical Literature, 2003), 265–95.

41. Sheila Briggs, "Paul on Bondage and Freedom in Imperial Roman Society," in Horsley, *Paul and Politics*, 110–23.

the whole material and ideological domain. Of particular importance is her reading of the interplay among gender, sexuality, and slavery in Paul's rhetoric in Galatians 3–4 and 1 Corinthians 6–7. While scholars have used the baptismal formula in Galatians 3:28 to argue that Paul has a social egalitarian vision that abolishes all boundaries and differences, Briggs helpfully contextualizes the formula in the dual system of slaveholding patriarchy in Paul's time and highlights the plight of slave women living in such a society.[42] She notes that gender was always constructed through sexuality, and the inferior status of the slaves (both male and female) was marked by their sexual availability. Sexuality was deployed to maintain a hierarchical order and to denote legal and social status of persons. For example, the superiority of the free woman because of her honor and chastity was contrasted with the lack of honor and sexual degradation of the slave woman. Reading from such a context, Briggs eschews the consensual interpretation, which maintains that the baptismal formula speaks in parallel manner of three differences among human beings: ethnicity, class, and gender. Instead, she proposes that "an analogy is drawn between the common strife of Jew and Greek and the conflictual relationships inherent in the patriarchal dual system of slavery and gender."[43] The baptismal formula, for Briggs, sought to replace ethnicity in civic life and the household as sources of identity and conflict with the new identity in Christ.

Briggs notes that Paul did not draw the egalitarian and emancipatory import from the baptismal formula in his construction of meaning of the Sarah and Hagar story, which he used to symbolize the two covenants (Gal. 4:21–31). He pitted Sarah against Hagar, and Sarah's children against Hagar's children, in the dual system of gender and slavery. While Christians were regarded as the true descendants of Abraham and shared in the covenant, the children of Hagar, born out of slavery, could not share the inheritance of God's promise. And in 1 Corinthians, Briggs finds it problematic that Paul used the discourse of evasion when he addressed but evaded the social institution of slavery. In particular, he condemned going to prostitutes (1 Cor. 6:15–16) as incompatible with Christian behavior, but did not criticize the sexual uses of slaves, which was seen as acceptable in the Roman moral and legal codes. In fact, most prostitutes were usually slaves coerced into this dishonorable occupation.[44] Paul also used slavery as a theological metaphor to describe Christians' relationship with Christ, asserting that Christians "were bought with a price"

---

42. Sheila Briggs, "Slavery and Gender," in *On the Cutting Edge: The Study of Women in the Biblical Worlds*, ed. Jane Schaberg, Alice Bach, and Esther Fuchs (New York: Continuum, 2003), 171–92.

43. Ibid., 182.

44. Briggs, "Paul on Bondage and Freedom," 114–15.

(1 Cor. 6:20; 7:23). Such a metaphor would sound very different to the free-born than to the enslaved. What would it mean to a slave woman who would have experienced double slavery?

Having raised all these questions about Paul's position on the empire, women, and slavery, these feminist scholars insist that Paul was but one of the many voices in early Christianity. Elisabeth Schüssler Fiorenza argues for a hermeneutics of *ekklesia* that "seeks to displace the politics and rhetorics of subordination and otherness which [are] inscribed in the 'Pauline' correspondence with a hermeneutics and rhetorics of equality and responsibility."[45] Antoinette Clark Wire lifts up the submerged "voices within Paul's voice" and highlights the women prophets in Corinth.[46] Sheila Briggs reminds us to read gender and slavery as a dual system and to bear in mind the silent voices of the slave woman in the text. Early Christianity was a plurivocal movement of women and men from many social locations, and a postcolonial reading helps us to raise new questions and make connections.

POSTCOLONIALISM, FEMINISM, AND ANTI-JUDAISM

Postcolonial feminist interpreters of the Bible need to pay attention to deep-seated anti-Jewish biases in Christian thought and their manifestations in different contexts. Amy-Jill Levine has charged that anti-Jewish readings can be found in the writings of Third World theologians and biblical scholars working out of a feminist-liberationist framework.[47] To make Jesus look like a feminist, the first-century Jewish context was described and labeled as blatantly misogynist. Jewish feminists, most notably Judith Plaskow and Susannah Heschel, have challenged such anti-Jewish tendencies in white Christian feminist biblical interpretation in the 1970s and early 1980s.[48] Levine is concerned

45. Elisabeth Schüssler Fiorenza, "Paul and the Politics of Interpretation," in Horsley, *Paul and Politics*, 54.

46. Wire, *The Corinthian Women Prophets*.

47. Amy-Jill Levine, "Lilies of the Field and Wandering Jews: Biblical Scholarship, Women's Roles, and Social Location," in *Transformative Encounters: Jesus and Women Re-viewed*, ed. Ingrid Rosa Kitzberger (Leiden: Brill, 2000), 329–52. A version that focuses on Third World women's writings is found in Amy-Jill Levine, "The Disease of Postcolonial New Testament Studies and the Hermeneutics of Healing," *Journal of Feminist Studies in Religion* 20, no. 1 (2004): 91–99.

48. Judith Plaskow, "Blaming the Jews for the Birth of Patriarchy," *Lilith* 7 (1980): 11–12, 14–17; and idem, "Anti-Judaism in Feminist Christian Interpretation," in *Searching the Scriptures*, vol. 1, *A Feminist Introduction*, ed. Elisabeth Schüssler Fiorenza (New York: Crossroad, 1993), 117–29; Susannah Heschel, "Anti-Judaism in Christian Feminist Theology," *Tikkun* 5, no. 3 (1990): 25–28, 95–97.

about the resurfacing of such biases in the global feminist biblical discourse in the 1990s.

There has not been much conversation and dialogue between Third World feminist scholars coming out of postcolonial contexts, on the one hand, and Jewish feminists, on the other. Judaism and Christianity exist as two distinct traditions and operate within very separate orbits in the Third World. Even where there is a local Jewish population, there are few opportunities for Christian and Jewish feminists to mingle and work together. In most cases, the writings of Jewish feminists and other Jewish sources on first-century Judaism are not easily available, and there are few who have adequate training in using these materials. Further, combating anti-Judaism has not been a priority within global Christian feminist networks and in the ecumenical circles. And most importantly, Third World feminists may see the holocaust as the burden for Europeans only. Since their countries have not participated directly in persecuting the Jews, they have not been as pressed to see anti-Judaism as a critical issue to reckon with. Furthermore, in the continual Middle East conflict, they tend to stand in solidarity with the Palestinians, who are driven from their land and suffer under the military might of the state of Israel, supported by the government of the United States.

But Third World feminists and Jewish feminists have a lot to learn from one another to understand on a deeper level how anti-Semitism intersects with colonial discourse, especially during the nineteenth century and early twentieth century—how, for example, the Jews were treated by the Christian colonists as the Others within, who were persecuted and suppressed, while the colonized were the Others from without, who were enslaved and conquered. When Christianity was brought to other parts of the world from the West, it was almost completely purged of its Jewish context, such that the universal tradition initiated by Jesus was seen as a new religion, supplanting the old tradition of Judaism. A postcolonial analysis will help Third World scholars see more clearly how such a mystification of Christian origins supports both anti-Semitism and Christian imperialism. If we were to see the Jesus movement not as an innovation of Jesus, but as a reform or emancipatory movement within Judaism, Christian feminists from the Third World could dialogue with Jewish feminists about how to assess the emancipatory nature of this movement.[49]

49. Elisabeth Schüssler Fiorenza had earlier characterized the Jesus movement as "renewal or reform movement," but has changed it to an "emancipatory" or "*basileia*" movement, to indicate that the reference point of such emancipation was not Judaism but Roman imperial domination. See "Of Specks, Beams, and Methods: Anti-Judaism and Antifeminism," in idem, *Jesus and the Politics of Interpretation* (New York: Continuum, 2000), 119.

It is important, therefore, to pay attention to what Levine identifies as problematic and anti-Jewish in Third World women's biblical interpretation. First, there is often a blanket and monolithic portrayal of the Jewish tradition as patriarchal. Jewish women were depicted as marginalized and excluded from religious leadership and public roles, a view that has long been challenged by feminist historians who have studied that period. Second, against this negative foil of Judaism, Jesus is seen as either not influenced by or rejecting his Jewish context, a countercultural radical who befriended women, healed, and preached to them. Third, the demand of Jewish laws for ritual purity and cleanliness is highlighted, which is regarded as biased against women and non-Jews. Against such taboos of pollution and impurity, Jesus is seen as transgressing the boundaries between the clean and the unclean, and between Jews and Gentiles. Fourth, women's oppression and powerlessness in their modern social location was projected into Jewish antiquity, as if transcultural and transhistorical comparisons could be made. Fifth, Third World women who are outside the guilds of biblical studies and have no access to biblical scholarship tend not to reproduce anti-Jewish readings.[50]

When we examine these charges, we can see that some of them bear a close resemblance to what missionaries have taught the "native" Christians. Levine also astutely observes that "much of the anti-Judaism named in this paper thus appears to be another colonial product of global symbol capital, exported along with cured tobacco and DDT."[51] The claim that Jesus was a liberator of women who broke from Jewish tradition was first introduced to the Third World not by Western academic scholarship but by missionaries who wanted to convert native women to Christianity. For example, missionaries cited Jesus' befriending women, teaching profound spiritual truths to them, his healing the woman who suffered from hemorrhage, his sympathy for the woman caught in sin, and his appearance to women after his resurrection.[52] The subordination of women in the native traditions was regarded as symptomatic of the inferiority of their cultures. Many native women who leave their tradition to become Christians believe that Jesus does not discriminate against women and that Christianity offers women a better chance for life. Because of this long history of hailing Jesus as an iconoclastic hero in missionary and also native Christian women's discourses, I am not persuaded that only Western-educated Third World feminists are making anti-Jewish remarks, and that ordinary readers who are not theologically trained are not. Since ordinary readers tend to read the Bible more

50. Levine, "Lilies of the Field," 331–50.
51. Ibid., 348–49.
52. Kwok Pui-lan, *Chinese Women and Christianity, 1860–1927* (Atlanta: Scholars Press, 1992), 47–51.

literally, it is difficult to believe that anti-Jewish statements found in the text itself, especially in the passion narratives, would not influence them.

So what are the causes of anti-Jewish readings in Third World feminist writings that Levine identifies as problematic? I agree with her that it is possible that Third World feminist theologians may simply reinscribe the colonialist position and internalize the colonizers' abjection of the Jews. Or they may have repeated the kind of argument that "Jesus was a feminist" found in Western Christian feminist interpretation in the 1970s. But to lay blame on the colonists, missionaries, and early feminists may lead us to overlook some deeper cultural politics at work. Unlike in the West, the cultures in the Third World do not harbor a long animosity toward the Jews. Few Third World feminists have had sufficient sustained contact with the Jewish people or dialogue with Jewish feminists to know how they feel about the Jewish tradition. Levine suggests that the reproduction of anti-Jewish discourse by Third World feminists can be interpreted as a colonial mimicry and a repetition of what they have learned from their Western teachers. I want to highlight the ambivalent nature of mimicry, which Homi Bhabha has described as "almost the same, *but not quite.*" Bhabha emphasizes the indeterminacy and double articulation of mimicry: on the one hand, it may reinscribe colonial authority (trying to be white); on the other hand, it may be a complex strategy to challenge identity and difference constructed by "normalized" knowledges ("*but not quite*") and to appropriate, fracture, and displace the dominant discourse for resistance.[53] Whereas Levine looks at mimicry as a repetition and reinscription of Western Christian anti-Jewish discourse (trying to be white), I want to probe in what ways Third World feminist writings are different ("almost the same but not white")[54] from those of their colonial masters and mistresses.

I suggest the critique of patriarchy in Jewish culture may have served as a rhetorical device not just to make Jesus look good, but also to bring into sharp relief patriarchy in their own cultures. As Jesus critiqued his own culture (some aspects of it, not all), these women find support and encouragement to challenge their own culture. As Elsa Tamez has said:

> The sometimes sharp criticism that Jesus thrusts at his own Jewish culture does not reflect an anti-Jewish stance. As we know, Jesus is a Jew and therefore places himself in a position of self-critique with respect to the patriarchy of Judaism and Roman culture as enacted in oppressive practices. Importantly, in this same way, women today engage in constructive criticism of their religious and social culture.[55]

53. Homi K. Bhabha, "Of Mimicry and Man: The Ambivalence of Colonial Discourse," in idem, *The Location of Culture* (London: Routledge, 1994), 85–92.

54. Ibid., 89.

55. Elsa Tamez, *Jesus and Courageous Women* (New York: Women's Division, United Methodist Church, 2001), viii.

From a liberationist perspective, Jesus is seen as attacking not only patriarchy alone, but also imperialism, colonialism, and militarism. Thus, these Third World feminists may not have engaged in a simple kind of colonial mimicry, but may have tried to refashion the dominant colonial discourse in order to create a language of resistance that challenges both patriarchy in native cultures and imperialism at once.

Still, we must question the ethics of portraying Judaism as blatantly sexist to serve as a negative foil to criticize patriarchy in native cultures. To heed Levine's call, we must avoid using generalized and monolithic descriptions about the Jewish tradition or about indigenous cultures. An important postcolonial insight is that what is so-called national culture is always constructed, contested, forged through debate, negotiation, and sometimes confrontation. This will require us to know much better the different groups and factions of first-century Judaism: their daily practices, local histories, and religious and political ideologies. Instead of singling out the patriarchal practices of the Jews, we need to place them in the wider contexts of the Roman imperial rule.

Levine has noted that Third World feminists have identified "the Jews" transhistorically and transculturally with their oppressors, but rarely with "the Romans." One plausible reason is that, in the colonial setting, the oppression of the colonialists is often not felt intimately and immediately, for the colonialists, as members of the upper class, rarely mix with the people. It is the disciplinary power of the indigenous elites employed as colonial agents and accomplices that is most keenly felt. At this juncture, postcolonial criticism may provide a corrective to a one-sided blaming of "the Jews," since postcolonial biblical studies focus on the impact of the empire, both ancient and modern, and on its representations in the text. For example, postcolonial feminist studies of the Bible can examine how Roman imperial rule had shaped and changed Jewish cultures and customs, especially regarding gender relationships and women's roles in their faith community. And, if the conflicts of Jesus with the Pharisees and the Jewish leaders were not Christian-Jewish conflicts but intra-Jewish arguments, it would be productive to explore the political implications of such conflicts under the shadow of the empire. A postcolonial interpretation will highlight the roles these religious leaders played in maintaining the traditional ways of Jewish life, while also serving as mediators between the Jewish people and the Roman order.[56] Furthermore, the Jesus movement must be recognized as a movement within the context of Judaism, and postcolonial feminists are interested to know if this movement

56. Horsley, *Paul and Empire*, 207–8.

provided opportunities for Jewish women to challenge not only patriarchy but also imperial rule.

Levine places the burden of detecting and correcting anti-Jewish interpretation on the shoulders of those who have been theologically trained, noting that mainstream New Testament scholarship has perpetuated and even promoted such readings. In the Third World, this problem is particularly acute, as some of the theological schools are still using "standard" Western dictionaries and commentaries published a generation ago. Some of these texts not only contain anti-Jewish remarks, but also present an outdated and skewed picture of Christian origins. For example, Susannah Heschel has noted that Rudolf Bultmann's highly negative depictions of Judaism's legalism had influenced New Testament scholarship after the Second World War, especially in the new quest for the historical Jesus.[57] Before the Third World libraries are updated, we must exercise caution and discretion in using these resources and maintain a healthy dose of suspicion whenever Jewish culture is portrayed in a negative light.

I support many of Levine's strategies for conscientizing people about anti-Jewish biases in biblical and theological studies: learning more about Jewish history, avoiding making generalized negative statements about Judaism, the inclusion of Jewish voices in anthologies, updating libraries (especially in the Third World) with Jewish resources, and naming the problem when we see it. Relating to the process are pedagogical issues regarding teaching the body of Third World feminist writings. Levine is concerned that the teaching of these multicultural voices with anti-Jewish contents will infect the next generation of students, and the infection would have global effects. I think these Third World writings must be taught with an understanding of the history and cultures of their contexts and the rhetorical strategies they use. At a time when American imperialism is on the rise, those of us teaching in the United States must insist on including voices outside the United States to challenge "sanctioned ignorance" perpetuated by the dominant white educational system, the mass media, and the state apparatus. A roundtable discussion of Levine's work by some of the authors she criticizes can be used to help students understand the complex and multifaceted dimensions of the issues and to illustrate that those feminists are not afraid to dialogue on difficult issues across differences.[58]

---

57. Susannah Heschel, "The Image of Judaism in Nineteenth-Century Christian New Testament Scholarship in Germany," in *Jewish-Christian Encounters over the Centuries: Symbiosis, Prejudice, Holocaust, Dialogue*, ed. Marvin Perry and Frederick M. Schweitzer (New York: Peter Lang, 1994), 234.

58. "Anti-Judaism and Postcolonial Biblical Interpretation," *Journal of Feminist Studies in Religion* 20, no. 1 (2004): 91–132.

I welcome Levine's invitation to feminists to read the biblical texts in community, so that we can confront our prejudices and be aware of how our social location influences our reading practices.[59] Reading in company with those who have not been our constant dialogical partners has the added benefit of shifting our location within a changing configuration of social relationships. For example, Levine, as a North American, is concerned that her critique of the work of an Asian, African, Australian, or Latin American woman might be seen as "patronizing racism."[60] But outside the United States, where the issues of racism and anti-Semitism are understood differently, her partners in conversation may respond to her in ways different from her American audiences. Similarly, her Asian, African, Australian, and Latin American colleagues will have an opportunity to redefine their hybridized Christian identity as they encounter diasporic Jewish feminists.

Feminist interpretation of the Bible has come a long way since the day when the Chinese woman excised from her Bible those Pauline passages that she considered misogynous. It has become a global movement, as women with different histories and cultures challenge patriarchal readings and articulate their faith and understanding of God. If the Bible has been the "great code" undergirding Western civilization as Northrop Frye has said,[61] women from all over the world are claiming the power and authority to retell, rewrite, and reinterpret this important document. In particular, they have pointed to the intersection of anti-Semitism, global racism, and sexism in the colonialist imagination. Women can benefit from reading together with others in community in order to challenge our own biases and investment in a particular interpretive method. We have the challenge to turn the postcolonial "contact zones" into places of mutual learning, and places for trying out new ideas and strategies for the emancipation of all.

59. Levine, "Lilies of the Field," 350.
60. Ibid.
61. Northrop Frye, *The Great Code: The Bible and Literature* (New York: Harcourt Brace Jovanovich, 1982).

4

Finding Ruth a Home

Gender, Sexuality, and the Politics of Otherness

My daughter, should I not seek a home for you, that it may be well with you?

Ruth 3:1 (RSV)

When is the word "home" shrunk to denote the private, domestic sphere and when is the "domestic" enlarged to denote "the affairs of a nation"?

Rosemary Marangoly George[1]

A young widowed woman left her homeland because of economic hardship. Living among strangers, she resorted to extraordinary means, including using her sexuality, to survive and to take care of her ailing mother-in-law. Sound familiar? Except that this is not a modern story, but a story about Ruth dated back to ancient biblical times. The stories of Ruth the Moabite,[2] the Syrophoenician woman (Matt. 15:21–28; Mark 7:24–30),[3] and Rahab the Canaanite prostitute

---

1. Rosemary Marangoly George, *The Politics of Home: Postcolonial Relocations and Twentieth-Century Fiction* (Cambridge: Cambridge University Press, 1996), 13.

2. Laura E. Donaldson, "The Sign of Orpah: Reading Ruth through Native Eyes," in *Vernacular Hermeneutics*, ed. R. S. Sugirtharajah (Sheffield: Sheffield Academic Press, 1999), 20–36; Musa W. Dube, "The Unpublished Letters of Orpah to Ruth," in *Ruth and Esther: A Feminist Companion to the Bible*, 2nd ser., ed. Athalya Brenner (Sheffield: Sheffield Academic Press, 1999), 145–50.

3. Kwok Pui-lan, *Discovering the Bible in the Non-Biblical World* (Maryknoll, N.Y.: Orbis Books, 1995), 71–83; idem, "Overlapping Communities and Multicultural Hermeneutics," in *A Feminist Companion to Reading the Bible: Approaches, Methods, and Strategies*, ed. Athalya Brenner and Carole Fontaine (Sheffield: Sheffield Academic Press, 1997), 103–18; Musa W. Dube, *Postcolonial Feminist Interpretation of the Bible* (St. Louis: Chalice Press, 2000), 127–95; R. S. Sugirtharajah, "The Syrophoenician Woman," *Expository Times* 98 (October 1986): 13–15.

(Josh. 2)[4] have captured the attention of postcolonial feminist critics because they illustrate the intersections among gender, class, race, ethnicity, and sexuality in cultural contacts and border crossings. The book of Ruth is especially significant because it is one of the two books in the Bible in which the protagonist is a woman (the other is the book of Esther).

My reading of the book of Ruth is tied to my interests in the history of immigration, the discussion of the foreigners and new immigrants, and the larger politics of identity formation in the United States. When I open the advertisement section of the *World Journal*, the best-selling Chinese newspaper in the United States, I can find almost every day advertisements of women in China looking for men with American citizenship to begin a relationship or with marriage in mind. These advertisements remind me of the heart-wrenching history of the Asian mail-order brides, the prostitutes around American foreign bases who dream of coming to America, and others who use fake marriages or marrying an American GI as a ticket to the United States. Some of these marriages have a happy ending, but some eventually end up in domestic violence, divorce, poverty, and neglected children.

In the book of Ruth, the Judahite mother-in-law, Naomi, wants to find a home for her Moabite daughter-in-law, Ruth. The Hebrew word translated as "home" (*mānôach*) can also mean a place where one can find rest and a sense of security. For many readers, the word "home" connotes the private sphere of domesticity, shelter, comfort, nurture, rest, and protection. It is, therefore, not surprising that the story of Ruth has been a favorite of Christians and Jews throughout the centuries, because it can be read as a romantic story with a happy ending.[5] Indeed, if taken as an idyllic tale, the book of Ruth can offer readers some comfort and respite in the midst of war, murder, violence, disloyalty, rebellion, and unfaithfulness in the Scriptures.

But the harsh realities of United States immigration history and the global displacement and dispersal of huge numbers of people challenge the cozy picture of home defined by family romance and a perfect middle-class nuclear family. In the case of the United States, gender, sexuality, and marriage have been much tied with the powerful propaganda of the "American dream" and the national narrative of the United States as an immigrant country open to all. Thus, "home" cannot be read through the myopic lens of the warmth and comfort of the private sphere without taking into consideration how the private intersects with national identity, ethnicity, citizenship, law, and women's rights. In the global scene—where war, violence, ethnic strife, political instability, and

4. Dube, *Postcolonial Feminist Interpretation*, 76–80, 121–24; Donaldson, "The Sign of Orpah," 29–30.

5. Katherine Doob Sakenfeld, *Ruth* (Louisville, Ky.: John Knox Press, 1999), 1.

the global market combine to drive many people into homelessness, migrancy, and diaspora—home is not a fixed and stable location but a traveling adventure, which entails seeking refuge in strange lands, bargaining for survival, and negotiating for existence. Such a destabilized and contingent construction of home dislodges it from its familiar domestic territory and questions the conditions through which the cozy connotations of home have been made possible and sustained.

In this chapter I use the expression "finding a home" for Ruth as a metaphor and a heuristic device to describe and interrogate the different ways scholars have constructed meanings and mobilized data from their respective reading strategies. In the beginning of her book *The Politics of Home*, Rosemary Marangoly George discusses various ways in which "home" has been conceived:

> Today, the primary connotation of "home" is of the "private" space from which the individual travels into the larger arenas of life and to which he or she returns at the end of the day. And yet, also in circulation is the word's wider signification as the larger geographic place where one belongs: country, city, village, community. Home is also the imagined location that can be more readily fixed in a mental landscape than in actual geography.[6]

For postcolonial critics, the interrogation of the construction of the "home" is significant because home often reveals our desire, our construction of identity, even our sense of longing and belonging. Furthermore, the home and the outside—or the home and the world—must be read together simultaneously because these categories are mutually constitutive and contingent, whose content and meaning cannot be predetermined in advance without examining how they are deployed in specific discourses.[7]

In the first section I interrogate from a postcolonial perspective three ways that "home" has been read in the story of Ruth: home understood in the contexts of kinship, patriarchal household, and hospitality to the strangers. My interest is not to use these categories to demonstrate three distinct modes of readings, or to classify scholars into different camps, because many scholars do think about home in more than one way. For example, feminist scholars may critique the oppression of home in a patriarchal context and at the same time affirm the offering of hospitality to strangers. My intention, rather, is to show that implicit or explicit assumptions of "home" have led scholars to pay attention to certain parts of the story and to activate certain registers of reading, even though these scholars may come from distinct academic backgrounds utilizing

6. George, *The Politics of Home*, 11.
7. Aparajita Sagar, "Homes and Postcoloniality," *Diaspora* 6 (1997): 237; Homi Bhabha, "The World and the Home," *Social Text* 31 and 32 (1992): 141–53.

different methodologies. Furthermore, I want to investigate what is suppressed or ignored in order to allow a certain interpretation to be inscribed as a coherent or authoritative narrative. This is to trace what Gayatri Chakravorty Spivak has called "the itinerary of the silencing." For her, the deconstructive project provides us with a view "where we see the way in which narratives compete with each other, which one rises, which one falls, who is silent, and the itinerary of the silencing rather than the retrieval."[8] In the second section I elaborate some postcolonial feminist reading strategies of the Bible, using the insights provided by Regina Schwartz and Laura Donaldson. In the conclusion I offer some observations on the link between finding a home for Ruth and scholars' finding a home for themselves in the academic and religious community.

Such a postcolonial reading is made possible not only by the availability of postcolonial theories that introduce some of the most exciting and illuminating strategies for reading literary texts, but also by the emergence of diverse biblical interpretive paradigms. Indeed, scholars have used a wide array of methods to illuminate different parts of Ruth's story, including sociological analysis, narrative theory, feminist criticism, intertextuality, and analyses of realist fiction, the arts, and popular media. These new and divergent approaches do not emerge in a vacuum, but are made possible by the change of contours in the field of biblical studies. In the past several decades scholars have challenged the hegemony of traditional methods and proposed new paradigms of interpretation, such as reader-response criticism, rhetorical criticism, feminist criticism, cultural studies, postcolonial criticism, and vernacular hermeneutics. The understanding of "Scripture" has shifted from the sacred Word of God and a historical document from the past to a relational concept involving interaction with interpretive communities.[9] The meaning of the Bible is no longer seen as located in the authorial voice of God, or in the intention of the author or the redactor, but increasingly in the interpretive community, whether it is the religious community or the academic guild. Collectively, these new paradigms have shifted the emphasis from the world *behind the text* (historical criticism) to the world *in the text* (literary criticism informed by critical theories) and the world *in front of the text* (reader-response). As I discussed in the last chapter, Fernando Segovia traces the proliferation of new paradigms to two factors: theoretical shifts introduced into the discipline by

8. Gayatri Chakravorty Spivak, *The Post-Colonial Critic: Interviews, Strategies, Dialogues* (New York: Routledge, 1990), 31; see also Bart Moore-Gilbert, *Postcolonial Theory: Contexts, Practices, Politics* (London: Verso, 1997), 85.

9. Wilfred Cantwell Smith, *What Is Scripture? A Comparative Approach* (Minneapolis: Fortress Press, 1993).

literary and cultural criticisms, and a crucial demographic shift in the discipline, namely, the increasing presence and influences of "outsiders," including Western women and non-Western critics residing in both the West and the Third World.[10]

POSTCOLONIAL INTERROGATION OF HOME MAKING FOR RUTH

Based on different constructions of "home," the story of Ruth has been interpreted in many different ways. Read as a novella, the story can focus on love, courtship, seduction, female subjectivity, the new home, and the birth of the child. As such, the story has no historical reference and is irrelevant to the larger picture of national destiny and political salvation. If, however, we relate the home to the broader contexts of tribe, community, people, and nation, then the short book of Ruth offers many interesting scenarios for readers to plot different interpretive trajectories. I would like to interrogate and trace three such trajectories, which by no means exhaust all the possibilities.

Home as Kinship

It is rather difficult to ascertain the date and purpose of the book of Ruth, as scholars differ in their opinions. A date before the exile suggests that the book is intended to establish the patrilineal genealogy of David (4:21–22) and to affirm the practice of levirate marriage (Deut. 25:5–10). For example, Kirsten Nielsen suggests that the original purpose of the book was to "champion the right of David's family to the throne."[11] A date after the exile would suggest quite a different purpose of the book, which is to show that a non-Israelite can become a faithful worshipper of the Lord. Counteracting the teachings of Ezra and Nehemiah that required Jewish men to divorce their non-Jewish wives, the book may be a response to the postexilic laws against intermarriages.[12] In both cases, the importance of kinship and the significance of the bloodline in defining insiders and outsiders in ancient societies are underscored.

Kinship is an important theme throughout the Hebrew Bible and forms the backdrop to the book of Ruth. The study of kinship systems is a well-

---

10. Fernando F. Segovia, *Decolonizing Biblical Studies: A View from the Margins* (Maryknoll, N.Y.: Orbis Books, 2000), 121–22.

11. Kirsten Nielsen, *Ruth: A Commentary* (Louisville, Ky.: Westminster John Knox Press, 1997), 29.

12. Sakenfeld, *Ruth*, 1–5.

established discursive field. In addition to the historical-critical method, biblical scholars have at their disposal many new tools from disciplines as diverse as anthropology, sociology, semiotics, structuralism, poststructuralism, and cultural studies. Whether the text is read as a means to provide historical data or as a literary product, the book of Ruth provides many interesting points for discussion, such as the characteristics and nature of levirate marriage in ancient Israel, the issues of endogamy versus exogamy and patrilocal versus virilocal marriages (in the former, the bride and groom stay with the bride's father; in the latter, the bride goes to stay with her husband), and the form and style of genealogies.

The book is narrated in a way that assumes knowledge on the part of the implied reader of the practice of levirate marriage, which enables the continuation of the family line and the protection of property within the family. Out of distress and frustration, Naomi sends her two daughters-in-law away, lamenting that she has no more sons that can become their husbands (1:11). The encounter of Ruth with Boaz and the climax at the threshing floor are facilitated by the fact that Boaz is a kinsman of Naomi's husband (2:1). The anticlimax takes place by way of the public witness and decision regarding the legitimate next of kin to redeem family property and to marry Ruth (4:7–10).

In her intertextual study of the book of Ruth with the Tamar story in Genesis 38, Ellen van Wolde points to the implied interest of establishing the male line, which frames the beginning and the end of the narrative.[13] Both stories begin with a man leaving his home country: in the Tamar story, Judah leaves his home; in the book of Ruth, Elimelech from Bethlehem goes to sojourn in Moab because of famine. The stories of Tamar and Ruth are told from the Judahite perspective, and not from a Canaanite or Moabite point of view. Although the two women attract attention through their daring actions, they are both absent from the concluding scene of the story: the Tamar story ends with an account of childbirth, with no mention of Tamar's name; the Ruth story concludes with the birth of Obed and his place as the ancestor of David. Van Wolde writes: "The female protagonists, Ruth and Tamar, are in the end absent; they disappear in favour of their sons."[14] In both stories, the woman involved is a foreigner, who has to take radical action so that the man in question exercises the responsibility of the next of kin. The men, Judah and Boaz, are much older than the female protagonists. When Ruth gives birth to Obed, he is nursed by and identified as the son of the Judahite Naomi and not of Ruth the Moabite. Phyllis Trible points out that it is noteworthy that the

13. Ellen van Wolde, "Texts in Dialogue with Texts: Intertextuality in the Ruth and Tamar Narratives," *Biblical Interpretation* 5 (1997): 8–9.
14. Ibid., 9.

child is named by the women and identified as the son of Naomi rather than of Elimelech.[15]

The anxiety of the next of kin to establish his progeny through levirate marriage does not escape the notice of scholars. In Tamar's case, the closest kin, Onan, agrees to sleep with her, but safeguards his seed and decides to "do it his way."[16] In Ruth's case, the closest kin agrees to redeem the property for Naomi, but refuses to marry a foreign woman. He is willing to follow the law of redeemer but not the law of levirate.[17] This opens a possibility for Boaz to act against established customs and social roles: "He searches for ways to maximize his own advantage while maintaining his proper family honor; his solution bends the social rules about marriage while adhering to and exceeding the redemption law."[18] Since Boaz is an older man, his response to being sexually awakened by Ruth at the threshing floor and his concern about his virility are highlighted by some readers. Washed, perfumed, and dressed in her finest clothes, Ruth wakes Boaz, literally and figuratively, challenging Boaz to leave behind his pious public respectability. "The younger woman," states Francis Landy, "comes to sleep with the older man at a site marked symbolically by decision and fertility and temporally by the suspension of social norms."[19]

The story touches on endogamy and exogamy as well as on patrilocal versus virilocal marriages. The Israelites were admonished not to marry foreign women and worship their gods. This was one of the reasons why the immediate next of kin refused to marry Ruth, because she was a Moabite. In fact, according to some rabbinical interpretations, Naomi's two sons, Mahlon and Chilion, were struck down by God because they had committed the sin of marrying foreign women.[20] But Boaz was able to cross the boundary and hence became the ancestor of David. Following Mieke Bal's study of the transition from patrilocal to virilocal marriage in Judges, David Jobling argues that the book of Ruth reads "like an apology for virilocal marriage."[21] Here Ruth disassociates herself from her father's family and joins her husband's family, and

15. Phyllis Trible, *God and the Rhetoric of Sexuality* (Philadelphia: Fortress Press, 1978), 194–95.

16. Van Wolde, "Texts in Dialogue with Texts," 10, 15.

17. Mieke Bal, *Lethal Love: Feminist Literary Readings of Biblical Love Stories* (Bloomington: Indiana University Press, 1987), 80.

18. Jon L. Berquist, "Role Dedifferentiation in the Book of Ruth," *Journal for the Study of the Old Testament* 57 (1993): 34.

19. Francis Landy, "Ruth and the Romance of Realism, or Deconstructing History," *Journal of the American Academy of Religion* 62 (1994): 292.

20. Katheryn Pfisterer Darr, *Far More Precious than Jewels: Perspectives on Biblical Women* (Louisville, Ky.: Westminster John Knox Press, 1991), 62–63.

21. David Jobling, "Ruth Finds a Home: Canon, Politics, Method," in *The New Literary Criticism and the Hebrew Bible*, ed. J. Cheryl Exum and David J. A. Clines (Sheffield: JSOT Press, 1993), 133.

participates in establishing the monarchy. Although Ruth gives birth to the baby and the women name the newborn, the child is reckoned according to Boaz's family line in the closing genealogy. The genealogy leaves out Judah and starts with his son Perez, so that Boaz will occupy the honorable seventh position and David the tenth. Katherine Doob Sakenfeld suggests that the formal and official genealogy serves several purposes in the book.[22] The genealogy demonstrates that the blessing prayer for Boaz (4:12) is fulfilled and provides a literary link to 1 Samuel, in which the establishment of the monarchy and David's kingship is told. It also reminds Christian readers of another important genealogy in Matthew, namely, the genealogy of Jesus as a descendant of David. While the genealogy in the book of Ruth does not include any women, the Matthean genealogy includes four women (Tamar, Rahab, Ruth, and the wife of Uriah).

Finding a home for Ruth within the kinship system, either in terms of continuation of the male line in the family saga or in the political narrative of the rise of monarchy, has been criticized by feminist critics.[23] Yet, as we have seen, both the narrative structure and the framing of the book lend themselves to such a reading. As a matter of fact, before the advent of feminist criticism, many women's stories in the Bible had been read as serving some grand purpose, such as the salvation of God or the political liberation of the people. From a postcolonial feminist perspective, we must also ask what is suppressed in the reading of home as kinship. A postcolonial feminist reading will highlight the significance of a foreign woman being used as the boundary marker to define difference in the contact zone of different cultures. The recuperation of David's patrilineal genealogy is done with the effective effacing of the name of the foreign woman in the family history and of her own family heritage. Furthermore, as Marcella Althaus-Reid has helped us to see, the foreign woman's sexuality has been appropriated figuratively both in the texts and in economic and political systems that treat her body as commodity or instrument. Here, Ruth's sexuality is not a private matter but is intimately related to finding security and a means of survival for her and Naomi, as well as to the preservation of family land and property. Using the critical insights of Althaus-Reid, we can discern an omnipresent heterosexual system operating in the story through different economic and political arrangements, and supported by theological discourse.[24] Such critical observations lead us to the next clusters of issues when we consider home as patriarchal household.

22. Sakenfeld, *Ruth*, 85–86.

23. Esther Fuchs, "The Literary Characterization of Mothers and Sexual Politics in the Hebrew Bible," *Semeia* 46 (1989): 151–66.

24. Marcella María Althaus-Reid, "On Wearing Skirts without Underwear: 'Indecent Theology Challenging the Liberation Theology of the Pueblo': Poor Women Contesting Christ," *Feminist Theology* 20 (1999): 40.

Home as Patriarchal Household

The story presents problems for feminist scholars because the narrative does not challenge patriarchal and heterosexual familial structures: a widow can find economic security only through remarriage; marrying a man with some means (no matter the age difference) guarantees financial gain; giving birth to a son is the greatest responsibility of women; a male child is more valuable than a female child; and the authority of the mother-in-law is over the daughter-in-law.[25] Armed with the hermeneutics of suspicion, feminist scholars want to retrieve liberating moments in the story, since it is rare to find women with such major roles in a book in the Bible. In the following, I discuss the reading strategies of feminist scholars and demonstrate how their focus on the role and character of female protagonists, female friendship, decent/indecent female sexual behavior, and lesbian love might have left out important power dynamics of race, nation, and ethnicity at work in the story. Instead of retrieval, my concern is to show what is silenced, suppressed, or glossed over.

Borrowing insights from feminist literary criticism, biblical scholars accentuate the roles, character, and subjectivities of female protagonists. Phyllis Trible, for example, stresses the courage and determination of Naomi and Ruth in "their struggle for survival in a patriarchal environment."[26] In the midst of poverty, famine, and dislocation, Naomi invokes the promise of Yahweh and Ruth chooses life over death. In this way, they have changed from nonpersons toward personhood.[27] In keeping with her narratological method, Mieke Bal looks at women's speech, focalization, and action as portrayed in the narrative.[28] Susan Reimer Torn suggests that the book of Ruth preserve the ancient matriarchal tradition, in which powerful women forge their own identity and take initiative.[29] It seems to me that many white feminist readings are interested in the recovery of the authoritative self associated with the modern female subject. Following the important insights of Gayatri Chakravorty Spivak in her "Three Women's Texts and a Critique of Imperialism,"[30] I argue that such overemphasis on individualist female subjectivity downplays the ethnicity

25. Sakenfeld, *Ruth*, 11; Amy-Jill Levine, "Ruth," in *The Women's Bible Commentary*, ed. Carol A. Newsom and Sharon H. Ringe (Louisville, Ky.: Westminster John Knox Press, 1992), 78–79.

26. Trible, *God and the Rhetoric of Sexuality*, 166.

27. Ibid., 168.

28. Bal, *Lethal Love*, 77–79.

29. Susan Reimer Torn, "Ruth Reconsidered." in *Reading Ruth: Contemporary Women Reclaim a Sacred Story*, ed. Judith A. Kates and Gail Twersky Reimer (New York: Ballantine Books, 1994), 345–46.

30. Gayatri Chakravorty Spivak, "Three Women's Texts and a Critique of Imperialism," *Critical Inquiry* 12 (1985): 243–61.

of the woman and suggests that the heroic acts of the protagonist can solve all problems.

Besides personal virtue and character, feminist commentators also elaborate on the interpersonal relationship between women. Some suggest that the book might stem from women's culture because the relationship of Naomi and Ruth is sharply different from the stereotypical biblical image of women as rivals.[31] It is rare in the Bible to find two women who commit their life and future to each other at such a deep level. For Ruth Anna Putnam, the story provides a model of female friendship, which sometimes requires stepping outside one's moral tradition (Ruth's "leaving home") and the courage to share the hardship in a friend's life.[32] From the Taiwanese context, where mothers-in-law exercise great authority, Julie Chu cherishes the respect and devotion of these two women, who struggle together against patriarchal culture.[33] My earlier reading of Ruth emphasizes "the covenant between Naomi and Ruth, two women of different races and religions, [that] exemplifies the deepest commitment and solidarity between persons."[34] However, I have begun to see that such readings, though helpfully accenting female friendship and bonding, have a tendency to decontextualize the story, while trying to lift up moral ideals or universal truths for appropriation in other situations. For example, such readings gloss over the difficulties of Ruth's "leaving home," and do not suggest how this liberal-humanist construction of female friendship could undermine in a concrete way patriarchal power.

By far the most interesting discussions center on Ruth's desire and sexuality, because in the process deep-seated assumptions about family, gender relation, and women's appropriate behavior are revealed. Scholars differ greatly in interpreting the unconventional action of Ruth at the threshing floor, because Ruth's behavior presses against what white, middle-class people considered as female decency. Susan Reimer Torn came to Ruth's defense by suggesting that there is no reason why women cannot take matters in their own hands, "even steering their male protagonists toward their chosen course of action."[35] She continues: "These biblical women, rather than bowing to some external,

31. Fokkelien Van Dijk-Hemmes, "Ruth: A Product of Women's Culture?" in *A Feminist Companion to Ruth*, ed. Althalya Brenner (Sheffield: Sheffield Academic Press, 1993), 136.

32. Ruth Anna Putnam, "Friendship," in Kates and Reimer, *Reading Ruth*, 53–54.

33. Julie L. C. Chu, "Returning Home: The Inspiration of the Role Dedifferentiation in the Book of Ruth for Taiwanese Women," *Semeia* 78 (1997): 47–53.

34. Kwok Pui-lan, "The Future of Feminist Theology: An Asian Perspective," in *Feminist Theology from the Third World: A Reader*, ed. Ursula King (Maryknoll, N.Y.: Orbis Books, 1994), 71.

35. Torn, "Ruth Reconsidered," 344.

foreign authority embodied in the father, fully appropriate their preroga-tives. They themselves seduce fathers and father figures. The importance of their directing—rather than submitting to—the father cannot be over-looked."[36] For Amy-Jill Levine, the issue at hand, however, is not defining decent and indecent behavior of women in general, because the gender of Ruth must be read together with her ethnicity. Reading this scenario as a Jew-ish scholar, Levine particularly cautions that the story can be used to preach that Gentile women are bad models for Israelite women because they are sex-ually manipulative and dangerous. She states: "It is the reader's task to deter-mine whether this book affirms Ruth or ultimately erases her, whether she serves as a moral exemplar or as a warning against sexually forward Gentile women."[37] Levine's warning should be heeded because of the long history of stereotypical views of the sexuality of "foreign" women—black, colonized, native, and indigenous—as seductive, lustful, and promiscuous. The binary construction of decent/indecent women has served both to control white women's sexuality and to facilitate the creation of fantasy-driven racial and sex-ual stereotypes.

A radical debunking of the ideology of the patriarchal household is pre-sented by lesbian readers, who focus on the love between Naomi and Ruth instead of the liaison between Ruth and Boaz. For Rebecca Alpert, a Jewish rabbi, the book of Ruth is an important source for the location of women who are lovers of women in Jewish history. The story provides important role mod-els for female friendship for Jewish lesbians: committed relationship across the boundaries of age, nationality, and religious tradition; commitment to main-taining familial connections and raising children together. But Alpert goes a step further to ask readers to "read between the lines of the text and imagine Ruth and Naomi to be lovers," because for her "without romantic love and sexuality, the story of Ruth and Naomi loses much of its power as a model for Jewish lesbian relationships."[38] To the critics who feel unease with reading it as a lesbian love story, Alpert retorts that much sexual love between women is hidden from public view. Even though Ruth married Boaz in the end, she might have done so to protect herself and Naomi, for it was difficult for women to survive without male protection in biblical times.[39] Alpert issues two chal-lenges in proposing such a reading. The first one is epistemological: whether the reader can interpret the story without using a patriarchal heterosexual lens.

36. Ibid.
37. Levine, "Ruth," 79.
38. Rebecca Alpert, "Finding Our Past: A Lesbian Interpretation of the Book of Ruth," in Kates and Reimer, *Reading Ruth*, 95.
39. Ibid.

The second one is ethical: can enough room be made for lesbian interpretations of the book of Ruth as a way of welcoming lesbians?

I respect such a reading because of the relative silence among feminist biblical scholars on the oppression of compulsory heterosexuality both in ancient and modern societies. But coming from an Asian society where the mother-in-law has historically wielded so much power over the life of the daughter-in-law, it is difficult for me to imagine an egalitarian and even passionate friendship between the two. Thus, I hope Alpert will elaborate on the power differentials between these two women, so that her readers will not simply focus on their female friendship or love, while easily glossing over the thorny issues of ethnicity. The work of Audre Lorde, for example, has lifted up the difficulties of loving, living, and raising children as interracial lesbian couples.[40] The fairy tale that Ruth and Boaz live happily ever after serves to assert patriarchal and heterosexual power; a romantic tale about Ruth and Naomi can equally cover up ethnic differences, as well as the difficulties of maintaining an interethnic or interracial relationship.

Home as Hospitality for Strangers

In the Jewish tradition, the book of Ruth is read during Shavuot, the Feast of Weeks in May, which is connected with the acceptance of Torah by the children of Israel. During the harvest of late-spring crops, the festival reminds the Jewish people of their covenantal relationship with God. Since they were brought out of the land of Egypt by God, they were exhorted to be merciful to the stranger, the orphan, and the widow among them. In the story, Naomi and Ruth embody all these marginalized qualities and challenge the Jewish world to live up to Torah ideals.[41] For some commentators, the story exhibits a model of loyal living, in which the care and concern for others are reciprocated. The three major characters—Naomi, Ruth, and Boaz—act in ways that promote the well-being of others, and they are in turn praised in the book.[42] The attitude of Boaz is especially contrasted with that of the closest kin. Thus, Boaz protects and takes care of Ruth when she gleans in his field; exhibits moral rectitude and does not take advantage of the young woman at the threshing floor; and agrees to marry Ruth, even though she belongs to an enemy people.

But such a liberal reading of compassion toward the strangers living in our midst masks the fact that the people at home do not accept all strangers equally.

40. Audre Lorde, *Sister Outsider: Essays and Speeches* (Trumansburg, N.Y.: Crossing Press, 1984), 72–80.
41. Kates and Reimer, *Reading Ruth*, xix.
42. Sakenfeld, *Ruth*, 11.

Reading the story from a Jewish nationalist perspective, Cynthia Ozick argues that the story offers two examples of strangers—Orpah and Ruth—whose destinies are quite different. Although Orpah might have been more daring than other women by marrying a Jew, she is no iconoclast and chooses to return to her mother's land and her gods.[43] For ten years she has been with Naomi's family, but she has not fully absorbed the Hebrew vision.[44] When given a chance to return to her homeland, no one would blame her for choosing the normal course, which most people would have taken. On Orpah, Ozick comments: "She is no one's heroine. Her mark is erased from history; there is no Book of Orpah. And yet Orpah *is* history. Or, rather, she is history's great backdrop. She is the majority of humankind living out its usualness on home ground."[45] The real heroine is Ruth, whom Ozick characterizes as a visionary, for she thinks beyond exigency and is willing to commit herself to a monotheistic god. Contrasting Ruth with Orpah, Ozick says: "Ruth leaves Moab because she intends to leave *childish ideas* behind. She is drawn to Israel because Israel is the inheritor of the One Universal Creator."[46]

Without questioning the powerful ideology of assimilation, Ozick praises Ruth for her successful assimilation into the Jewish community and her conversion to the God of the Israelites. Her interpretation is criticized by Bonnie Honig, who argues that Ozick has neutralized the differences Ruth the Moabite represents, making her a model émigré without threatening the identity of the Israelites. Honig notes:

> The contrast between Ruth and Orpah highlights the extraordinariness of Ruth's border crossing, as Ozick points out. But the contrast also has another effect: it suggests that Ruth's migration to Bethlehem does not mean that Israel is now a borderless community open to all foreigners, including even idolatrous Moabites. Israel is open only to the Moabite who is exceptionally virtuous, to Ruth but not Orpah.[47]

Honig has called attention to the imagined boundary created by interpreters between the home and strangers, the dangerous alien and the assimilated immigrant, a kinship-style (national) identity and a challenged and contested democracy.[48] For her, Ruth's incorporation into the Israelite order is not without complications and ambivalence.[49] She further argues that Israel,

---

43. Cynthia Ozick, "Ruth," in Kates and Reimer, *Reading Ruth*, 222.
44. Ibid., 223.
45. Ibid., 221.
46. Ibid., 227. Emphasis mine.
47. Bonnie Honig, "Ruth, the Model Emigrée: Mourning and the Symbolic Politics of Immigration," in Brenner, *Ruth and Esther*, 55–56.
48. Ibid., 74.
49. Ibid., 60–61.

as the chosen people, needs to construct the foreignness of the Other, but that, at the same time, the foreign Ruth also threatens the very definition of the identity of Israel.

Honig's reading has direct implications for the current discussion of immigrants and aliens in the United States. As the melting pot analogy has been criticized by many as an ideology of false inclusion, the cultural identity of the United States has been hotly debated, whether it is framed in terms of offering bilingual education to immigrant children, the teaching of Ebonics in schools, or the nature of multiculturalism. Such contemporary issues lead us to questions such as: How is the stranger to be defined? Should the stranger be assimilated and under what terms? What are the ways the stranger is continually kept on the margin without threatening the power at the center? Furthermore, we need to question the powerful myths of home, nation, people, and bloodline on which a common "origin" of belonging is generated, leading sometimes to the violent exclusion of others. In the next section, I will turn to some recent discussions that further interrogate the very definition of "home."

HOME AND ITS DISCONTENTS

As new paradigms of interpretation emerge, the Bible is not only read for its religious and theological meanings, in the context of the development of biblical scholarship, but also for its broader cultural and political impact on shaping the values, norms, and actions of society. Mieke Bal, for example, explicitly states that she does not attribute moral, religious, or political authority to the biblical texts, but is interested in the "cultural function of one of the most influential mythical and literary documents" of Western culture.[50] Literary critic J. Cheryl Exum foregrounds the textuality of biblical literature and examines the Ruth-Naomi-Boaz triangle through paintings, Hollywood films, and novels as metatexts.[51] Postcolonial critics deploy different theoretical tools to question the relation between culture and empire and how the Bible has been interpreted to facilitate violence, genocide, slavery, and other atrocities done in the name of God.

Although Jewish scholar Regina Schwartz does not identify herself as a postcolonial critic, she makes the explicit connection between, on the one hand, the function of religious and national identities through the deployment of covenant, land, kinship, "nation," and memory in the Hebrew Bible, and,

50. Bal, *Lethal Love*, 1.
51. J. Cheryl Exum, *Plotted, Shot, and Painted: Cultural Representations of Biblical Women* (Sheffield: Sheffield Academic Press, 1996), 129–74.

on the other, the modern history of colonial expansion of the West. I will first discuss the contribution of her important book *The Curse of Cain* before turning to a postcolonial reading by Laura Donaldson.

Home, Violence, and Identity Formation

Regina Schwartz begins her controversial book *The Curse of Cain* by sharing an encounter she had with a student while discussing the exodus story. To the student's simple question, "What about the Canaanites?" Schwartz replies:

> Yes, what about the Canaanites? and the Amorites, Moabites, Hittites? While the biblical narratives charted the creation, cohesion, and calamities befalling a people at the behest of their God, what about all the other peoples and their gods? Having long seen the Bible put to uses that I could not excuse—hatred of Blacks, Jews, gays, women, "pagan," and the poor—I now began to see some complicity, for over and over the Bible tells the story of a people who inherit at someone else's expense. . . . Through the dissemination of the Bible in Western culture, its narratives have become the foundation of a prevailing understanding of ethnic, religious, and national identity as defined negatively, over against others.[52]

Schwartz notes that the themes of "covenant," "chosen people," and "promised land" have been used repeatedly by the Christian West to justify the colonization of non-Christians and the annihilation of Native peoples of the Americas. But the same belief system also undergirded the rise of modern Zionism and the displacement of Palestinians from their homeland. Schwartz's book emerged from the larger discourse of a critical scrutiny of modern Jewish collective identity. In his Jewish theology of liberation, Marc Ellis insists that Jews should never use the painful memory of holocaust as a pretext to oppress other people.[53] Along the same vein, Jonathan Boyarin raises the links between Zionism and European nationalism, questions the grounding of Jewish identity in a territory, and challenges the attempt to "escape history by a return to a mythic past."[54]

Schwartz makes several bold claims at the outset of her book. She argues that the acts of identity formation are themselves acts of violence, because for

---

52. Regina M. Schwartz, *The Curse of Cain: The Violent Legacy of Monotheism* (Chicago: University of Chicago Press, 1997), ix–x. Hereafter page references will be given in parentheses in the text.

53. Marc H. Ellis, *Toward a Jewish Theology of Liberation: The Uprising and the Future* (Maryknoll, N.Y.: Orbis Books, 1989).

54. Jonathan Boyarin, *Storm from Paradise: The Politics of Jewish Memory* (Minneapolis: University of Minnesota Press, 1992), 116–29.

her "imagining identity as an act of distinguishing and separating from others, of boundary making and line drawing, is the most frequent and fundamental act of violence we commit" (5). At the center of her interest is how identity is related to monotheism—thus the subtitle of her book, *The Violent Legacy of Monotheism*. She explains: "Monotheism is a myth that grounds particular identity in universal transcendence. And monotheism is a myth that forges identity antithetically—against the Other" (16). But why would identity formation based on a monotheistic God spawn violence? The answer, she claims, is the principle of scarcity, which is also found in the Bible. This principle—encoded as one people, one nation, one land, and ultimately one God—demands exclusive allegiance and threatens with the violence of exclusion. Schwartz finds a paradigmatic account of the "original violence" in the story of Cain and Abel, wherein Cain kills Abel as a result of God's acceptance of the sacrifice of Abel, but not his.

With these broad theoretical interests, Schwartz argues that the book of Ruth demonstrates that the principle of scarcity is at work and that kinship is attached to monotheism (90–91). The story associates the foreigner Ruth with the principle of scarcity. During a time of famine in her homeland, she travels with her mother-in-law into the land of Israel, and is fed by a generous Israelite who takes care of her and later marries her. Throughout the story, the themes of fertility of the land and human fecundity are interwoven with the threat of famine and barrenness. On the surface, the fact that Ruth is generously treated would seem to suggest the inclusion of a foreigner within the kinship system and a broadening of the vision of monotheism. On closer scrutiny, however, one finds that the principle of plenitude and generosity is compromised, because Boaz is providing not for a complete stranger but for his kin Naomi, and for the continuation of his family line. While Ozick commends Ruth for her conversion to monotheism, Schwartz regards the adoption of the God of Israel as precondition for embracing the foreigner as highly problematic. Ruth's vow, "Your people shall be my people, and your God my God," binds kinship with monotheism by linking a people with one God and excluding other identities.

While Schwartz's reviewers have raised questions concerning the relation between identity formation and violence and the necessary link between monotheism and scarcity,[55] I am interested in the reading strategies she

---

55. Walter Brueggemann, "The Curse of Cain: The Violent Legacy of Monotheism," *Theology Today* 54 (1998): 534–37; Miroslav Volf, "Jehovah on Trial," *Christianity Today* 27 (April 1998): 32–35; Brian K. Smith, "Monotheism and Its Discontents: Religious Violence and the Bible," *Journal of the American Academy of Religion* 66 (1999): 403–11.

proposes to lessen the infliction of violence. First, she persistently demonstrates that in the Bible identity (people, nation, land) is a question and not an answer, provisional and not reified. As such, the Bible cannot be used unambiguously to justify nationalism, imperialism, and the persecution of the Other (142). Second, she does not see the Hebrew Bible as offering a coherent, unified, and developmental history to which Jewish people can unequivocally lay claim. She argues that the preoccupation with collective identity as God's chosen people and chosen nation was colored by German nationalism, which emerged at the same time as the historical-critical method (10–11, 122–23). Following Foucault, she regards history in the Hebrew Bible as a series of discontinuities, ruptures, and incoherences, in which identities need to be remade and re-formed. Third, she pays attention to the triad of sex, power, and transcendence. There are many incidents in the Bible where sexual violation begets violence and war (e.g., the rapes of Dinah and the Levite's concubine). Sexual fidelity is related to divine fidelity in the attempt to construct kinship, nationhood, and monotheism (141). Fourth, she draws out contradictory biblical narratives on group identity so as to destabilize the definition of the stranger or the foreigner. She writes: "What I have been exploring here is not a single view of the Other that is somehow 'in the Bible,' but instead pursuing a strategy of reading the Bible that makes any single consistent ideological viewpoint difficult to defend" (103). Fifth, she suggests that, apart from the principle of scarcity, there is also the principle of plenitude and generosity in the Bible, though she does not concretely spell out how this will affect identity formation.

Home, Women's Sexuality, and the "Pocahontas Perplex"

In certain ways, Laura Donaldson's reading of the book of Ruth complements that of Schwartz. While Schwartz is interested in debunking the identities of kinship, chosen people, and monotheism, Donaldson lifts up the themes of projected sexual stereotypes of the Other and assimilating the Other into the same. Both Schwartz and Donaldson are trained not primarily in the Bible and biblical studies but in English literature and literary criticism, and engage a wide range of reading strategies in their works. Donaldson also begins by making some bold claims. She maintains that the Bible has been introduced to Native cultures in the context of a colonizing Christianity and has facilitated "culturecide" of Native peoples. Yet she argues that, through the long history of victimization, Native peoples have also read the Bible on their own terms.[56]

---

56. Donaldson, "The Sign of Orpah," 20–21. Hereafter page references to Donaldson will be given in parentheses in the text.

Donaldson's intervention focuses on women's sexuality in the story and interprets it through the lens of the encounter between Native women and European colonizers. Her reading is significantly different from that of Schwartz on this point. Schwartz pays attention to sexual violation, rape, and adultery in the Hebrew Bible because she is interested in the relation between violence and identity formation. In Ruth's story, there is seemingly no sexual violence involved, and the sexual relationship between Ruth and Boaz does not matter much to Schwartz, except that they get married and a son is later born. Donaldson, on the other hand, sees the "voluntary" interethnic marriage as an assimilationist strategy that has wreaked havoc on her people. Placing women's sexuality beyond the sex/gender framework, Donaldson differentiates herself from those feminist biblical critics who challenge the ideology of home as patriarchal household, whether by exposing its masculinist and heterosexist bias or by constructing a woman-identified love between Ruth and Naomi (23).

While traditional interpretations emphasize the genealogy of Boaz, David, and Jesus, Donaldson constructs another matrilineal genealogy, from Lot's daughters to Rahab and Ruth. The Moabites allegedly are descendants of Lot and his daughters from incestuous encounters (Gen. 19) and are excluded from the assembly of the Lord even to the tenth generation (Deut. 23:3). Moabite women are portrayed not only as worshipping idols but also as hypersexualized and presenting enormous threats to Israelite men. Such stereotypical images of Moabite women, Donaldson argues, would have fitted the profiles of indigenous women held by European Christians (24). Ruth's other mother-in-law is Rahab, Boaz's Canaanite mother, whose family is spared by Joshua during the fall of Jericho because she has collaborated with the spies. Rahab's destiny foreshadows that of Ruth, because "Rahab embodies a foreign woman, a Canaanite Other who crosses over from paganism to monotheism and is rewarded for this act by absorption into the genealogy of her husband and son" (30). Here, Donaldson echoes the point of view expressed by Musa Dube, who argues that the story of Rahab cannot be reclaimed for women's roles without paying close attention to the imperialistic agenda. Dube characterizes the story of Rahab as "a script about the domestication of the promised land. She reflects the colonizer's desire to enter and domesticate the land of Canaan."[57]

For Donaldson, the narrative figures of Rahab and Ruth are best understood as the Israelite versions of Pocahontas in Native history. In what Cherokee scholar Rayna Green has termed the "Pocahontas Perplex," the beloved daughter of Powhatan saves and falls in love with John Smith, the white colonist in Jamestown, Virginia, thus enabling the settlement of the English pilgrims. The mythology of Pocahontas prescribes that a "good Indian

---

57. Dube, *Postcolonial Feminist Interpretation of the Bible*, 77.

woman" is one who loves and aids white men, while turning her back on her own people and wisdom tradition. In the biblical stories, Salmon and Boaz stand in for John Smith, and the loyalty of Ruth, the good Moabite, is praised by generations of biblical scholars, while Orpah is scorned as the bad Moabite.

Postcolonial critics have increasingly paid attention to the role sexuality plays in the representation of the Other in colonial discourse. By subjecting the story of Ruth to a sexualized reading, Donaldson helps us to discern more clearly how the representation of otherness is achieved through both sexual and cultural modes of differentiation. This does not mean simply paying attention to how Moabite woman or Moabite sexuality is represented. It also entails deciphering the ways in which representations of the Other are interwoven through sexual imageries, unconscious fantasies, and desires, as well as fears. As Meyda Yeğenoğlu has argued, to fully understand the double articulation of colonial discourse, we must explore the "articulation of the historical with fantasy, the cultural with the sexual, and desire with power."[58]

Homi Bhabha argues that the difference between the colonizers and the colonized is never static or fixed, so that colonial discourse is never closed or unidirectional. In fact, colonial authority is always ambivalent, contested, and conflictual, characterized not only by the manifest power of domination but also by latent dreams, fantasies, myths, and obsessions.[59] Using psychoanalytic theory, Lacan's in particular, Bhabha articulates the colonizer's consistent and unconscious need or demand for psychic affirmation. The Pocahontas Perplex belongs to a genre of myths about an indigenous or native woman falling in love with a white man, longing for his return, and even willing to die for him. Other cultural specimens that represent the white male fantasy of sexy Asian woman falling for heroic white man include such figures as Madame Butterfly, Suzie Wong, and Miss Saigon.

Donaldson's reading of the book of Ruth illustrates several useful reading strategies. First, in this example as well as in her book *Decolonizing Feminisms*, she insists that gender and sexuality must be examined in the wider contexts of race, class, culture, colonialism, conquest, and slavery. In her book, she finds that interpreters of nineteenth- and twentieth-century novels and movies produced from these books tend to focus on white women characters without questioning the imperial textual construction and white authority and rule. She warns against using "anti-sexist rhetoric to displace questions of colonialism, racism, and their concomitant violence."[60] Second, she pays attention to

58. Meyda Yeğenoğlu, *Colonial Fantasies: Towards a Feminist Reading of Orientalism* (Cambridge: Cambridge University Press, 1998), 26.

59. Homi K. Bhabha, *The Location of Culture* (London: Routledge, 1994), 71.

60. Laura E. Donaldson, *Decolonizing Feminisms: Race, Gender, and Empire-Building* (Chapel Hill: University of North Carolina Press, 1992), 62.

the tangents of the texts, minor characters, subplots, and marginalized motifs. For example, she lifts up the voices that are marginalized in the text and in the history of interpretation. Orpah, who returns to her mother's house, becomes for Donaldson the story's central character, for Orpah does not abandon her mother's house and thus becomes a sign of hope for Native women. In sharp contrast to Ozick's reading, Donaldson questions the premature narrative foreclosure, or violence, done to the figure Orpah. Third, she demonstrates that Native people must take response-ability for their own reading and inter-face the biblical text with their own history and struggles. In this particular case, reading against the grain means conferring positive value to a figure that has been censored in traditional interpretations.[61] Fourth, the meaning of the text can be determined only with reference to specific cultural and historical contexts. In the Native American communities, the convergence of the his-tory, biblical text, and social and political situation is sharply different from white and Jewish women's situations. Much of the complexity of interethnic and interreligious encounters in the Bible can be fruitfully interpreted with the help of theories of the contact zone.

REFLECTION ON METHOD

Several decades ago, when the historical-critical method was the reigning par-adigm in the field, biblical scholars belonged to the same tribe, shared the same habitus, and read the same genealogy of scholars. Today, biblical scholars belong to many different tribes, and each tribe has its own sources of author-ity and its own genealogy of founding fathers and mothers. The fact that schol-ars can construct so many different "homes" for Ruth points to the radical expansion of the field and the diversity of reading interests. The "home" for biblical studies is fixed no more, but is constantly shifting and changing, being remade and re-created.

One important consequence of such a change is that the Bible is seen not only as a religious or historical product, but also increasingly as a cultural and ideological product. Its interpreters are not limited to those within the faith community or teachers in divinity schools, but are likely to include cultural and postcolonial critics coming from many disciplines in the secular univer-sity. Their research interests are not so much motivated by the search for reli-gious truths as for cultural and political meanings promoted and endorsed by the Bible. Unlike the historical critic who traces the meaning of the texts diachronically to their original settings, the cultural critic is more interested

61. Darr, *Far More Precious*, 62.

in constructing meaning synchronically through reading the Bible with other cultural metatexts. While the former asks what the Bible said to its original audience, the latter asks what the Bible is saying to our contemporary situation. Since both the Bible and the contemporary contexts can be read in so many different ways, the issues of the ethics and accountability of interpretation are brought to the forefront. As Elisabeth Schüssler Fiorenza stated in her 1987 presidential address to the Society of Biblical Literature:

> If the Bible has become a classic of western culture because of its normativity, then the responsibility of the biblical scholar cannot be restricted to giving "the readers of our time clear access to the original intentions" of biblical writers. It must also include the elucidation of the ethical consequences and political functions of biblical texts and their interpretations in their historical as well as in their contemporary sociopolitical contexts.[62]

Both Regina Schwartz and Laura Donaldson raise critical questions regarding the political functions of biblical texts and trace the problem not only to the history of its interpretation but to the text itself.

As a Jew, Schwartz challenges the ways in which the Hebrew Bible has been read for millennia as a book defining the special identity of Jews as God's chosen people and Israel as the chosen nation. She notes that during the exile, when Jews lost their homeland and their temple, the memory of the exodus and of Israel as the chosen people became paramount in defining their identity. After the holocaust, many Jews linked their identity to a specific territory and evoked the memory of the past in justifying the establishment of the nation of Israel. Schwartz takes upon herself the responsibility of interpreting the Hebrew texts so that they will not perpetuate the violent ways that national, ethnic, and religious boundaries have been drawn. Thus, she argues for a diasporic understanding of Jewish identity that is fluid, destabilized, and open to negotiation in specific circumstances. Schwartz's iconoclastic reading puts her at odds with much rabbinic teaching and modern Jewish politics. She says: "Freud's courage to write his *Moses and Monotheism* in the midst of Nazi persecution gave me strength to criticize the biblical legacy despite a continuing tragic climate of antisemitism" (xiv).

In her postcolonial and Native reading, Laura Donaldson calls our attention to how the Christian West has appropriated the Jewish text and used it against the indigenous and colonized peoples. Instead of reading the text from a Jewish perspective, she is compelled to reexamine the relationship between

---

62. Elisabeth Schüssler Fiorenza, *Rhetoric and Ethic: The Politics of Biblical Studies* (Minneapolis: Fortress Press, 1999), 28.

Israel and her neighbors and to interpret the text from a Moabite perspective. She debunks the triumphant Christian claim that Christians have replaced the Jews as the chosen people of God and are entrusted with the "civilizing mission" of the world. She writes: "I can only hope that my indigenization of Ruth has located new meaning in the interaction between biblical text and American Indian context—a meaning that resists imperial exegesis and contributes to the empowerment of aboriginal peoples everywhere" (36).

In the postcolonial era, when many of the world's boundaries are being remade and redrawn, Schwartz and Donaldson challenge us to read the Bible not from the cozy "home" of traditional Jewish or Christian interpretations but from the experiences of those whose lives have been marginalized and oppressed by the Bible. They demand biblical scholars leave their cozy habitus of "objective" and apolitical readings to engage in a world beset by warfare, anti-Semitism, ethnic strife, and racial bigotry. Such critical engagement will sometimes lead them to the unsettling place of questioning some of the foundational myths that they cherish and hold dear to their hearts, such as the exodus, the covenant, the promised land, and the chosen people.

In conclusion, as we search for new ways of interpreting the Bible for the contemporary world, it is important to pay attention to critical and prophetic scholarship, often coming from marginalized communities in our society. As biblical scholars and theologians entrusted with the task of interpreting and transmitting the tradition, it is imperative for us to recognize the violent legacy of biblical interpretation in the past and in the present. The Bible has fueled such beliefs as the "heavenly kingdom in America," the "manifest destiny" of the United States, and the "one country, under God" of the national motto. Since the United States has become the single superpower in the world, it is significant to look for ways to read the Bible that will help us to destabilize all hegemonic claims and that will make room for others to share the planet as their "home."

PART 2

Postcolonial Feminist Theological Vision

5

Postcolonial Feminist Theology

What Is It? How to Do It?

My research for emancipatory knowledge over the years has made me realize that ideas are always communally wrought, not privately owned.

Chandra Talpade Mohanty[1]

Analyses of the sacred have been one of the most neglected, and may be one of the most rapidly expanding areas of post-colonial study.

Bill Aschroft, Gareth Griffiths, and Helen Tiffin[2]

The term "postcolonial" was applied to a body of Commonwealth literature written during and after colonialism by authors from the former colonies of the British Empire in Asia and Africa.[3] One of the pioneering works on postcolonial literary criticism is entitled *The Empire Writes Back*, which derives from a phrase of Salman Rushdie: "The Empire writes back to the Centre."[4] This title captivates me because "writing back" connotes the power of the written word

---

1. Chandra Talpade Mohanty, *Feminism without Borders: Decolonizing Theory, Practicing Solidarity* (Durham, N.C.: Duke University Press, 2003), 1.
2. Bill Aschroft, Gareth Griffiths, and Helen Tiffin, *The Empire Writes Back: Theory and Practice in Post-colonial Literatures*, 2nd ed. (London: Routledge, 2002), 212.
3. For the interesting story of how a publisher changed Commonwealth literature to postcolonial literature, see R. S. Sugirtharajah, "A Postcolonial Exploration of Collusion and Construction in Biblical Interpretation," in *The Postcolonial Bible*, ed. R. S. Sugirtharajah (Sheffield: Sheffield Academic Press, 1998), 92.
4. Laura Chrisman, "The Imperial Unconscious? Representations of Imperial Discourse," in *Colonial Discourse and Post-colonial Theory*, ed. Patrick Williams and Laura Chrisman (New York: Columbia University Press, 1994), 498.

as well as the location and posture of the writing subject. The act of writing back implies an oppositional stance, of claiming the power to narrate, to contest and reconstruct meanings, and to play with language and imagination. The subject writing back is the colonized Other, whose text and context have been shaped by the colonial process, and whose experiences become the focal point of postcolonial literature and narration. Doing postcolonial feminist theology, it can be argued, is akin to the "writing back" process in postcolonial literature—only that this time, the writing subjects are the formerly colonized Christian women, and the matter to be discussed is theology.

Third World and indigenous Christian women have been writing theology for some time, though they may not have called their theological works postcolonial feminist theology. Since I have not construed "postcolonial" primarily in a chronological sense, I shall not label all writings by Christian women from the former colonies postcolonial feminist theology. For some of them, the term "feminist" is a nonstarter in their context, because it connotes the kind of separatist feminism defined by the interests of radical middle-class women in the West. For others, postcolonial theory is still too new to them, and they have yet to utilize its insights in analyzing their postcolonial condition and in interrogating Christian doctrines. Some may even be suspicious that postcolonial theory is the product of Third World and diasporic intellectuals in the Western academy, with little relevance to the burning issues they face.

This does not mean, however, that the theological writings of Third World and indigenous women have little in common or show no affinities with what I envisage as postcolonial feminist theology. For although these women have not used the label "postcolonial," their writings reflect an acute understanding of the social, cultural, and political impact of colonialism and neocolonialism on women's lives and on the Christian communities. As I have demonstrated elsewhere, Ghanaian feminist theologian Mercy Amba Oduyoye's concept of "crossroads Christianity," which signals multiple strands of cultures coming into contact in African Christianity, shows similarities to the postcolonial concept of hybridity.[5] But in order to recognize the diverse theoretical frameworks these feminist theologians have employed, I hesitate to call their works postcolonial feminist theology if the authors have not self-proclaimed that they are working out of such a perspective. In fact, postcolonial feminist theology is still in the gestation process, for its theoretical horizon, its subject matter, and its future direction have yet to be defined. As can be expected, there is no one single postcolonial feminist theology that is adequate or comprehensive enough to cover the pluralistic postcolonial con-

5. Kwok Pui-lan, "Mercy Amba Oduyoye and African Women's Theology," *Journal of Feminist Studies in Religion* 20, no. 1 (2004): 7–22.

texts, as the experiences of colonialism are far from homogeneous. There will need to be a rainbow of colors, pluriphonic voices, and multiple rhythms, following different heartbeats.

Who are the people who can do postcolonial feminist theology? Let us first recall that there has been a long debate on whether men can do feminist theory and theology. For some, men are incapable of doing feminist theory and theology because they lack the experiences that women go through because of their sex and gender and, therefore, cannot speak about feminist issues with authority. But for others, feminism is a political stance rather than an embodied experience, and men can certainly contribute to the fight against women's oppression and to the promotion of women's rights. I am more inclined to think that the development of feminist theory and theology is primarily the responsibility of feminists, though profeminist men can indeed be allies in the movement and struggle. This is not to deny that men have a significant role to play, but since women as a group have been sidelined for so long in terms of knowledge production, they should be given a preeminent role representing themselves.

The next question that immediately comes to mind is, Who are the women who can do postcolonial feminist theology? Only the colonized others, the female subalterns, and their descendants? Or should we include women who benefit from colonialism and still reap the plenty of neocolonialism? These are not simple questions, because the term "postcolonial" is highly contested and hard to define. As I have argued, following Stuart Hall, that the colonial process is doubly inscribed, affecting both the metropolitan centers and the colonies, the postcolonial process must involve both the colonizers and the colonized. This means that not only do the colonized need to disengage from the colonial syndrome, the colonizers have to decolonize their minds and practices as well. To complicate the issue at hand, it is not always clear-cut as to who are the postcolonials and who are not. Should white feminists in the United States identify themselves as "postcolonial," since the United States was a former colony of Britain, or would it be better for them to claim their privileged status as members of the dominant group in the world's superpower? And what about the women in the industrialized nations of the Asian Pacific Rim, whose countries suffered during the colonial era but are now enjoying both the benefits of economic growth and the possibilities of oppressing men and women of other poorer nations? Because of all these multiple social locations and subject positions, I will argue that both the (former) female colonizers and the (former) colonized women are able to do postcolonial feminist theology, although they will have different entry points, priorities of issues, accents, and inflections. I also insist that female subalterns who experience the intersection of oppressions in the most immediate and brutal way have epistemological privileges in terms of articulating a postcolonial feminist theology that will be more inclusive than others.

From my particular vantage point, I see the task of postcolonial feminist theology as revolving around three loci, which are closely linked to one another: resignifying gender, requeering sexuality, and redoing theology. In the following, I attempt to bring postcolonial theory to bear on a critical reflection of feminist theology and queer theology, with the goal to provide some guideposts to chart the unexplored terrain called "postcolonial feminist theology." While gender and sexuality are much linked, as queer theorists have pointed out, I have separated the discussion into two sections, because they are taken up separately in theology. This separation is not satisfactory, but it allows me to handle the diverse materials in their discursive contexts. This is, I must admit, only one of the many ways of applying postcolonial theory to what Serene Jones has called "*specific* imagistic patterns of reflection."[6] There are many other possible ways of mapping, and I invite the readers to try out their own.

RESIGNIFYING GENDER

The first book on feminist theology published in the United States at the brink of the second-wave feminist movement was Mary Daly's *The Church and the Second Sex* (1968).[7] As the title suggests, the work builds on Simone de Beauvoir's *The Second Sex* and draws inspiration from the European Enlightenment discourse of equality and liberty to argue for the inclusion of women. The use of gender as a critical category of analysis of the theological tradition and practices of the church was the point of departure for white feminist theology. Mary Daly's classic text *Beyond God the Father* critiqued the androcentrism of Christian language and symbols and raised the consciousness about the use of inclusive language in the church and liturgies.[8] Rosemary Radford Ruether's question "Can a male savior save women?" named the theological paradox and conundrum that many churchwomen felt at the time when the Vatican reaffirmed that women could not be ordained because only men could represent Christ.[9] The gender of Christ and its implication for women's redemption became a focal point of sustained debates between Euro-American and Euro-

6. Serene Jones, *Feminist Theory and Christian Theology: Cartographies of Grace* (Minneapolis: Fortress Press, 2000), 11.
7. Mary Daly, *The Church and the Second Sex* (New York: Harper and Row, 1968). She devotes the first chapter to discussing de Beauvoir's *The Second Sex*.
8. Mary Daly, *Beyond God the Father: Toward a Philosophy of Women's Liberation* (Boston: Beacon Press, 1973).
9. See Rosemary Radford Ruether, *To Change the World: Christology and Cultural Criticism* (New York: Crossroad, 1981), 45–56; and idem, *Sexism and God-Talk: Toward a Feminist Theology* (Boston: Beacon Press, 1983), 116–38.

pean feminists. Observing that women and nature were considered inferior to men and culture, Ruether further made the connection between the subordination of women and nature in the Christian tradition, which she traced to the dualistic tendency in Greek philosophy.

The central questions raised by these early pioneers—masculine language about God, the gender of Christ, and women's relationship to nature—defined to a large extent the *Problematik* and shaped the imagistic pattern of reflections of feminist theology. Goddess thealogy as represented by Carol P. Christ, which arose somewhat in opposition to the predominantly androcentric nexus of Christian symbolism, shared the same episteme, in Foucauldian parlance, although with different emphases—the focus on the feminine symbol of the Goddess and women's closeness to both the Goddess and nature.[10] While acknowledging the contributions of these thinkers in challenging the patriarchal tradition and breaking new grounds, I would like to examine the construction of gender in different phases of white feminist theology in order to argue for a resignification of gender in postcolonial feminist theology.

The early writings of feminist theologians and thinkers in the United States follow a binary construction of gender, as if gender is stable and fixed, not open to question or negotiation. Gender is further naturalized and universalized through the history and experiences of white, middle-class Euro-American women. With the advent of queer theory in the 1990s, and especially with the publication of Judith Butler's *Gender Trouble*, feminists began to see the limitations of gender binarism, which has to be destabilized in order to avoid reinscribing gender hierarchy in our thought patterns and social practices.[11] Daly's famous maxim that seems to have captured the sin of patriarchal Christianity, "If God is male, then the male is God,"[12] raises more theoretical puzzles today than it did some thirty years ago.

Although feminist theologians such as Ruether and Letty Russell have consistently paid attention to women's social and political struggles, much of white liberal middle-class feminist theological discourse concentrates on challenging the construction of gender at the cultural and symbolic levels. The disproportionate amount of time and energy paid to inclusive language and the gender of God is a case in point. I certainly understand the argument that the change in language is necessary, because language shapes consciousness and has the power to constitute reality. I also do not want to underestimate the hurt

10. See especially Carol P. Christ, *The Laughter of Aphrodite: Reflections on a Journey to the Goddess* (San Francisco: Harper and Row, 1987).

11. Judith Butler, *Gender Trouble: Feminism and the Subversion of Identity* (New York: Routledge, 1990).

12. Daly, *Beyond God the Father*, 19.

many Christian women feel when God is constantly referred to by masculine pronouns and metaphors. Still, I want to heed the advice I have repeatedly heard in ecumenical circles that inclusive language has *not* been a primary concern of women in the Third World. The struggle for gender justice, for those without safe water to drink and adequate food to put on the table, cannot be fought primarily at the cultural-symbolic level, without simultaneously attending to sociopolitical struggles.

This leads to my next point, which is closely related. Many white feminist theorists and theologians give priority to gender oppression over other forms of discrimination, such as racism, classism, heterosexism, and colonialism. They blame patriarchy as the root cause for societal problems, and see white women as victims rather than as oppressors. Such a complicit attitude, which does not take into consideration the interlocking nature of oppression, can easily obscure how power actually operates in society. History has repeatedly shown that white feminism does not automatically challenge, and even may camouflage, racial prejudice, class division, compulsory heterosexism, and Western colonialism. With her characteristic sharpness, Gayatri Chakravorty Spivak issues this stark chastisement of Western feminism: "Mainstream project of Western feminism . . . both continues and displaces the battle over the right to individualism between women and men in situations of upward class mobility."[13] And in his historical introduction to postcolonialism, Robert J. C. Young makes this poignant observation: "Feminism is not intrinsically anti-imperialist."[14]

If I may extend Young's argument, I would argue that feminist theology, especially as it has been done by white feminists, is not intrinsically anti-imperialist. If we look back to some forty years of history of Euro-American feminist theology, we cannot say that anticolonialism and anti-imperialism have been its major concerns. While people outside America have protested American imperialism for decades, those inside, feminists included, have been slow in debunking American empire building, except during the last several years with the government's declaration of a "war against terrorism" and the invasion of Iraq. Why is this so? Given the international influence of Euro-American feminist theology, a diagnosis of its problems, in the spirit of inviting critical dialogue rather than assigning blame, is very urgent and necessary.

Meyda Yeğenoğlu, a Turkish feminist sociologist, has analyzed the contradictions of Western women's attempt to challenge the masculinist stance on

13. Gayatri Chakravorty Spivak, *A Critique of Postcolonial Reason: Toward a History of the Vanishing Present* (Cambridge, Mass.: Harvard University Press, 1999), 282.
14. Robert J. C. Young, *Postcolonialism: An Historical Introduction* (Oxford: Blackwell, 2001), 369.

the one hand and their effort to construct an imperial subject for themselves on the other. She notes:

> Although feminist theory has successfully revealed the phallocentric bind of the claims for neutrality and universality, it has nevertheless, by privileging sexual difference to other forms of difference, itself remained blind to the imperialist and ethnocentric bind of such a gesture. . . . The apparently benign appeals to a common good for universal womanhood and the presumption that all women are being spoken for in the same global sisterhood are not free from colonial and masculinist fantasies of attaining a sovereign subject status.[15]

Such an epistemological position circumscribes the way white feminists have done feminist theology. Though they have criticized the masculinist God, a simple change of gender does not automatically challenge an imperialistic construction of God as the benefactor and patron of white people. In fact, many have argued that the constructions of God as the Mother, the Goddess, or the God/dess merely reinscribe sexual difference if only her maternal and nurturing roles are stressed. And I would add that this may be yet another attempt of white feminists to avoid social antagonism by projecting a benign spiritual figure who is supposed to provide comfort and consolation for all. Progressive Christian women in the Third World are astute enough to know that a mere change of the gender of God will not suffice, because gender is only *one* of the problems of Christian imperialism.

In response to mounting criticism in the 1980s, white feminist theologians have paid much more attention to the plurality of women's experiences. Ruether, in her new introduction to *Sexism and God-Talk*, acknowledges the need for "multicontextualization of feminist theology across ethnic, cultural, and religious lines,"[16] and specifies that her work is only one voice arising from an Anglo-American Christian context. Ruether, Letty Russell, and Elisabeth Schüssler Fiorenza have collaborated with Christian women in the Third World in the production of new theological knowledge and in political organizing.[17]

---

15. Meyda Yeğenoğlu, *Colonial Fantasies: Towards a Feminist Reading of Orientalism* (Cambridge: Cambridge University Press, 1998), 105–6.

16. Rosemary Radford Ruether, *Sexism and God-Talk: Toward a Feminist Theology, with a New Introduction* (Boston: Beacon Press, 1993), 13.

17. Rosemary Radford Ruether, ed., *Women Healing Earth: Third World Women on Ecology, Feminism, and Religion* (Maryknoll, N.Y.: Orbis Books, 1996); idem, ed., *Gender, Ethnicity, and Religion: Views from the Other Side* (Minneapolis: Fortress Press, 2002); Letty M. Russell et al., eds., *Inheriting Our Mothers' Gardens: Feminist Theology in Third World Perspective* (Philadelphia: Westminster Press, 1988); Kwok Pui-lan and Elisabeth Schüssler Fiorenza, eds., *Women's Sacred Scriptures*, Concilium 1998, no. 3 (Maryknoll, N.Y.: Orbis Books, 1998).

These so-called first-generation feminist theologians have taken steps to deal with difference in their own ways and moved beyond their positions articulated some thirty years ago. In fact, both Russell and Schüssler Fiorenza have increasingly paid attention to postcolonial perspectives and adopted some of the insights in their work on Christian mission and biblical interpretation.[18]

Several of the second-generation white feminist theologians turn to poststructuralist theory to theorize about difference and interrogate the liberal universal subject in European humanism. Two books make critical contributions in opening up spaces for rethinking the female subject. In *Changing the Subject*, Mary McClintock Fulkerson argues that feminist theology cannot be based on a universalist claim of women's experience. Following the poststructuralists, she argues that the female subject is constructed through a dense web of signification and formed at the intersection of different and sometimes competing discourses. At a time when the usage of such terms as "woman" and "gender" are contested, Fulkerson writes: "The point is not to lose the subject 'woman,' but to *change the subject* in the sense that the complex production of multiple identities becomes basic to our thinking."[19] The multiple subject positions of women enable Fulkerson to make two strategic theoretical moves: to debunk the construction of a unified modern self, thus opening the way to respect difference, and to discover that our identity is rendered by the others it creates. For her, feminist theology must always "turn to the others" (to borrow a term from Joerg Rieger)[20] and ask, "Who is the stranger?" and "Who is 'unintelligible' now?"[21]

Ellen Armour's *Deconstruction, Feminist Theology, and the Problem of Difference* intends also to subvert the liberal humanist subject and faces head-on the question of white feminists' failure to take race seriously.[22] As the title of her work suggests, Armour turns to deconstruction as a remedy, and in particular

---

18. Letty M. Russell, "Cultural Hermeneutics: A Postcolonial Look at Mission," *Journal of Feminist Studies in Religion* 20, no. 1 (2004): 23–40; Elisabeth Schüssler Fiorenza, "The Ethos of Interpretation: Biblical Studies in a Postmodern and Postcolonial Context," in *Theological Literacy for the Twenty-first Century*, ed. Rodney L. Petersen (Grand Rapids: Wm. B. Eerdmans, 2002), 211–28.

19. Mary McClintock Fulkerson, *Changing the Subject: Women's Discourses and Feminist Theology* (Minneapolis: Fortress Press, 1994), 7.

20. Joerg Rieger, *God and the Excluded: Visions and Blindspots in Contemporary Theology* (Minneapolis: Fortress Press, 2001), 99–127.

21. Mary McClintock Fulkerson, "*Theologia* as a Liberation Habitus: Thoughts toward Christian Formation for Resistance," in *Theology and the Interhuman: Essays in Honor of Edward Farley*, ed. Robert R. Williams (Valley Forge, Pa.: Trinity Press International, 1995), 174.

22. Ellen T. Armour, *Deconstruction, Feminist Theology, and the Problem of Difference: Subverting the Race/Gender Divide* (Chicago: University of Chicago Press, 1999).

to the works of Jacques Derrida and Luce Irigaray for theoretical guidance. Basic to Derrida's deconstruction is the concept of *différance*, which subverts the phallocentric regime, destabilizes the economy of sameness, and enables the emergence of alterity. Armour spends the bulk of her book discussing the usefulness of deconstruction for feminist theory and theology, and reading race and woman in the works of Irigaray and Derrida individually and in relation to each other. Such close readings enable her to argue that it is difficult for white feminists to handle both gender and race, because woman and race stand in supplementary relation to each other vis-à-vis man—both as sites of lack and desire and as figures of man's boundaries. It is possible to concentrate on one of these supplements without encountering the other because of the distance maintained between them:

> The roots of whitefeminism's woman lie in man. Whitefeminism's white solipsism can now be read as a reflection of metaphysical humanism's dealing with race. If race and woman are supplements to each other as well as to man, then interrogating one will not necessarily involve interrogating the other. Whichever supplement is left unchallenged goes underground but continues its silent and invisible inscription of the text or context in question.[23]

Armed with such theoretical insights, Armour returns in her conclusion to engage African American feminist literary criticism and discusses the figures of raced women. Her book provides critical insights for white feminist theologians to heed the challenges of black theorists and theologians.

While the works of second-generation white feminist theologians have been characterized as "theoretically sophisticated"—which is a coded way of saying that they do feminist theology with a French inflection—I do not see their output as necessarily anti-imperialistic, for the following reasons. First, while Yeğenoğlu clearly adopts an anti-imperialist framework in her deployment of poststructuralist theory and deconstruction, the same cannot be said of the works of Fulkerson and Armour. Fulkerson is helpful in accounting for difference among women, by showing how three groups of women—academic feminist theologians, Presbyterian laywomen, and Pentecostal women—construct their subject positions and develop different registers in reading biblical texts. She is less successful in integrating race into her account of difference for these women[24] or in using an international framework to examine American women's position vis-à-vis that of women in other parts of the world. This is most evident when she fails to critique the colonial complicity of missionary literature

23. Ibid., 166.
24. Ibid., 27–30.

and its construction of "native" women, when she discusses the impact of missionary literature on Presbyterian women.[25] As for Armour, she has purposely restricted her problem of difference to race, though she is fully aware that postcolonial theory, gay and lesbian studies, and queer theory have shown that there are other differences to which white feminists have to attend.[26] Her argument for limiting her discussion to race is that she does not find all "differences" to be the same and substitutable for another. Still, I want to challenge her theoretical framework of whether one can separate discourses on race neatly from that of class, homophobia, and colonialism. It may also be myopic for her to limit the question of race primarily to the domestic context of the United States, without grounding it in the broader context of rising global racism during the time when she wrote the book in the 1990s.

Second, both Fulkerson and Armour concentrate on discourse and textuality, as this is the special forte of poststructuralist theory, though neither will go as far as saying that there is "nothing outside the text." Fulkerson rejects the dichotomy between ideas and reality.[27] Armour goes to great lengths to clarify the misconception around Derrida's idea of the "text" and concludes the book by saying that she is not interested in providing "a merely textual therapy."[28] She insists that without subverting the gender/race divide in white feminist discourse, it will be more difficult to form alliances with women of color to deconstruct political and social systems of violence against women. I agree that attention to discourse is important, as there is a whole body of insightful works on colonial discourse analysis. But the discursive aspect of colonialism is inseparable from the material conditions of political and economic domination. Likewise, I would have hoped that both Fulkerson and Armour might attend more to materialist analysis, in addition to discourse, in the books.[29]

Third, I am not persuaded that American white feminists have to learn to speak French, though this is not a bad thing, or turn primarily to the French for help in creating what counts as sophisticated theory, when there are exciting homegrown womanist theory, borderland theory, contact-zone cultural

25. Fulkerson, *Changing the Subject*, 207–9.
26. Armour, *Deconstruction*, 5.
27. Fulkerson, *Changing the Subject*, 86–88.
28. Armour, *Deconstruction*, 184.
29. Fulkerson includes a short discussion on "materialism" in *Changing the Subject*, 91–93, and some analyses of class in shaping the subject positions of women. Using the work of Raymond Williams, she discusses a materialist analysis of culture in "Toward a Materialist Christian Social Criticism: Accommodation and Culture Reconsidered," in *Changing Conversations: Religious Reflection and Cultural Analysis*, ed. Dwight N. Hopkins and Sheila Greeve Davaney (New York: Routledge, 1996), 43–57.

analysis, and much more. This love for the French may count as yet another incidence of Eurocentrism. Furthermore, as Terry Eagleton has pointed out, European postmodernist and poststructuralist theorists emerged out of intense debates and creative dialogue with Marxism as both an intellectual theory and social strategy.[30] This context is nonexistent in the United States, and the kind of postmodernist and poststructuralist theories circulated in the American academy are not known for their social critique. The attention to language, desire, and bodies in poststructuralism risks the danger of being easily appropriated into a highly individualistic, eroticized consumer culture of American late capitalism.

Fourth, those who apply poststructuralist theory to feminist theology are better at performing deconstruction than at constructing new discourses about God. Unless I am able to see what theological directions their works will lead to, it is premature to say that their theology will be anticolonial and antiimperialist. The only book-length constructive attempt using poststructuralist theory available today is Catherine Keller's *Face of the Deep*, a theology of becoming that is both innovative and dazzling. But if we follow Armour's lead, Keller has unfortunately separated the discussion of race and gender into two chapters as if they do not inform each other.[31] And when we turn to the chapter in which she puts her "tehomic theology" to the test of gender, we will be hard-pressed to find the figures of the raced woman or the colonized woman in the midst of "tehomic waves," "the ocean of divinity," and "deep-end feminism." These figures must be still groaning at the margin of the text, with "sighs too deep for words."[32]

If the buzzword in feminist theorizing and theologizing was "difference" in the 1990s, feminist theorists have begun to rethink the feminist agenda for the twenty-first century because of the challenges of late capitalism and globalization.[33] Chandra Talpade Mohanty, whose widely quoted essay "Under Western Eyes: Feminist Scholarship and Colonial Discourses" (1986) elucidates the obfuscation of difference in Western feminist scholarship, argues now that the shifts in both global restructuring and the academy will not allow us to dwell on the notion of difference. In *Feminism without Borders*, she challenges feminist studies to create a paradigm of historically and culturally specific "common differences" as a basis for social analysis and solidarity, because the local and the global exist simultaneously and mutually constitute

30. Terry Eagleton, *After Theory* (New York: Basic Books, 2003), 34–36.
31. Catherine Keller, *Face of the Deep: A Theology of Becoming* (London: Routledge, 2003), chaps. 12, 13.
32. Ibid., 213–28.
33. See, e.g., Elisabeth Bronfen and Misha Kavka, eds., *Feminist Consequences: Theory for the New Century* (New York: Columbia University Press, 2001).

each other.[34] She articulates a transnational feminist project that is anticapitalist and gives consideration to racialization at the same time. By transnational, Mohanty and her colleague M. Jacqui Alexander refer to three interlocking elements:

> 1) a way of thinking about women in similar contexts across the world, in *different* geographical spaces, rather than as *all* women across the world; 2) an understanding of a set of unequal relationships among and between peoples, rather than a set of traits embodied in all non-U.S. citizens . . . ; and 3) a consideration of the term "international" in relation to an analysis of economic, political, and ideological processes which foreground the operations of race and capitalism.[35]

This transnational project needs to resignify gender, so that it will not be imprisoned by essentialized gender binarism or lost in the poststructuralist play of difference. It will locate gender not only in local, regional, and national cultures, but also in the relations and processes across cultures. It will ask, What sort of female gendered bodies and subjects are produced by the globalization process in the households, workplaces, churches, academy, or military? For example, some scholars have turned their attention to the global teenage female workers in sexual, domestic, and service industries, Third World and poor migrant workers in richer countries, women of color in prisons, female refugees, and victims of war.[36]

At the same time, this resignifying process examines and makes visible the aspect of gender in cross-cultural and transnational social movements. For example, in the demonstrations against global capitalism during the meeting of the WTO in Seattle and other cities, what were the feminist issues raised? In the movements against the bombing of Iraq in major capitals and cities across the globe, how did feminist organizations and grassroots groups respond? Where are local grassroots women's efforts to resist the tendrils of globalization? And how can we narrow the gap between what academic feminists are debating and what is happening in politics? Judith Butler, for example, has noted that feminist debates on gender are woefully out of sync with the contemporary political usage of the term—for example, in Vatican statements and in United Nations resolutions after the 1995 Beijing conference.[37]

---

34. Mohanty, *Feminism without Borders*, 244.

35. M. Jacqui Alexander and Chandra Talpade Mohanty, "Introduction: Genealogies, Legacies, Movements," in *Feminist Genealogies, Colonial Legacies, Democratic Futures*, ed. M. Jacqui Alexander and Chandra Talpade Mohanty (New York: Routledge, 1997), xix.

36. Mohanty, *Feminism without Borders*, 245–47.

37. Judith Butler, "The End of Difference?" in Bronfen and Kavka, *Feminist Consequences*, 424.

The resignification of gender will place gender in the wider context of cross-cultural and transnational networks of relations and will eventually lead to a new way of conceptualizing feminist theology, as I will outline in this chapter's last section.

REQUEERING SEXUALITY

In the spring of 2004, pictures and videos depicting the sadomasochistic abuse of Iraqi detainees at Abu Ghraib prison sent shock waves around the world. These naked detainees were forced to masturbate, simulate homosexual sex, pile on top of one another in a pyramid, and wear female underwear on their heads. Young female, white American soldiers were shown among the perpetrators. In one image, a female soldier was holding a dog leash that encircled the neck of a naked Iraqi detainee lying on a cellblock floor. While the White House and the world media hastened to condemn such grotesque violations, the case brings into sharp relief the need to do transnational feminist analysis and to engage in requeering sexuality in the long tradition of colonialism.

Queer theory, particularly through the work of Judith Butler, has made two special contributions to feminist theory.[38] The first is destabilizing a binary construction of gender and any forms of identity politics based on fixed notions of "gay" and "lesbian," through the theory of performativity. The second is bringing sexuality to the foreground when discussing sexual difference and thus challenging the mainstream feminist paradigm that sex is in some significant ways distinguished from gender. This move is necessary, queer theorists argue, because feminists have either left out sexuality and pleasure from their analysis or, even worse, harbored hidden heterosexist biases. Queer theorists are unafraid to metaphorically lift up the skirts of these feminists to expose their heterosexist assumptions.

Queer theory is quite useful for analyzing the power dynamics displayed in the pictures from Abu Ghraib prison as well as the responses from viewers. To those viewers who are shocked that women soldiers could be perpetrators, queer theory would say that they are steeped in a binary gender construct: women are good and men are bad. We may never be able to ascertain the sexual orientation of the Iraqi detainees shown in the pictures. We only know that they were forced to put up a gay sexual performance because the soldiers wanted to humiliate and "soften" them. Homosexual acts performed in such a context did not subvert the heterosexist regime, but played into the homophobia in both American and Muslim cultures. This public spectacle was

38. Butler, *Gender Trouble*.

meant to shame the detainees, because homosexual behaviors are against Islamic law, and homosexual men have stereotypically been portrayed as effeminate and less than men. To add to the insult, the detainees were forced to go naked and masturbate in front of American female soldiers in a position of subordination. Homophobia, gender, religion, and nationality intertwine intimately in this particular scenario, which must not be seen as the aberrations of a few American soldiers, but scrutinized in the historical context of colonialism.

Lest we have forgotten, the concept "homosexuality" was derived in Europe as part and parcel of the colonial discourse. As Jeffrey Weeks has pointed out, the term can be traced to two closely related discourses: first, the work of sexologists such as Magnus Hirschfeld, Iwan Block, and Havelock Ellis, whose categorizing and labeling led them outside their culture, and, second, anthropological and ethnographical accounts of sexual practices from various cultures, especially those regarded as primitive.[39] These two discourses intersected in the construction of inversion as a form of disorder and dread, a neuropsychological counterevolution and also a historical and cultural regression. Psychiatrist Vernon Rosario points out: "Inversion was theorized as a retreat from the intellect to the passions, from the real to the imaginary, from the civilized to the primitive—typically feminine regressions consonant with the effeminacy associated with male hysteria and sexual inversion."[40] Christianity was implicated in such a construction, because the French doctors Alexandre Lacassagne and Julien Chevalier portrayed inversion as a regression to pre-Christian moralities.[41]

The association of homosexual acts with other religious practices has deep roots in the Bible and in Christianity. The only direct references to male homosexual acts in the Hebrew Bible appear in Leviticus 18:22 and 20:13; and in both cases, there is a close parallel between the condemnation of idolatry and of a male lying with another male. Leviticus 18:21–22 says: "You shall not give any of your offspring to sacrifice them to Molech, and so profane the name of your God: I am the LORD. You shall not lie with a male as with a woman; it is an abomination." John Boswell points out the close proximity of these two injunctions: "The prohibition of homosexual acts follows immediately upon a

39. Jeffrey Weeks, *Against Nature: Essays on History, Sexuality and Identity* (London: Rivers Oram Press, 1991), 11. Havelock Ellis found that there was a widespread natural instinct toward homosexual relationship among the "lower races." See Havelock Ellis and John Addington Symonds, *Sexual Inversion* (1897; reprint, New York: Arno Press, 1975), 4.

40. Vernon A. Rosario, *The Erotic Imagination: French Histories of Perversity* (New York: Oxford University Press, 1997), 88.

41. Ibid.

prohibition of idolatrous sexuality."[42] His purpose of highlighting this connection is to argue that the condemnation of these homosexual acts is best seen in the context of temple prostitution involving idolatry. These passages are part of the Jewish purity code, he surmises, which is meant to distinguish the Jews from the neighboring peoples, and the word "abomination" denotes something that is "ceremonially unclean rather than inherently evil."[43] Boswell tries to distinguish between what was culturally specific to the Jews and what was applicable to Christianity in general, as Gentile Christians were not asked to abide by Jewish law. But Boswell and others influenced by him have not questioned how the religious Other has been represented in the passages concerned. For instance: How much do we know about the worship of Molech, the deity of the Ammonites? Why is this foreign tradition reduced to and signified by child sacrifice or temple prostitution? Do the religious Other and the sexual Other mutually constitute each other, serving as placeholders for the boundaries of religion, purity, and sexuality?

The same pattern of close linkage between idolatry and homosexual acts can be found in Romans 1:23–27 and 1 Corinthians 6:9. The passage in Romans contains the only reference in the Bible about female homoeroticism. Much work has been done by William Countryman, Dale Martin, Robin Scroggs, Tom Hanks, and others to defend and rehabilitate Paul or to show that the Bible is not against homosexual relations: Homoerotic acts were part of an unclean Gentile culture of his time; the Greek terms used in 1 Corinthians have been mistranslated and misapplied to homosexuality; Paul was referring to pederasty in the Greco-Roman world; Paul had in mind heterosexual oral or anal sex as unnatural intercourse, and he was probably fearful of his own sexual desires.[44] On the other hand, Bernadette Brooten has shown that the injunction against female homoeroticism is closely related to Paul's understanding of gender roles. What is not acceptable to Paul, Brooten says, is that women exchanged the passive, subordinate sexual role for an active dominant role.[45] These laudable and meticulous studies link sex with gender, body anatomy, Jewish purity codes, Greco-Roman sexual practices, pederasty, nature, asceticism, and idolatry, but do not raise the issue of sex and representation of religion. It is surprising that these progressive Christian scholars have questioned the sexual episteme of the Bible, but left the religious

42. John Boswell, *Christianity, Social Tolerance, and Homosexuality* (Chicago: University of Chicago Press, 1980), 100.

43. Ibid., 102.

44. See the discussion of these scholars' work in Robert E. Goss, *Queering Christ: Beyond Jesus Acted Up* (Cleveland: Pilgrim Press, 2002), 198–202.

45. Bernadette J. Brooten, *Love between Women: Early Christian Responses to Female Homoeroticism* (Chicago: University of Chicago Press, 1996), 216.

episteme intact. They follow willingly the classification system offered by biblical writers and historians that other people's religious traditions are idol worship, that Gentiles are unclean and are associated with what are perceived to be abominable sexual acts. In short, they have spent much energy queering sex; I wish they had spent a little more time querying religion.

In various periods of the history of Christianity, the intersection of homophobia, ethnocentrism, and other religious practices has led to grave consequences, and sometimes deadly results. Mark Jordan has shown that in the medieval tales of the martyrdom of the young and beautiful of St. Pelagius, the Muslim king was shown to have been corrupted by "Sodomic vices." He also alludes that Paul of Hungary's *Summa of Penance*, written shortly after the Fourth Lateran Council (1215), might have in mind that people in Islamic regimes engage in sin against nature.[46] This fits the general representations of the Muslims as infidels and Islam as a carnal religion that fueled the furor and justified the Crusades. Later, in the encounter with the Native peoples of the Americas, Columbus's first remark and one of his most frequent comments about the Indians refers to their lack of clothes. The voyeuristic aspect of such observations is evident, because it is clear that certain girdles or loincloths were worn.[47] Europeans steeped in Christian morality were curious about the sexual behaviors of Native peoples, condemning those behaviors they saw strange and unusual as abominable. Nineteenth-century anthropologists noticed that there were Native men who cross-dressed, possessed spiritual powers, and lived with men and had sexual relations with men. They called them *berdaches*. While these *berdaches* were seen as strange people in former times, the figure has been recovered and exploited in contemporary white gay culture, as examples of homosexuals who did not fit nicely in a two-gender system.[48]

Homophobia and illicit homoerotic desire intertwined in fascinating ways in colonial India, especially because of certain Hindu religious practices. Hindu men were frequently constructed as less than masculine in colonial discourse, as Sharada Sugirtharajah notes: "Hindu devotion to the divine feminine shocked the Victorian morality and Puritan sensibilities of colonial administrators and missionaries, who not only derided it but perceived it as a

46. Mark D. Jordan, *The Invention of Sodomy in Christian Theology* (Chicago: University of Chicago Press, 1997), 15, 20, 99. I am grateful to Mark Jordan for pointing me to these references.

47. Nicholas Thomas, *Colonialism's Culture: Anthropology, Travel, and Government* (Princeton, N.J.: Princeton University Press, 1994), 72, see also 212, n. 15.

48. Will Roscoe, "We'wha and Klah: The American Indian Berdache as Artist and Priest," in *Que(e)rying Religion: A Critical Anthology*, ed. Gary David Comstock and Susan E. Henking (New York: Continuum, 1997), 89–106; George E. Tinker, "American Indian Berdaches and Cross-Cultural Diversity," *Journal of the American Academy of Religion* 57 (1989): 607–15.

sign of degeneration. Bengali Hindu men who worshiped the feminine were seen as effeminate. . . . Such effeminate men, in the view of colonialists and missionaries, lacked a strength and toughness which only British masculinity could provide."[49] Such a characterization, on the one hand, bolstered the superiority of British men, who looked down on their Hindu counterparts as weak, vulnerable, and passive. On the other hand, it greatly increased Hindu men's appeal to the homosexual cravings of some British colonizers, often to the dismay of their British wives and unleashing their racism.[50] The discourse of effeminacy points to the complications of gender in the construction of empire, the role of homoeroticism in colonial desire, and racist projections in the narratives of colonialism.[51]

The manifold and entangled relations of homophobia and homoerotic desire to gender, race, religion, and colonialism scarcely surface on the pages of white queer theology, either in the United States or Britain. Robert Goss's *Queering Christ* makes significant contributions to queer theology and hermeneutics, but its vision is not inclusive enough for people of color. The book contains a very significant chapter that traces what he has called homo-devotion to Jesus from the New Testament through the centuries.[52] From the mysterious youth in Mark (Mark 14:51–52) and the beloved disciple in John to contemporary gay men like himself, Goss constructs a gay homoerotic tradition dominated by Europeans and Euro-Americans. The poets of this tradition include Richard Crashaw, John Donne, and George Herbert; the philosopher is best represented by Jeremy Bentham; and the artists are the Renaissance masters who dared to exhibit Jesus' genitals in their paintings. The fact that Goss's construction of this genealogy is so white reinforces the popular bias that gay means white in the United States, and further silences the voices of gay men of color. Although he is aware of the problem and cites the works of gay men and lesbians of color elsewhere in his book, he has not integrated race into his queer theology.[53] Moreover, he ignores the fact that the sexuality of European and Euro-American men has been much shaped by the colonial impulse and cannot be read in the metropolitan center alone. At the end of the chapter, Goss claims Jesus as "a penetrated male, a bottom violating the masculine code of penetration and phallic domination. He is an outsider, transgressing the normative borders of heteronormativity and experiencing forbidden love between

49. Sharada Sugirtharajah, "Hinduism and Feminism: Some Concerns," *Journal of Feminist Studies in Religion* 18, no. 2 (2002): 103.

50. Ashis Nandy, *The Intimate Enemy: Loss and Recovery of Self under Colonialism* (New Delhi: Oxford University Press, 1983), 9–10.

51. Sara Suleri, *The Rhetoric of English India* (Chicago: University of Chicago Press, 1992), 16.

52. Goss, *Queering Christ*, 113–39.

53. Ibid., 225, 253.

men."[54] This sounds rather puzzling to me: Is Goss reinscribing colonial homo-eroticism between a white and a Mediterranean Jewish man?

Elizabeth Stuart's *Religion Is a Queer Thing: A Guide to the Christian Faith for Lesbian, Gay, Bisexual, and Transgendered People* is written by authors residing in Britain and published by an English press.[55] As a primer to queer theology, the book introduces the work of first-generation queer theologians such as Carter Heyward, Robert Goss, and Gary David Comstock. It positions queer theology as emerging in the 1990s after liberation theology, black theology, and feminist theology, and never specifies that the book is mainly dealing with white queer theologians. While the book frequently alludes to the existence of different forms of oppression, such as patriarchy, racism, heterosexism, and disabilities, it does not analyze how these oppressions intersect with one another. The book fails to interrogate the British context from which the authors speak, partly because of its heavy reliance on the works of American theologians. Nowhere can I find mention of British colonial history of the past or neocolonial interests in the present. The book gives the erroneous impression that the struggles of gay, lesbian, bisexual, and transgendered people are transhistorical and everywhere the same. As a theological resource for queer people, it is lamentable that the book mentions only three non-Western theologians, in passing or at a chapter's conclusion.[56]

Given white queer theologians' propensity to separate sexual oppression from the broader network of power relations, postcolonial feminist theology needs to engage in requeering sexuality. We can begin by constructing what I will call a "new genealogy of morals," following the hint from Nietzsche.[57] By this I mean tracing the origin and development of moral teachings about sexuality and their religious justification in the wider framework of the cultivation of the bourgeois self and national and international politics. The histories of sexuality, the histories of race, and the histories of colonialism are so much intertwined, that tracing one history while neglecting the other two leads to a complete mystification of their intricate relations. Foucault's *The History of Sexuality* examines the genealogy of sexuality without taking into account race and colonialism.[58]

---

54. Ibid., 138.

55. Elizabeth Stuart et al., *Religion Is a Queer Thing: A Guide to the Christian Faith for Lesbian, Gay, Bisexual and Transgendered People* (London: Cassell, 1997).

56. Ibid., 25, 84–85.

57. Friedrich Nietzsche, *On the Genealogy of Morals*, trans. Douglas Smith (New York: Oxford University Press, 1996).

58. Michel Foucault, *The History of Sexuality*, vol. 1, *An Introduction*, trans. Robert Hurley (New York: Vintage, 1978), and the critique of his work in Ann Laura Stoler, *Race and the Education of Desire: Foucault's History of Sexuality and the Colonial Order of Things* (Durham, N.C.: Duke University Press, 1995).

Judith Butler's *Gender Trouble* traces what she calls "a feminist genealogy of the category of women,"[59] again without discussing racial gender norms and colonialism. Edward Said's *Orientalism* analyzes colonial discourse with little reference to either sex or gender. This new genealogy of morals will need to show that sexuality and intimate relations are not private matters, but critical sites for investigating the surveillance of colonial boundaries and production of desire. Ann Laura Stoler has noted in *Carnal Knowledge and Imperial Power* that the management of the sexual practices of colonizer and colonized is fundamental to the colonial order of things and that discourses on sexuality aim to shape bourgeois subjects, while at the same time policing domestic recesses of imperial rule.[60]

This means that the new genealogy of morals must be read through multiple lenses at the same time. It would not only be interested in describing continuity and discontinuity of the colonialist, racist, masculinist, heterosexist regimes of power, but would also need to signal possibilities of inversion, subversion, and displacement of these regulatory practices. In this Butler's work proves to be insightful. For after troubling gender, she turns to alternative performances of gender, especially homosexual practices such as drag and butch-femme roles, as instances that counteract gender normativity and open up ways for resignification.[61] She says the task is to "redescribe those possibilities that *already* exist, but which exist within cultural domains designated as culturally unintelligible and impossible."[62] Her work prompts us to ask, Which are those critical sites of resistance that requeer sexuality, subvert colonial desire, and refuse to naturalize race?

One of the projects that is interested in looking at these "unintelligible" sites is Marcella Althaus-Reid's *Indecent Theology*.[63] In her work she charges that much of liberation theology, feminist theology included, has remained trapped in the binary and dualistic construction of gender and in decent heterosexual norms. At the same time, much of the queer theology has separated sexuality from political economy, and speaks only on behalf of middle-class queer interests. By refusing to separate the sex/gender system from economic

59. Butler, *Gender Trouble*, 5.

60. Ann Laura Stoler, *Carnal Knowledge and Imperial Power: Race and the Intimate in Colonial Rule* (Berkeley: University of California Press, 2002), 145.

61. Butler clarifies that her use of drag is not to suggest that this is a paradigm of subversive action or political agency, but to show that naturalized gender norms hold deep in our minds. See her "Preface (1999)" in *Gender Trouble* (New York: Routledge, 1999), xxii.

62. Butler, *Gender Trouble* (1990 ed.), 148–49.

63. Marcella Althaus-Reid, *Indecent Theology: Theological Perversions in Sex, Gender, and Politics* (London: Routledge, 2001).

and political structures, Althaus-Reid's indecent theology makes the connection among sex, politics, and liberation theology. And she has rightly pointed out that sexuality has much to do with the globalized economic structures, political terror, and violence, as well as with maintaining colonial and neo-colonial power. The disturbing abuse at Abu Ghraib, as we have seen, unfortunately substantiates her claim. While I have hoped that she would be more sensitive to racism and especially the racial biases of the North American theologians she cites, her works open room for dialogue between queer theory and postcolonial thought. She has used sexual stories, which have hitherto been deemed perverse and unfit for theological data, as a source for theological imagination. Given that sexual theology is an area crying for attention in the global South, her work encourages us to take bold steps outside the norm to explore the unthinkable and unimaginable.

REDOING THEOLOGY

The resignification of gender and requeering of sexuality in this transnational and intercultural feminist project will require us to think of the methodology and horizon of feminist theology in some new ways. Postcolonial feminist theology does not undermine the contributions of white feminist theology, but goes beyond the universalist female subject of liberal feminism and the unending subject-in-process of poststructuralism. Together with Third World feminist theologians, womanists, *mujeristas*, Latinas, and other feminists of color, postcolonial feminist theologians write back to a masculinist theological tradition defined by white, middle-class, Eurocentric norms. Postcolonial feminists invite and welcome men who are profeminist and share the postcolonial optics to contribute to this exciting new venture.

The most important contribution of postcolonial feminist theology will be to reconceptualize the relation of theology and empire through the multiple lenses of gender, race, class, sexuality, religion, and so forth. As a postcolonial feminist from Asia, I think there are three issues that require urgent attention. The first concerns the circulation of theological symbols and cultural capital in the colonial period and its permutations in late capitalism. An important theological agenda will be to analyze the use of theological symbols for the colonization of women's minds and bodies, as well as the reappropriation of such symbols for resistance, subversion, and empowerment. Postcolonial feminist theologians trace the interesting itinerary of the symbols of Mary or Jesus when they migrated from the colonial center to the colonies, and assumed a darker face (as in the Virgin of Guadalupe) or a flattened nose (as in some Asian Christs) on the journey. Yet, this is only part of the circulation process. The other concerns the ways feminist theological works from the former colonies are being brought back and consumed in the metropolitan centers by white feminist scholars to bolster their cosmopolitanism. The imbalance of power of both of these cultural and symbolic circuits must be studied with a materialist analysis of culture in order to do justice to the complexity of issues.

The second issue relates to how we conceptualize the religious difference that has fueled much colonial discourse. Postcolonial theory calls into question the construction and maintenance of religious boundaries and the assumptions behind much of interreligious dialogue. This has particular relevance for Asian Christian theology because Asian theologians have been in the forefront of interreligious, sometimes called interfaith, dialogues. While the Christocentrism of much of these dialogues has been challenged, Asian theologians need to contribute to the theoretical rethinking and postcolonial discussions of religious difference. Asian feminist theologians have particular roles to play, because they are known in the ecumenical circles for their "syncretism" and their defying rigid and stable religious identities.

The third issue has to do with environmental degradation and its impact on the lives of marginalized women who bear the major brunt of its effects. While the damage to the environment in both settler colonies and colonies of occupation has brought havoc to many peoples and their habitats, the global reach of late capitalism has exacerbated the situation. A postcolonial feminist theology debunks the myths of sustainable development and the green revolution, and points out its contradictions. Apart from evaluating ecofeminist theology formulated in the First World, Asian feminists have turned to their rich cultural resources, including their indigenous traditions, to articulate a theological vision that God's creation is a gift to be shared by all, and not monopolized by a few.

In assessing the relation between theology and empire, postcolonial feminist theologians need not reinvent the wheel or create theology ex nihilo. Although they are not bound by the Western tradition, they will be ill advised to dismiss it if they want to speak to a larger audience to push for theological and institutional changes.[64] The Western theological tradition is not monolithic, nor is its interpretation and organization fixed. A postcolonial feminist perspective will help open the theological texts to new inquiries and negotiations. For example, Augustine has long been criticized for his views on original sin and sexuality, but few have broached these issues from the perspective

---

64. I find Kathryn Tanner's discussion helpful to think through feminist use of patriarchal theology; see her "Social Theory Concerning the 'New Social Movements' and the Practice of Feminist Theology," in *Horizons in Feminist Theology: Identity, Tradition, and Norms*, ed. Rebecca S. Chopp and Sheila Greeve Davaney (Minneapolis: Fortress Press, 1997), 185–97.

that Augustine as a bishop represented the church at the Imperial Court, especially when he pursued rivals such as the Arians and Pelagians.[65] Feminist theologians are interested in Friedrich Schleiermacher's gender politics, but it will be productive to inquire how his understanding of the feminine, religion, and senses was informed by his conception of German character and piety when faced with the threats of the French Empire.[66] Karl Barth will be a very interesting figure in postcolonial feminist thought: on the one hand, he was against Nazism and was instrumental in drafting the Barmen Declaration; on the other hand, his gendering of men and women was blatantly hierarchical. While Serene Jones has staged a brilliant dialogue between Barth's "God" and Irigaray's "woman,"[67] it would be interesting to pursue the discussion further to invite the figure of the "female subaltern" to join the conversations.

Besides reading Western theological texts, postcolonial feminist hermeneutics can also be applied to liberation theologies, which purport to be anti-imperialistic. Let me cite Latin American liberation theology as an example. I agree with liberation theologians that the sociopolitical circumstances that have called liberation theology into existence have not improved, but have gotten worse. However, the social analysis of Latin American liberation theology, based primarily on class, needs to be reformulated to catch up with new forms of economic control and oppression in our globalized world. The "preferential option for the poor" requires much unpacking if we are to avoid a monolithic construction of "the poor." As I have already indicated, Althaus-Reid has subjected Latin American liberation theology to a queer critique, and elsewhere I have also discussed liberation theology with reference to postmodernity, non-Western religious traditions, and gender.[68]

A postcolonial feminist interpretation will expose the historical contingency of theological thoughts and show that they are not timeless. It will show that the authority of the past is established through repetitious citation and continuous interpretation using the same framework. Kathryn Tanner has tactfully suggested various ways of contesting the authorizing past of patriarchal theological discourse: "by reinterpreting and rearticulating the cultural

---

65. R. S. Sugirtharajah, *The Bible and the Third World: Precolonial, Colonial, and Postcolonial Encounters* (Cambridge: Cambridge University Press, 2001), 33.

66. Patricia E. Guenther-Gleason, *On Schleiermacher and Gender Politics* (Harrisburg, Pa.: Trinity Press International, 1997).

67. Serene Jones, "This God Which Is Not One: Irigaray and Barth on the Divine," in *Transfigurations: Theology and the French Feminists*, ed. C. W. Maggie Kim, Susan M. St. Ville, and Susan M. Simonaitis (Minneapolis: Fortress Press, 1993), 109–41.

68. Kwok Pui-lan, "Liberation Theology in the Twenty-first Century," in *Opting for the Margins: Postmodernity and Liberation in Christian Theology*, ed. Joerg Rieger (New York: Oxford University Press, 2003), 71–88.

elements so designated, by disputing their purported continuity with what has gone before, and/or by transforming the archaic into a rival authorizing past by establishing its own connections with present practices and future possibilities."[69] She encourages us to see the past as an open book, rather than a closed canon, that both women and men can selectively use to construct new emancipatory discourses.

What will be the scope, themes, and organization of a book on postcolonial feminist theology? There are different ways of conceptualizing this: The first approach is to adopt traditional Christian themes as a way to think through theology, such as God, Christ, atonement, church, and eschatology. The advantage of this reformist approach is that this can appropriate and rearticulate as many patriarchal elements of traditional theology as possible, both to contest their discursive power and to provide alternative ways of thinking. Rosemary Radford Ruether's *Sexism and God-Talk* employs such a strategy, and the book remains a valid resource for feminist theology.[70] The disadvantage, of course, is that it gives too much power to the theological categories established by the patriarchal tradition and limits creative ways of reconceptualizing the whole discipline.

The second approach may be more daring, for it starts not from the established theological tradition, but from a feminist analysis of the postcolonial condition, and then articulates theological issues and themes from such an analysis. This method is similar to what Delores Williams has suggested for womanist theology: for her the intention is for "black women's experience to provide the lens through which we view sources, to provide the issues that form the content of our theology, and to help formulate the questions we ask about God's relation to black American life and to the world in general."[71] The advantage is that it is inductive and culturally specific, for the issues and themes will not be predetermined, but derived from concrete experiences of social struggles. But the disadvantage is that it may continue to be marginalized, because it may not have significantly engaged and contested the theological mainstream. Moreover, we have few models to follow at this point to see how this may be done.

I imagine that these two approaches are not diametrically opposite, and many postcolonial theological projects will be a hybrid of the two. Postcolonial theologians will not shy away from reconstructing certain Christian doctrines if they are still significant for their communities, while adding other themes and

---

69. Tanner, "Social Theory," 194.

70. Ruether, *Sexism and God-Talk*.

71. Delores S. Williams, *Sisters in the Wilderness: The Challenge of Womanist God-Talk* (Maryknoll, N.Y.: Orbis Books, 1993), 12.

concerns they deem appropriate. An example is the book *A Native American Theology*, which includes several traditional categories such as creation, deity, Christology, theological anthropology, and sin and ethics, in addition to trickster and land, two categories with specific meanings for Native Americans. The authors state: "Our argument, however, goes beyond simply 'revisioning' conventional categories of Western systematic theology. It also means considering new categories from Native thought-worlds."[72] The Christian categories of the book may look deceptively familiar on the surface, but they are rearticulated through the thought form, myths, and stories of Native peoples in dialogue with the Bible and tradition.

Marcella Althaus-Reid's two provocative volumes, *Indecent Theology* and *The Queer God*, represent the other end of the theological spectrum. Her work is to rediscover God outside heterosexist theology and to "facilitate the coming out of God by a process of theological queering."[73] She uses witty and shocking subheadings for such purposes, such as "French kissing God," "A story of fetishism and salvation," "Rahab in a brothel in Paris," and "Sade and holiness." She demonstrates in her works "the magnitude of the law [in this case totalitarian theology] by portraying the magnitude of the transgression necessary to eliminate it."[74] Yet, it is her engagement with Christian categories, such as Mary, Christ, Trinity, and Holy Spirit that makes her books particularly interesting for theologians. Reading her books is a demanding intellectual exercise, but erotically enticing, because she satisfies the voyeuristic gaze of theologians who always wish to lift up Mary's skirt, to know with whom Jesus goes to bed, and (heaven forbid) to imagine the size of God's penis.

Who will be interested in these theological hybrids, and for whom is postcolonial feminist theology written? Let me be clear that postcolonial feminist theology is not written primarily for the poor, the peasants, the subalterns, and other marginalized people who may or may not have the language or education to read it, though I certainly hope that some of them may find such a project interesting and beneficial. This disclaimer is to be honest about possible readership and make less grandiose marketing claims. The readers are likely to be an "imagined community," made up of intellectuals interested in the relation between theology and empire building and having the commitment to subvert the use of sacred symbols to oppress people. These may be theologians, scholars in religion, and intellectuals working in different disciplines using postcolonial theory, and Christians in progressive religious communities.

---

72. Clara Sue Kidwell, Homer Noley, and George E. "Tink" Tinker, *A Native American Theology* (Maryknoll, N.Y.: Orbis Books, 2001), 113.

73. Marcella Althaus-Reid, *The Queer God* (London: Routledge, 2003), 2.

74. Ibid., 169.

Will postcolonial feminist theology be a temporary fad, ascendant for the moment because words with the prefix "post-" are currently in vogue? The question has an implicit value judgment—that some theologies are classic and have enduring power, while others will last only for a short while. But, as I have argued, theologies become "classic" only because we repeatedly cite them and give them power, and when Aquinas or Schleiermacher first put down their thoughts on paper they were considered "the new kid on the block." It is a pity if postcolonialism is considered a "fad" in theology, which would only show how insular the field of theology is, because we are lagging almost a generation behind postcolonial studies in other fields.

I would like to conclude this chapter by going back to the book *The Empire Writes Back*. In a new chapter written for the second edition of the book, the authors conclude:

> Few would deny that the concept of the post-colonial has been one of the most powerful means of re-examining the historical past and re-configuring our contemporary world-wide cultural concerns. More than any other concept, the post-colonial has facilitated the gradual disturbance of the Eurocentric dominance of academic debate, and has empowered post-colonial intellectuals to redirect discussion towards issues of direct political relevance to the non-Western world.[75]

Given this vast potential of postcolonial inquiry, I sincerely hope that more theologians will participate in it and that the "analyses of the sacred" will as the authors say be "one of the most rapidly expanding areas of post-colonial study."

75. Aschroft, Griffiths, and Tiffin, *The Empire Writes Back*, 219.

6

Political Theology

Voices of Women from the Third World

Beginning to think in a different way requires us to take different positions on the subject of knowing: to open up spaces for new ways of thinking and to consider our own thinking in terms of how our goals affect our perceptions.

Ivone Gebara[1]

Until women's views are listened to and their participation allowed and ensured, the truth will remain hidden, and the call to live the values of the Reign of God will be unheeded.

Musimbi R. A. Kanyoro and Mercy Amba Oduyoye[2]

Political theology in the Third World emerged from the struggle for political independence after the Second World War and the critique of neocolonialism and the ideology of development. Third World theologians decried the theological hegemony of Europe and North America and reclaimed the right to speak about God as subjects of their own destiny. They developed different forms of contextual theologies to address concrete social and political concerns and to relate the Christian tradition to the lived experiences of the people. While the male theologians might be adamantly against imperialism and corrupt dictatorial regimes, they have not concomitantly denounced patriarchal privileges and the subjugation of women and children, who are the most vul-

1. Ivone Gebara, *Longing for Running Water: Ecofeminism and Liberation* (Minneapolis: Fortress Press, 1999), 21.
2. Musimbi R. A. Kanyoro and Mercy Amba Oduyoye, "Introduction," in *The Will to Arise: Women, Tradition, and the Church in Africa*, ed. Mercy Amba Oduyoye and Musimbi R. A. Kanyoro (Maryknoll, N.Y.: Orbis Books, 1992), 1.

nerable in society. Feminist theologians have to create an alternative space to articulate the theological vision of the hope and aspiration of women.

Because of the multiple oppressions of gender, race, and class, the struggles of women in the Third World often operate from positions of extreme marginality, outside the established channels of national politics.[3] Women's movements focus on practical social and political issues affecting women, such as education and reproductive rights, specific localized struggles, coalition building with other oppressed groups, and community efforts to address particular needs. Living in such an environment, feminist theologians understand "politics" in a comprehensive and multifaceted sense not limited to state power, participation in government, or political representation and rights. "Politics," for them, concerns the collective welfare of the whole people in the *polis*. Their political theology aims to promote the survival, health, and well-being of the whole community, taking into account how the social, cultural, and psychological dimensions intersect with gender and the politicoeconomic base.

Since the 1970s, feminist theological movements have gathered momentum in the Third World through the establishment of national, regional, and global ecumenical networks. Since the "Third World" is a mental construct covering a vast territory with many cultures, languages, and peoples, we must not homogenize the diverse regions or generalize feminist theologies from radically different backgrounds. Liberation theologians from the Third World take seriously the contexts from which theology emerges, and begin their theological reflection with social analysis. I shall follow their methodology and present a brief discussion of the differences and commonalities of the regions.

SOCIOPOLITICAL CONTEXTS OF FEMINIST THEOLOGY IN THE THIRD WORLD

In *Feminism and Nationalism in the Third World*, Kumari Jayawardena documented the history of women's participation in anti-imperialist movements in Asia and the Middle East since the 1880s.[4] The emergence of feminist consciousness in the Third World took place in the wider political climate of national struggles, the fight against economic exploitation, and the quest for cultural self-definition. The rapidly changing social and political circumstances and the mobilization of the masses enabled women to step outside their

3. Robert J. C. Young, *Postcolonialism: A Historical Introduction* (London: Routledge, 2001), 361.
4. Kumari Jayawardena, *Feminism and Nationalism in the Third World* (London: Zed Books, 1986).

domestic spheres and experiment with new roles traditionally denied them. The nature of feminist politics in the Third World does not narrowly focus on gender inequality and on the freedom and liberation of women. Instead, feminist struggles are generally seen as a part of the overall liberation of the whole people, but with a distinct focus and strategies. Mary John Mananzan of the Philippines writes: "There is no total human liberation without the liberation of women in society. And this is not an automatic consequence of either economic development or political revolution. In other words, the women's movement is an essential aspect of the very process of societal liberation."[5]

Because of the divergent historical, cultural, and economic situations of the southern continents, feminist theologians have different emphases and priorities in their social analyses and theological agendas. As Latin American countries won their independent struggles in the nineteenth century, liberation theologians focused on neocolonialism, the failure of the Western development model, and problems of political and military dictatorship. Informed by Marxist social theory, they stressed the preferential option for the poor, liberation, and redemption in history, the integration between theology and praxis, and the church's transformative role in bringing about the kingdom of God. Developed in the late 1970s, feminist theology in Latin America shared these concerns, while highlighting the oppressions of machismo cultures and violence against women. The feminist theological agenda has been gradually broadened to include racism, multiple levels of cultural oppression in a continent with various forms of racial hybridity, and environmental justice.

Asian and African feminist theologians tend to highlight the cultural and religious dimensions of oppression because of the impact of entrenched cultural myths, rituals, and traditions on women's roles in society. They are interested in assessing Christianity's role in supporting colonialism and patriarchy, because political independence for many of them happened only a generation ago. Postcolonial interpretation of the Christian past involves new readings of the missionary enterprise, attention to cultural hybridity and resistance, demystifying racial hierarchy, and critical evaluation of the use of the Bible as a tool of oppression. Cultural studies and postcolonial theories have been employed to assist in building more comprehensive frameworks of analysis.

There are also particular concerns for Asian feminist theologians. The economies of countries on the Pacific Rim have developed at a phenomenal rate in the past thirty years. In fact, the twenty-first century has been hailed as the Pacific Century, and the "Asian miracle" was touted as a model for other devel-

---

5. Mary John Mananzan, "Redefining Religious Commitment in the Philippine Context," in *We Dare to Dream: Doing Theology as Asian Women*, ed. Virginia Fabella and Sun Ai Lee Park (Maryknoll, N.Y.: Orbis Books, 1989), 105.

oping countries. While Max Weber has attributed capitalistic development in Europe to Calvinistic ethics, Asian feminists point out the East Asian miracle has been sustained by a political oligarchy, transnational capital, and the revitalization of elements of patriarchal neo-Confucian ethics.[6] While the focus has been on the glistening Pacific Rim, countries in the Asian subcontinent are still suffering from abject poverty, compounded by the caste system and violent ethnic clashes. Sexual exploitation of women, especially in the form of sex tourism in Southeast Asia, domestic violence, dowry, the fast spread of HIV/AIDS, and child prostitution are also significant concerns for Asian feminists.

On a continent where many die from famine, malnutrition, unclean water, diseases, and warfare, African feminists have focused on survival, just distribution of resources, and the quality of life. Much of their theological writing has been devoted to the cultural, ritualistic, and religious customs that disempower women, such as the issue of polygamy, the stigma of the pollution of blood, widowhood and rituals of mourning, and female circumcision. At the same time, apartheid in South Africa, as well as racial and ethnic strife in Rwanda, Zimbabwe, Sudan, and other African countries have heightened their concerns for racial oppression and the use of religious ideology in social conflicts. African feminist theologians express the "will to arise" as women on their continent continue their strides to gain collective power and respect in their societies.

Because of globalization, women across the Third World face similar socioeconomic challenges: women's subsistence economy crushed by larger-scale industries and multinational corporations, the social and economic consequences of large national debts, and in some cases the constant threats of instability and war. The realignment of world powers according to their geopolitical interests and the economic structural adjustments imposed on poorer countries both lead to less political autonomy and less democratic participation. In the transnational movement of capital and the "race to the bottom" for cheaper resources and labor, countries in the South have to compete with one another to be exploited by corporations in the North. In the age of information technology, many women have found that they are totally left out in the postindustrial and technological restructuring process because of lack of access and training.

FEMINISM, COLONIALISM, AND CHRISTIANITY

The encounter between Western colonizing culture and indigenous cultures often involved thorny questions pertaining to women's roles and female

6. Kwok Pui-lan, "Business Ethics in the Economic Development of Asia: A Feminist Analysis," *Asia Journal of Theology* 9, no. 1 (1995): 133–45.

sexuality, notably veiling, polygamy, child marriage, foot binding, and *sati*. As an integral part of the colonialist agenda, saving colonized women from their oppression, ignorance, and heathenism appealed to the compassion of Westerners and garnered support for Christian missions. To challenge the collusion of Christianity with colonialism and the predominantly Eurocentric interpretation of the missionary movement, feminist political theology from the Third World uses several methodologies: questioning missionary sexual theology, unmasking the impact of monotheistic and androcentric theology on religiously pluralistic cultures, and ideological critique of Christian symbolism.

While the missionary movement has been credited with bringing about the emancipation of women by introducing female education, health care, and monogamous marriages, Third World feminist theologians charged that the imposition of a colonial system and patriarchal structure actually reinforced a sexual ideology that prescribed a dualistic and hierarchical ordering of the sexes. Mananzan observes that the Roman Catholic Church, accompanying the arrival of the Spaniards, curtailed women's freedom by confining them to the church, kitchen, and children, and the social status of Filipino women became lower after colonialism.[7] The gender ideology of the church exerted pressure in Filipino communities, where the relations between the sexes had hitherto been more inclusive and egalitarian and where matrilineal heritage predominated. During the nineteenth century, Victorian assumptions of sexual prudence and female domesticity influenced missionary sexual theology and ethics. With deep-seated fear of women's bodies and sexuality, colonial Christianity limited women's leadership in religious and communal activities. Mercy Amba Oduyoye of Ghana has observed that while Akan women play significant roles in rituals associated with birth, puberty, marriage, and death, their participation in Christian rituals has been marginalized.[8] Marcella Althaus-Reid further charges that colonial sexual theology was not only sexist but also heterosexist, lending its support to the sexual control of women and the policing of sexualities that were considered outside the established norm.[9] The sexual ideologies of the colonizers were forced on other peoples through violence of the so-called civilizing mission.

While Western feminist theologians have challenged this androcentric Christian symbolic structure, their counterparts in the Third World investigated the impact of the introduction of a monotheistic and male-dominated

7. Mary John Mananzan, "The Filipino Woman: Before and after the Spanish Conquest of the Philippines," in *Essays on Women*, ed. Mary John Mananzan (Manila: Institute of Women's Studies, 1991), 6–35.

8. Mercy Amba Oduyoye, "Women and Ritual in Africa," in *The Will to Arise*, 9–24.

9. Marcella Althaus-Reid, *Indecent Theology: Theological Perversions in Sex, Gender, and Politics* (London: Routledge, 2001).

symbol order into their cultures, which had maintained inclusive representations of the divine. Christian mission undermined the myths and practices associated with female divine power. For instance, Musa Dube points out that among the Ibgo people in Nigeria, women used to enjoy certain economic and social privileges in terms of ownership of property and inheritance, and their gender construction was supported by a spiritual world that recognized female religious imagery and power. Allusion to these powerful goddesses allowed women to carve out their own social space and sphere of influence. But the Christian church and the mission schools systemically condemned devotion to the goddess, such that the symbolic structure that bolstered women's self-esteem was shattered.[10] Among the Asian religious traditions, the worship of goddesses and the feminine images of the divine has a long history, dating back to the prehistoric period. Worshipped by women and men, the prevalent goddesses of Ina, Guanyin, Durga, Kali, and Sita, as mothers, consorts, daughters, and protectors, have not been superseded by the male gods as in Mesopotamia and prehistoric Europe. Thus, the propagation of a monotheistic Christian God imaged as a male being, modeled after the father, king, and lord, introduced gender asymmetry into the religious symbolic system and reinforced male domination.[11]

The most sustaining demystification of the colonial misuse of Christianity is the ideological critique of Christian symbolisms, focusing particularly on the figures of Jesus and the Virgin Mary. Teresa M. Hinga from Kenya explains how the imperialistic images of Christ arrived in Africa:

> During the period of colonial and imperial expansionism, the prevailing image of Christ was that of the conqueror. Jesus was the warrior King, in whose name and banner (the cross) new territories, both physical and spiritual, would be fought for, annexed, and subjugated. An imperial Christianity thus had an imperial Christ to match. The Christ of the missionaries was a conquering Christ.[12]

With little respect for the cultures and wisdom traditions of the African peoples, the missionaries created alienation and confusion in the Africans, for their culture and identity were to be erased and supplanted by a foreign religious tradition that belonged to the colonizers.

---

10. Musa Dube, "Postcoloniality, Feminist Spaces, and Religion," in *Postcolonialism, Feminism, and Religious Discourse*, ed. Laura E. Donaldson and Kwok Pui-lan (New York: Routledge, 2002), 111.

11. Kwok Pui-lan, *Introducing Asian Feminist Theology* (Cleveland: Pilgrim Press, 2000), 72–73.

12. Teresa M. Hinga, "Jesus Christ and the Liberation of Women in Africa," in *The Will to Arise*, 187.

But Hinga notes that the Christ of the missionary enterprise also contained emanicipatory impulses, which attracted African followers. African women were able to perceive more liberating images of Christ when they went back to the biblical sources and discovered empowering and healing images from the New Testament. They asserted their theological agency when they interpreted the Bible through their experiences in the African churches and their own cultural lenses. Hinga offers three popular images of Christ in the African context. Some see Jesus as a personal friend, savior, or healer who does not demand women's subjugation, but accepts them as they are and accompanies them in their suffering. Among the African Independent Churches where women are more vocal and less inhibited than those in the established churches, the image of Christ as the embodiment of the Spirit, the power of God, is prominent. Christ becomes the voice of the voiceless and the power of the powerless in this pneumatic Christology. Another popular image of Christ is that of the iconoclastic prophet, who subverts existing power relations and challenges the status quo. Hinga opines that, to be relevant for women's emancipation, Christ must be a concrete figure who brings hope and courage to the oppressed and vindicates the marginalized in society.

A further dimension of Christology, which has been used to solidify colonial rule, was the glorification of the suffering and sacrifice of Jesus. Mananzan noted that during Spanish colonization, the suffering Christ was highlighted during the annual Holy Week procession, complete with the reenactment of the nailing to the cross. The emphasis on the passion and submission of Christ was meant to inculcate both loyalty to Spain and a passive acceptance of the destiny of this life. While Good Friday was dramatized, there was not a concomitant celebration of Easter Sunday: the resurrection and the beginning of new life. The depiction of a beaten, scourged, and defeated Christ and the direction of salvation toward another world functioned to pacify the people under the colonial masters. Furthermore, women were exhorted to model themselves after the sacrifice and obedience of Christ and to internalize passive and resigned endurance of their own pain and suffering.[13]

To counteract Christian imperialism, Mananzan and other feminist theologians in Asia rediscovered the subversive and revolutionary power of the Christ symbol. While the Spaniards used Jesus' suffering as a tool for oppression, the Filipino people combined the passion narrative with their own millennial beliefs to construct a language of anticolonialism in the nineteenth century. For subjugated women, salvation and the good news does not imply

---

13. Mary John Mananzan, "Paschal Mystery from a Philippine Perspective," in *Any Room for Christ in Asia*, ed. Leonardo Boff and Virgil Elizondo, Concilium 1993, no. 2 (Maryknoll, N.Y.: Orbis Books, 1993), 86–94.

a life of passive suffering and endless sacrifice and denial. The suffering of Jesus was not to be used to condone state terror or domestic violence. Filipino feminists reinterpret Jesus as a fully liberated human being, who confronts the wrongs of society and stands up for justice to bring about the reign of God, while feminists in other Asian contexts experiment with new images of Christ, using their cultural and religious resources, as discussed below.

The image of the Virgin Mary, the dominant feminine symbol in the Christian tradition, has been subject to careful scrutiny both for its oppressive impact and for its revolutionary significance. The Roman Catholic Church has largely portrayed Mary as a gentle and docile model for women, whose submissiveness was idealized to serve colonial and patriarchal interests. Tracing the development of Mariology in Latin America, Ivone Gebara and María Clara Bingemer point out that in the colonial period Mary was worshipped as the great protector of the conquistadors against the Indians, whom they regarded as infidels. The largely male-centered, dualistic, and idealistic interpretations of Mary did not help women to develop their self-esteem and assert their power. But alongside such colonial images of Mary are other stories of the Virgin, who appears to people in numerous ways and intermingles with the poor. Most noteworthy is Our Lady of Guadalupe, who first appeared in 1531 to the Indian Juan Diego, and has been widely venerated as the patroness of the continent. In that story the dark-skinned Virgin adopted the natives as her children and pledged to hear their prayers and offer her loving favor and compassion. In the continuous struggle against neocolonialism and other oppressions, Gebara and Bingemer suggest reclaiming Mary as the mother of the poor, who denounces injustice, announces the coming of the kingdom, and reveals a God who does not cease to perform wonders on behalf of the poor.[14]

Asian feminist theologians have also reclaimed more liberating images of Mary. Mary has been acknowledged for her historical consciousness and for her prophetic anger against the injustice of the rich and powerful. Instead of being set on a high pedestal, Mary is brought down to earth to be a fully liberated human being. Her virginity signals her autonomy and independence, not subjection to others; her mothering role points to her role as a giver of life to God and new humanity. As one of the founders of early Christianity, Mary is remembered for modeling the true discipleship of discernment, risk, and resistance for liberation. She is also seen as the coredeemer with Christ for the salvation of humankind, because of her role as a model of liberation and her mediating role for the redemption of humanity.[15]

---

14. Ivone Gebara and María Clara Bingemer, *Mary: Mother of God, Mother of the Poor* (Maryknoll, N.Y.: Orbis Books, 1989).

15. Chung Hyun Kyung, *Struggle to Be the Sun Again: Introducing Asian Women's Theology* (Maryknoll, N.Y.: Orbis Books, 1990), 74–84.

In the ideological critique of Christian symbols, these theologians pay attention to the rhetorical and political functions of theology. Christianity has never been proclaimed in a vacuum, but is always situated within cultural and political discourses of power and authority, particularly so in a colonial context where power is so lopsided. The aim is the recovery of more positive and emancipatory symbols to mitigate the devastating effects of colonial Christianity and to create a new culture and consciousness for Christian women.

CULTURAL POLITICS AND THEOLOGY

As gender became a contested site in the colonial encounter, male national elites responded by upholding male superiority as a long-standing and sacred tradition. In many parts of the Third World, feminist struggle has been enmeshed in the uneasy intersection of colonialism, nationalism, and Westernization. In some cases, these elite males hark back to a pristine period before colonization when their cultures were unpolluted, and staunchly resist social changes required by "modernization." The revival of fundamentalism and the concomitant restriction of women's social participation are familiar examples. And even when "modernization" is deemed necessary, some national elites hope only to imitate Western scientific and technological development, while keeping intact the spiritual and familial spheres, where they can still find a sense of belonging.

Feminist theology in the Third World entered the scene when these vigorous debates on cultural identity took place both in the secular sphere and in theological circles. For when male theologians tried to indigenize or contextualize Christianity into their native soils, many of them subscribed to an anthropological understanding of culture as unitary, holistic, and governing the value and behavior of the whole people.[16] The myths of homogeneous national or cultural identity often benefit those who hold power, and exclude women, minorities, and other diasporic communities; as Oduyoye sarcastically observes, "Each time I hear 'in our culture' or 'the elders say' I cannot help asking, for whose benefit? Some person or group or structure must be reaping ease and plenty from whatever follows."[17] Third World feminist theologians, on the one hand, have to counteract their male colleagues' assumption that feminism is a Western idea and not important to the theological agenda. On the other hand, they want to differentiate themselves from a Western, middle-class feminism, which

16. Kathryn Tanner, *Theories of Culture: A New Agenda for Theology* (Minneapolis: Fortress Press, 1997), 25–37.
17. Mercy Amba Oduyoye, *Daughters of Anowa: African Women and Patriarchy* (Maryknoll, N.Y.: Orbis Books, 1995), 35.

tends to essentialize women's experience, as if women everywhere are the same, and focus primarily on the sex/gender system of particular societies.

Theologically, this means attention to multiple layers of women's oppression and employing this insight as a critical lens to look at the Bible and tradition. A notable example is Elsa Tamez's rereading of the figure of Hagar, a woman she says complicates the history of salvation. As a slave, Hagar is probably sold to Sarah as her servant, out of extreme poverty. As an Egyptian, she is a minority living among the Hebrews, whose customs and culture are foreign and discriminate against her as a stranger. As a woman, her reproductive function is used to produce a male heir, and her mistress is jealous of her and oppresses her. Yet, God with mercy and compassion appears to her in the wilderness, and she not only experiences a theophany but also gives a name for God—the God who sees. Tamez's reading challenges a homogenization of the poor in Latin American theology, because she shows that the poor are always gender differentiated and culturally located.[18] Rather than following a Marxist understanding of the poor in an economic sense, her work demonstrates that sexism must be included in the liberation of the poor from the cycles of oppression.

Another methodological concern is to integrate analyses of race and gender. For some time, Latin American theologians have been accused by other Third World colleagues of leaving out racial oppression in their class analysis. Tamez addresses the issue by focusing on cultural violence among the three different levels of Latin American culture—indigenous, black, and mestizo-white. These different levels are interlocked in a complex web, for while the mestizo-white culture is influenced and dominated by that of the rich nations, it in turn marginalizes the black and indigenous women. Tamez advocates greater intercultural dialogue and solidarity among the racial groups.[19]

Feminist theologians on other continents also echo the need for adopting a more multilayered, fluid, and contestable notion of culture in theologizing. Musimbi Kanyoro urges African feminists to engage in a "cultural hermeneutics" that utilizes insights from cultural analysis in evaluating which traditions should be kept and which should be abandoned.[20] Oduyoye demonstrates how

18. Elsa Tamez, "The Woman Who Complicated the History of Salvation," in *New Eyes for Reading: Biblical and Theological Reflections by Women from the Third World*, ed. John S. Pobee and Bärbel von Wartenberg-Potter (Oak Park, Ill.: Meyer Stone Books, 1986), 5–17.

19. Elsa Tamez, "Cultural Violence against Women in Latin America," in *Women Resisting Violence: Spirituality for Life*, ed. Mary John Mananzan et al. (Maryknoll, N.Y.: Orbis Books, 1996), 11–19.

20. Musimbi R. A. Kanyoro, "Cultural Hermeneutics: An African Contribution," in *Other Ways of Reading: African Women and the Bible*, ed. Musa W. Dube (Atlanta: Society of Biblical Literature, 2001), 101–13.

this cultural hermeneutics works by providing a few principles in her critical evaluation of myths, folktales, and proverbs of Africa. She begins by asking how does the corpus of "folktalk" reflect women's lives, and what its rhetorical functions are in shaping women's attitudes and behavior. She then asks for whose benefit and interests are these proverbs and myths being told and perpetuated. She says women must be courageous enough to discard some of these myths if they are harmful to women, and begin to weave new patterns of meaning that sustain mutual dependence and reciprocity of the human community.[21]

Oduyoye's cultural hermeneutics is significant because of the primacy of oral resources in doing theology by African women: songs, storytelling, and impromptu lyrics sung to interpret the Bible events and proclaim a call to worship. African male theologians have overlooked this rich layer of cultural resources because they devote more time to the written elitist culture. Neither the inculturation theologians nor the black theologians fighting apartheid in South Africa have developed sufficient tools to analyze oral resources. In a recent collection of essays on African women and the Bible, the contributors propose the methodologies of storytelling, the use of divination as social analysis, interpreting with nonacademic women, and challenging patriarchal and colonizing translations.[22] Since the majority of African Christian women are oral hearers and readers, the storytelling method is of particular importance. Stories are told and retold to interpret social reality, to transmit values, and to pass on wisdom from generation to generation. Musa Dube has called for a new mode of interpretation, using an oral-spiritual framework: "In the feminist oral-Spiritual space, responsible creativity that involves attentive listening to many oppressed voices and empathy; active prophecy that speaks against oppression and seeks liberation; and intent praying that seeks partnership with the divine, can begin to hear, speak and write new words of life and justice."[23]

African feminist theologians are also concerned about cultural practices around rites of passage of women, and issues such as fertility, dowry, widowhood, sexuality, polygamy, and female circumcision. Western feminists have vehemently condemned the practices of polygamy and female circumcision from the perspective of sexual freedom and control of women, but Oduyoye and Kanyoro caution that these practices must be placed in the wider contexts of religious beliefs in Africa, the socioeconomic structure, and assumptions

21. Oduyoye, *Daughters of Anowa*, 19–76.
22. Musa W. Dube, "Introduction," in *Other Ways of Reading*, 1–19.
23. Musa W. Dube Shomanah, "Scripture, Feminism, and Post-Colonial Contexts," in *Women's Sacred Scriptures*, ed. Kwok Pui-lan and Elisabeth Schüssler Fiorenza, idem, Concilium 1998, no. 3 (Maryknoll, N.Y.: Orbis Books, 1998), 53.

about human sexuality.[24] While Western feminists advocate women's right to control their bodies, freedom to seek pleasure, and monogamous companionship between two individuals, African cultures may have different understanding of human sexuality grounded in their own beliefs. Polygamy sometimes arises out of dire economic conditions, and cannot be condemned outright without considering the situation. While some African feminist theologians call for an end to female circumcision, they are also mindful that some African women regard the practice as a part of their cultural heritage.

The relation between culture and religion also preoccupies Asian feminist theologians: they, too, need to address the issues of dowry, *sati*, widowhood, arranged marriage, and taboos against women on their continent. Indian theologian Aruna Gnanadason, in particular, has written on how these practices limit women and the long history of Indian women's quest for emancipation.[25] But Asian feminist theologians are also concerned about how Asian cultural elements, symbols, and images can be used in theologizing. The controversial presentation of Korean theologian Chung Hyun Kyung at the Seventh Assembly of World Council of Churches, in which she used East Asian philosophy, Buddhism, and Korean shamanism as resources for interpreting the Spirit, brought the issues of diversity and syncretism to the fore of the ecumenical debate.[26]

In the ensuing discussion, in which Western Christians raised the limits of diversity and the boundaries of Christian identity, Asian feminist theologians have made several points.[27] First, they have insisted that Christianity has never been pure and has continuously, from its beginning, adopted elements from different cultures. It is only when non-Western churches are doing so that more established churches and theologians label such practices as "syncretism" in a derogatory sense, to exercise control and power. In fact, the relation between gospel and culture has never been simply wholesale borrowing or outright rejection, but full of negotiation and contestation, as well as accommodation. If Asian theology is not to be simply the mimicry of Western theology, Asian theologians must be bold enough to experiment with many different forms of cultural dialogues and negotiations.[28] Second, Asian religious traditions are not

24. Oduyoye, "Women and Ritual," 22–23; Kanyoro, "Cultural Hermeneutics," 109–11.

25. Aruna Gnanadason, "Towards an Indian Feminist Theology," in Fabella and Park, *We Dare to Dream*, 117–26.

26. Chung Hyun Kyung, "Come, Holy Spirit—Renew the Whole Creation," in *Signs of the Spirit: Official Report, Seventh Assembly*, ed. Michael Kinnamon (Geneva: World Council of Churches, 1991), 37–47.

27. Kwok Pui-lan, "Gospel and Culture," *Christianity and Crisis* 51 (1991): 10–11, 223–24; Chung Hyun Kyung, "Asian Christologies and People's Religions," *Voices from the Third World* 19, no. 1 (1996): 214–27.

28. Kwok, *Introducing Asian Feminist Theology*, 33–36.

driven by belief systems, nor are they shaped primarily by claims to truth and falsity, and as a result doctrinal purity has never been the concern of the common people, especially women. In religiously pluralistic Asia, where religious identities are less clearly defined and tightly bound than in the West, there has been much fluid adaptation and interplay among the Confucian, Buddhist, Taoist, and Shinto traditions. A Chinese person, for example, can adopt Confucian, Buddhist, and Taoist practices at different moments, depending on particular circumstances and religious need. Asian feminist theologians often find themselves embodying several religious traditions at once as they claim multiple spiritual roots. Such religious experience allows room for cultural hybridity and cross-fertilization between different traditions. Third, while the church has found shamanistic practices troubling, these practices form part of the culture of women in Korea, especially among the lower class. Feminist theology needs to reexamine the liberating potential of marginalized women's cultures. Fourth, the critical norm of judging Christian claims is not defined by whether they conform to the theological system dictated by the West, but by the concrete Christian praxis of solidarity and liberation according to the demand of the gospel. Noting that poor women do not care much about orthodoxy and have approached many religious resources for sustenance and empowerment, Chung Hyun Kyung has challenged Asian feminist theology to move beyond doctrinal purity to risk survival-liberation-centered syncretism.[29] Some may not go as far as Chung, but her theological position challenges Asian Christians to go beyond their comfort zone to listen to the cries of people in Asia, the majority of whom (97 percent) are not Christians.

ECOJUSTICE AND THE STRUGGLE FOR LIFE

Colonization means not only the domination of people, but also the exploitation of natural resources for the development and benefit of the colonizers. In the 1920s Western powers controlled almost half the world's territory. With neocolonialism and globalization, national boundaries are less significant, and the whole earth becomes "fair game" for unbridled profiteering. Women in the Third World witness their subsistence and their role as managers of water and forest eroded and changed by the arrival of multinational corporations. Deforestation, pollution, environmental racism, and other ecological disasters have wreaked havoc on the livelihood of poor women who

---

29. Chung, *Struggle to Be the Sun Again*, 113.

simply dream of sufficient fuel and clean drinking water. When the Amazon forest disappears at an alarming rate and global warming threatens the basic fabric of life, the earth as a living organism has been undermined and its sustainability crippled. These life-and-death concerns necessitate theological reflections that take seriously consideration of ecological, feminist, and liberationist perspectives.

Known for her prophetic voice for poor women's rights, Ivone Gebara of Brazil has written the most poignant and comprehensive ecofeminist theology from a Latin American perspective. Her book *Longing for Running Water* both critiques the epistemological framework of traditional theology and offers resources for constructing new understanding of Trinity, Christology, and anthropology.[30] She criticizes the hierarchal, dualistic, and patriarchal worldview that creates the dichotomies of God/creation, mind/body, men/women, and culture/nature. Within such a framework, God is modeled after the male ruling class, outside of nature, and controls the whole universe. Anthropocentrism coupled with monotheism allows Christianity, from its imperialist stance, to destroy other religious expressions that it considers inferior and to marginalize women's claim to sacred power.

Gebara distinguishes her ecofeminism from that being developed by more individualistic, middle-class "new age" movements in the North through her attention to race, globalization, and the claims of the poor. She argues that the images of God as patriarchal father, all-powerful Lord, king of all persons and living things, and as omnipotent and omnipresent, have functioned to keep poor women and men dependent on the church and others. Proposing a God of immanence and relationality, she seeks to overcome the dualism of spirit opposing matter and to speak of the interconnectedness of all beings in the mysterious body of the universe. Such an understanding of the divine underlines the basic relatedness of human beings and our ethical responsibility toward one another and the planet.

Gebara accuses traditional Christologies, mostly hierarchal and anthropocentric, for separating Jesus from all other human beings and from the natural environment. Jesus has been imaged as the Messiah who comes in the guise of a superman, a heroic figure to save humans from their sins. Such atonement theory sustains the culture of dependence and focuses on human beings alone. Gebara invites us to consider a biocentric understanding of salvation, alluding to Jesus' actions on behalf of the sick, the hungry, the outcast, and the oppressed, and his call for creating new relationships between human beings and the earth. Jesus is not the powerful Son of God who dies on the

30. Gebara, *Longing for Running Water.*

cross and is resurrected as our "king," she opines, but is the symbol of the vulnerability of love and compassion:

> Jesus does not come to us in the name of a "superior will" that sent him; rather, he comes from here: from this earth, this body, this flesh, from the evolutionary process that is present both yesterday and today in this Sacred Body within which love resides. It continues in him beyond that, and it is turned into passion for life, into mercy and justice.[31]

While Gebara's ecofeminist theology draws from and reconstructs the Christian tradition, Asian and indigenous feminists borrow insights from and welcome the contributions of Asian wisdom traditions. While Chung has proposed a methodology that gives priority to and begins with Asian people's stories and religiosity,[32] I have opted for a reinterpretation of the Bible and traditional resources informed by Asian cosmological insights. My concern is that the Bible has enormous power in the Asian churches and great impact on Asian Christian women. I also believe that the Bible has rich insights for addressing our ecological crisis if it is not read in a predominantly androcentric way. For example, I have written on the possibility of developing an organic model of Christianity that understands sin and redemption not merely as disobedience or egotism of human beings, but as concepts and actions with significant cosmological consequences.[33] Such a model pays attention to the plurality of images of Jesus in the New Testament, including the natural symbols: bread of life, the vine and the branches, and the hen protecting her brood. Jesus often shares table fellowship with the outcast, the tax collector, and the marginalized in society, while the miracles of feeding the hungry thousands testify to his concern for concrete human needs. His messianic banquet is open to all and welcomes people of all races.

An organic model may also revision Jesus as the incarnated Wisdom within the larger cultural and religious matrix of the wisdom tradition in the Asian traditions. Western feminist theologians have highlighted the figure of Jesus as Sophia-God, who embodies creative agency, immanence, and the promise of shalom, justice, and salvation. The Wisdom tradition can be examined and reflected on from the vantage point of other wisdom figures and sages—such as Prajna, Guanyin, and Isis—in Asian and other religious traditions.[34] Thus,

---

31. Ibid., 190.
32. Chung, "Asian Christologies and People's Religions," 214–27.
33. Kwok Pui-lan, "Ecology and Christology," *Feminist Theology* 15 (1997): 113–25.
34. A constructive attempt can be found in a Korean Canadian theologian's book—see Grace Ji-Sun Kim, *The Grace of Sophia: A Korean North American Women's Christology* (Cleveland: Pilgrim Press, 2002).

an organic model allows us to encounter Christ in many ways and many cultures, without being limited to a finite, historically conditioned human figure. The importance of Jesus as one epiphany of God does not exclude other christic images that Christians have constructed because of their diverse religious experiences and cultural contexts.

Feminist theologians in the Third World also look for cultural and religious principles and resources to overcome a mechanistic, capitalistic, and Darwinian mind-set. Such cultural retrieval does not simply re-create a romantic past, but constructs a polemical discourse against the myth of globalization that proclaims no alternative exists. From the Indian background, Gnanadason lifts up the principle of Shakti, the feminine and creative source of the universe, characterized by harmony between humans and nature. Indian feminist ecotheology, she says, must draw from the well of the holistic vision based on their spiritual past, and not rely on the ideological and theological assumptions of Western paradigms. Citing the history of the Chipko movement, in which women protected the trees by hugging them, Gnanadason says ecofeminist theology must come out of women's lived experience, "not only weeping with nature for deliverance and freedom, but out of years of organized resistance against senseless destruction."[35]

Indigenous peoples have spoken decisively about the importance of the land in their sacred memory, rituals, and communal belonging.[36] The conquest and pollution of the land is a sin against Mother Earth and a form of cultural genocide, depriving indigenous peoples not only of their means of survival but also religious sites for cultural preservation. In their cosmological vision for theology and spirituality, Aboriginal and Pacific feminist theologians, such as Anne Pattel-Gray, have emphasized a profound reverence for nature, communal ownership and stewardship, and women's roles in ceremonies and in providing sustenance for life.[37] Similarly in Africa, religious scholars and theologians draw from the rich heritage of inclusive cosmological worldviews in different ethnic groups as resources for constructing a communal ethic of care, responsibility, and environmental justice.[38] In the past, Westerners often labeled African indigenous traditions pejoratively as animistic or "nature worship." Feminist theologians have challenged such biases and recovered the significance

35. Aruna Gnanadason, "Toward a Feminist Eco-Theology for India," in *Women Healing Earth: Third World Women on Ecology, Feminism, and Religion*, ed. Rosemary Radford Ruether (Maryknoll, N.Y.: Orbis Books, 1996), 79.

36. Jace Weaver, *Defending Mother Earth: Native American Perspectives on Environmental Justice* (Maryknoll, N.Y.: Orbis Books, 1996).

37. Anne Pattel-Gray, *Through Aboriginal Eyes: The Cry from the Wilderness* (Geneva: World Council of Churches, 1991), 1–12.

38. See the articles by African contributors in Ruther, *Women Healing Earth*.

of rituals and healing practices that teach about human beings' reliance on and collaboration with nature.

CONCLUSION

Compared to the feminist movement in the North, feminist struggle in the South has not been defined by the liberal politics of the women's suffrage movement, women's rights, and the demand for equal access to opportunities and privileges enjoyed by men. Feminists in the Third World do not have the luxury of attending to gender oppression alone, without simultaneously taking into consideration class, racial, colonial, and religious oppression. Their political theology takes many forms, including the option for solidarity with the poor, the critique of cultural alienation and racial repression, the challenge of globalized economy, and activism for ecojustice and protection of nature. Virginia Fabella and Oduyoye articulate the nature of such a theology:

> Our theology must speak of our struggles and the faith that empowers us. Our theology goes beyond the personal to encompass the community, and beyond gender to embrace humanity in its integrity. Our theology takes cognizance of academic studies but insists on the wider spectrum of women's experience and reality for its inspirations and insights. Being contextual in the Third World has meant that women's theology has embraced the religio-cultural besides the socio-economic and has engaged it in a living dialogue.[39]

In contrast to political theology by their male counterparts, Third World feminist political theologies do not lay so much emphasis on God as an actor in and judge of human history. Aware of the limitation of anthropocentric discourse about God, feminist theologians avoid portraying human history as the only arena for God. They also question the wisdom of projecting a God that is all-powerful and controlling, a protector and benefactor for women, modeled after privileged males. While male liberation theologians have exhorted the church to bring about social changes, female theologians are more realistic about ecclesial power and their optimism is more guarded. The church, steeped in male hierarchy and tradition, has to repent for its sexism before it can be a beacon of hope and an agent for change.

---

39. Virginia Fabella and Mercy Amba Oduyoye, "Introduction," in *With Passion and Compassion: Third World Women Doing Theology*, ed. Virginia Fabella and Mercy Amba Oduyoye (Maryknoll, N.Y.: Orbis Books, 1988), xi.

Third World feminist theologians welcome opportunities for dialogue and seek solidarity with women in the North because feminist struggles are increasingly interconnected and global. They have also engaged in cross-cultural conversation with women theologians from racial minorities in North America. With passion and compassion, they continue to articulate a new theological voice full of hope and joy, with reverence for life and respect for all things. Integrating theory and praxis, their political theology is rooted in the local, but connected to the global.

7

Engendering Christ

Who Do You Say that I Am?

> The Black Christ of Black Theology was obscene because it uncovered racism under the guise of a white Jesus. . . . The *Christa* is another example of obscenity. It undresses the masculinity of God.
> *Marcella Althaus-Reid*[1]

Is the gender of Christ important? For some time it has been said that colonialist Christianity preached the Christ as the Lord and Conqueror to the peoples of the world. Then came the white feminists who said that the central problems of Christianity were that the savior was male and that the foundational Christian symbol was androcentric.[2] The debate on the maleness of Christ has become so intense that some feminists have left the church and declared themselves post-Christians.[3]

For me, the central question is, How is it possible for the formerly colonized, oppressed, subjugated subaltern to transform the symbol of Christ—a symbol that has been used to justify colonization and domination—into a symbol that affirms life, dignity, and freedom? Can the subaltern speak about Christ, and if so, under what conditions? What language shall we borrow? Do we need to borrow from malestream theologies or feminist theories? What are the dangers of doing so? Alternatively, if we need to ground our reflections in the culture and religiosity of our people, how can we avoid the pitfalls of cul-

---

1. Marcella Althaus-Reid, *Indecent Theology: Theological Perversions in Sex, Gender, and Politics* (London: Routledge, 2001), 111.

2. Mary Daly, *Beyond God the Father: Toward a Philosophy of Women's Liberation* (Boston: Beacon Press, 1973).

3. Daphne Hampson, *Theology and Feminism* (Oxford: Blackwell, 1990), and idem, *After Christianity* (Valley Forge, Pa.: Trinity Press International, 1996).

tural essentialism, nativism, and nationalistic ideologies? What makes it possible to say something new about Jesus/Christ?

POSTCOLONIAL FEMINIST RETHINKING
OF JESUS/CHRIST

A postcolonial interpretation of Christ needs to push the boundaries, and asks the following critical questions: How does belief in the uniqueness of Christ justify the superiority of Christianity and condone colonization as the "civilizing mission of the West," often seen as the "white man's burden"? Why did the image of Jesus sent by the missionaries look more like a white man with a straight nose and blue eyes than a Jewish man? How does the Aryan Christ contribute both to the colonization of the Other living outside Europe and also to the oppression of the Other living inside Europe—the Jews? When feminist theologians such as Mary Daly and Rosemary Radford Ruether criticize the androcentric symbols of Christianity such as the maleness of Christ, why is it that only the gender of Jesus matters? What does Ruether's famous question, "Can a male savior save women?"[4] both reveal and suppress? In the liberation theological movements that emerged in the 1960s, why was the maleness of Christ revitalized to signify a masculinist liberator, without concomitant concerns about how such images might have marginalized women? What is at stake when the colonizers, the dominant theologians, and the Vatican all take for granted that the Christ figure must be masculine? How has the masculinity of Jesus been constructed? Even if Jesus' masculinity is presupposed, why has Jesus' sexuality been regarded as taboo?

As these explosive questions indicate, a postcolonial female theologian cannot simply accept the dominant positions about Christology in mainline Christianity, and neither can she subscribe to white feminist or liberationist formulations without some serious rethinking. I believe the task of a critical theologian is not so much to provide answers, but to raise new questions that have not been asked before or to point to new avenues of thought that may have been overlooked or suppressed. Indeed, the question of the gender of Christ has been so much a part of our common sense that "engendering Christ" has seldom been the substance of serious theological debate. Ruether's question "Can a male savior save women?" implicitly consents to the fact that the savior is male, and the question then becomes what has a male savior to do

4. See Rosemary Radford Ruether, *To Change the World: Christology and Cultural Criticism* (New York: Crossroad, 1981), 45–56; and idem, *Sexism and God-Talk: Toward a Feminist Theology* (Boston: Beacon Press, 1983), 116–38.

with women. If we problematize the gender of the savior, what kind of questions will we ask?

To ask about the gender of Christ is to press on the discursive limits of sex, gender, and sexuality in Christianity. Such issues are at the heart of Christian symbolics. Since they are so powerful, they are often treated as taboo in Christian circles. In this chapter, I should like to experiment with thinking at the limits of conventional theology and listen to some of the emergent voices that are shaping the christological debate at the beginning of the new millennium. Sometimes we need to get out of our comfort zone in order to encounter God anew and to listen to the gentle voice of God coming from the whirlwind. It is often at the margin of our consciousness that something new can be discerned that jolts us from our familiar habit of thinking. As postcolonial critic Homi Bhabha has noticed, it is at the epistemological "limits" of some of the dominant and ethnocentric ideas that a range of other dissonant, and even dissident, histories and voices—of women, the colonized, and racial and sexual minority groups—can be heard.[5]

One of the most significant developments of liberation theology is that marginalized communities have begun to use their own cultural idioms and religious imaginations to articulate their own understanding of salvation and the role of Jesus Christ in the salvific process. Instead of a monolithic understanding of Christ as the liberator, a plurality of images of Jesus has been offered, including the Black Christ, Jesus the Crucified Guru, Jesus the Corn Mother, Jesus the Priest of Han, Jesus the Feminine Shakti, Jesus the Sophia-God. Some of these images highlight the socioeconomic aspects of salvation, while others have more to do with the cultural-religious dimensions.

How can we, as theologians, begin to understand and theorize this seeming "sea of heteroglossia," as Mikhail Bakhtin would say, when people begin to use their own tongues and cultural idioms to speak about Christ? At the beginning of the twentieth century, Albert Schweitzer's book, which summarizes nineteenth-century scholarship on Jesus, was translated and published in English as *The Quest of the Historical Jesus*. I would suggest that an apt title for a book that summarizes theological reflections on Jesus in the twentieth century would be *The Quest of the Hybridized Jesus*. I think the concept of hybridity, as it has been vigorously debated among postcolonial theorists, offers some important hints to interpret the emergence of these images. First, hybridity is not simply the mixing of two languages or the juxtaposition of two cultures, as our liberal or "pluralistic" understanding presents it, as if the two were on equal footing. Rather, hybridity in postcolonial discourse deals specifically with the colonial authority and power of representation. As Homi Bhabha puts

5. Homi K. Bhabha, *The Location of Culture* (London: Routledge, 1994), 4–5.

it: "Hybridity is a problematic of colonial representation and individuation that reverses the effects of the colonialist disavowal, so that other 'denied' knowledges enter upon the dominant discourse and estrange the basis of its authority—its rules of recognition."[6] Second, Stuart Hall and others have insisted that colonization is a double inscription process, affecting the metropolis as much as the colonies. Thus, hybridity exposes the myths of cultural purity, the monologic discourse, unitary enunciation, and the collapse of difference that legitimize colonial authority. Third, hybridity destabilizes the frame of reference/frame of mind that sees things as binary opposites: black and white, here and there, East and West, European and the native. It critiques rigid boundaries, challenges the construction of the center and the periphery, and speaks of "interstitial integrity."[7] The subtle, nuanced differences in-between, the multidimensional temporalities, the pluriphonic voices of women and men, and the "fruitful ambiguity" offer new possibilities and open new space for creative theological imagination of Christ.

JESUS/CHRIST AS HYBRID CONCEPT

The most hybridized concept in the Christian tradition is that of Jesus/Christ. The space between Jesus and Christ is unsettling and fluid, resisting easy categorization and closure. It is the "contact zone" or "borderland" between the human and the divine, the one and the many, the historical and the cosmological, the Jewish and the Hellenistic, the prophetic and the sacramental, the God of the conquerors and the God of the meek and the lowly. Jesus' question "Who do you say that I am?" is an invitation for every Christian and local faith community to infuse that contact zone with new meanings, insights, and possibilities. The richness and vibrancy of the Christian community is diminished whenever the space between Jesus and Christ is fixed, whether, on the one hand, as a result of the need for doctrinal purity, the suppression of syncretism, or the fear of contamination of native cultures, or, on the other hand, on account of historical positivism and its claims of objectivity and scientific truths about Jesus.

The images of Jesus/Christ presented in the New Testament are highly pluralistic and hybridized, emerging out of the intermingling of the cultures of Palestine, the Hellenistic Jewish diaspora, and the wider Hellenistic world. As George Soares Prabhu, a biblical scholar from India, has noted:

6. Ibid., 114.
7. Rita Nakashima Brock, "Interstitial Integrity: Reflections toward an Asian American Woman's Theology," in *Introduction to Christian Theology: Contemporary North American Perspectives*, ed. Roger A. Badham (Louisville, Ky.: Westminster John Knox, 1997), 183–96.

> New Testament christology is inclusive and pluriform. Every com-
> munity evolves its own understanding of Jesus responding to its own
> cry for life. And because life changes christologies change too. The
> New Testament preserves all these christologies, without opting
> exclusively for any one among them, because it does not wish to offer
> us (as dogmatic theology pretends to do) a finished product, to be
> accepted unquestionably by all. Rather its pluralism indicates a chris-
> tological open-endedness, inviting us to discover our own particular
> christology, that is, specific significance of Jesus for our situation in the
> Third World today.[8]

However, such open-ended and fluid understanding of Christology became
a threat to the expanding Roman Empire, when imperial unity required some
kind of doctrinal uniformity. Under political pressure and amidst ecclesiastical rivalry, the early Christian councils sought to differentiate orthodoxy from
heterodoxy. But it is important to remember that the christological formulas
crafted in Nicaea, Ephesus, or Chalcedon were never accepted as normative
by all Christians. These credal and "orthodox" formulas never succeeded in
silencing the debates or shutting out the voices of dissent. At a later stage,
when missionaries promoted the interests of European empires and the
United States through their so-called civilizing mission, their prepackaged and
encapsulated Christ was also resisted and challenged. Bhabha relates an interesting story about how the Indians on the subcontinent could not understand
the meaning of eating Jesus' body and drinking his blood, because most of
them were vegetarians.

One of the most important insights I have learned from postcolonial critics is that colonization is a double and mutually inscribing process. Much has
been said about cultural hybridization in the colonies as a result of the forced
imposition of European and American cultures onto others. Less attention has
been paid to the equally profound hybridization going on in the metropolitan
centers. In doing research on the relationship between Christology and the
colonial imagination, I am fascinated by the fact that the quest for the historical Jesus always takes place in the metropolis. The quest for Jesus is a quest
for cultural origin, national identity, and racial genealogy. The first quest could
not have taken place without the new knowledge brought to Europe about the
myths, cultures, and wisdom traditions of the colonized peoples. Its epistemological framework was constructed out of a combination of Orientalist
philology, racist ideology, and Eurocentric study of other peoples' mythology
and traditions.

8. George Soares Prabhu, "The Jesus of Faith: A Christological Contribution to an
Ecumenical Third World Spirituality," in *Spirituality of the Third World*, ed. K. C. Abraham and Bernadette Mbuy-Beya (Maryknoll, N.Y.: Orbis Books, 1994), 146.

I have argued that the search for Jesus must be read against the search for "natives" who could be conquered.[9] The encounter with the natives created anxiety and necessitated the quest for European self-identity. David Friedrich Strauss's portrayal of Jesus as a hero, Ernest Renan's picture of him within French bourgeois culture, and the Anglo-Saxon Christ of social Darwinism are examples of cultural hybridization, attempts to interpret the Christ symbol through the lenses of the culture of imperialism.[10] Yet, the ambivalence about one's origin and culture must be concealed, split off, or displaced. These images of Jesus were thus offered as the results of the quest for scientific and objective truths, on which the origin of Christianity could be established and the foundation of European civilization maintained.

The first quest for the historical Jesus, however, took place not only in the search for the native to colonize but also in the suppression of the Other within—namely, the Jews. Jonathan Boyarin's work *Storm from Paradise* has helped me understand this point and to make the connection among colonialism, anti-Judaism, and feminism.[11] Susannah Heschel's important research on the study of New Testament scholarship in nineteenth-century Germany has shown how the Jewishness of Jesus was downplayed by a variety of scholars, who portrayed him as a rebel against Judaism, calling himself the Son of Man to avoid being associated with the Jews. Some even suggested that Jesus might not be Jewish in origin, while others actually tried to prove that Jesus was in fact an Aryan because he had come from Galilee rather than Judea. This Aryan Christianity wanted to distinguish itself from its Jewish roots and to justify the superiority of the Aryan race, following the racial theory current at the time.[12]

While the first quest took place in Europe, the newest quest has gathered momentum in the United States, as the United States is trying to create a Pax Americana. Because of the history of immigration, the natives are no longer outside but are already *inside* the metropolitan centers, and the dominant white culture does not know how to deal with the challenges of diversity

9. Kwok Pui-lan, "Jesus/The Native: Biblical Studies from a Postcolonial Perspective," in *Teaching the Bible: The Discourses and Politics of Biblical Pedagogy*, ed. Fernando F. Segovia and Mary Ann Tolbert (Maryknoll, N.Y.: Orbis Books, 1998), 75–80.

10. For the Anglo-Saxon Christ, see Alan Davies, *Infected Christianity: A Study of Modern Racism* (Kingston and Montreal: McGill-Queen's University Press, 1988), 73–88.

11. Jonathan Boyarin, *Storm from Paradise: The Politics of Jewish Memory* (Minneapolis: University of Minnesota Press, 1992), 77–115.

12. Susannah Heschel, "The Image of Judaism in Nineteenth-Century Christian New Testament Scholarship in Germany," in *Jewish-Christian Encounter over the Centuries: Symbiosis, Prejudice, Holocaust, Dialogue*, ed. Marvin Perry and Frederick M. Schweitzer (New York: Peter Lang, 1994), 215–40.

and multiculturalism. The images of Jesus as the sage, the healer, the Spirit-filled person, promoted in the popular quest books, look much like the modern-day gurus in the age of self-help and New Age movements. Billed as the first interdisciplinary quest and the most scientific search for Jesus, this current quest may also be a displaced and repressed quest for white male identity when the melting pot does not melt anymore. Stephen Moore has described this current quest for Jesus in a sarcastic way:

> Many of us have joined that manhunt for the Jew of Nazareth, many more of us cheering or yelling obscenities from the sidelines. Startled eyes turn as the hysterical Jesus suspects are dragged into the church by the triumphant band of scholars. To the dubious congregation in the pews, each Jesus seems more unlikely than the last. "Did you at any time claim to be the Christ, the Son of the living God?" each is asked in turn. "I did not," most of them reply.[13]

MARGINALIZED IMAGES OF JESUS/CHRIST

Theologians from marginalized communities have offered different images and understandings of Jesus/Christ, subverting the theological hegemony of Europe and white America and expressing little interest themselves in joining this manhunt for Jesus. I would like to discuss five such images that are relevant to the topic "engendering Christ": the Black Christ in the works of black and womanist theologians; Jesus as Corn Mother; Jesus as the Feminine Shakti in India; Jesus as the theological transvestite; and Jesus as the Bi/Christ. Afterward, I will present a number of critical observations and reflections.

The Black Christ

The Black Christ became a concrete symbol of the civil rights and black power movements of the 1960s with the advent of the black consciousness era. In response to Malcolm X's challenges to Christianity, as an oppressive tradition in which black people worship a white Christ, black theologians formulated the hybridized concept of a Black Christ. The space between black and Christ is hotly contested and debated among male black theologians, later joined by their womanist colleagues.

---

13. Stephen D. Moore, "Ugly Thought: On the Face and Physique of the Historical Jesus," in *Biblical Studies/Cultural Studies: The Third Sheffield Colloquium*, ed. J. Cheryl Exum and Stephen D. Moore (Sheffield: Sheffield Academic Press, 1998), 378.

Albert Cleage, for example, advocated a literal blackness, arguing that Jesus of Nazareth was ethnically black.[14] He based his argument on Jesus' lineage from Mary, who was from the tribe of Judah, which consisted of nonwhite people. Genealogically speaking, he claimed, Jesus was of African ancestry, just as black people could trace their ancestry to Africa. In this sense, Cleage argued that the black people were not worshipping a white Christ, as he tried to rescue Jesus from a white racist society. Writing in the 1960s, Cleage hoped that the figure of the Black Messiah could bring closer together the expectations of the black nationalist movement and Christianity, a tradition embraced by the majority of the black people.

Contrary to Cleage, James Cone opted for a symbolic blackness, for as he so eloquently puts it, "Christ is black, therefore, not because of some cultural or psychological need of black people, but because and only because Christ *really* enters into our world where the poor, the despised, and the black are, disclosing that he is with them."[15] For Cone, the claim that Jesus is black is not meant to exclude white people, but to enable black people to identify the presence of Jesus in their lives. Moreover, this assertion is rooted in Cone's understanding of the life and work of Jesus, who claimed to be the Christ, the one who revealed that God is for us. One basic characteristic of Jesus' life and ministry was his identification with the oppressed and downtrodden of his time. To transfer this to the contemporary situation, Jesus would have to be black if he were to identify with the oppressed in the white racist American society.

More recently, Garth Kasimu Baker-Fletcher presents an even more hybridized version, with Jesus as an Afro-Asiatic Jew, and implores the black churches to affirm both Jesus' blackness and his Jewishness. He surmises that the Hebrew people, the Semites, were not a "race," but a "mixed crowd" of various peoples, including Africans. He writes: "Jews, like many peoples who arose on the land bridge between Africa and Asia, were Afro-Asiatic people."[16] To reclaim the Afro-Asiastic heritage of Jesus' Jewishness is important for the black churches, given the centuries of the Europeanization of Jesus and Jews and the ubiquitous images of the white Jesus superimposed by white hegemony.

These black theologians are challenged by their female counterparts, who claim that a one-dimensional focus on Jesus' racial and ethnic background is not sufficient as long as the maleness of Christ is left unexamined. The image

14. Albert Cleage, *The Black Messiah* (Kansas City, Mo.: Sheed and Ward, 1969), 42. See also the discussion of Cleage and James Cone in Kelly Brown Douglas, *The Black Christ* (Maryknoll, N.Y.: Orbis Books, 1994), 55–60.

15. James H. Cone, *God of the Oppressed* (New York: Seabury Press, 1975), 136.

16. Karen Baker-Fletcher and Garth Kasimu Baker-Fletcher, *My Sister, My Brother: Womanist and Xodus God-Talk* (Maryknoll, N.Y.: Orbis Books, 1997), 98.

of the Black Christ contests the power behind the symbol of the blue-eyed, pale-skinned Christ in order to restore the dignity and manhood of black men. The subjugated and enslaved black man wants to confront the white man's power, while preserving his male privilege intact. To understand Christ in the life and struggle of black women, womanist theologians insist that we must move beyond limiting the experience of Christ to the historical Jesus, and risk seeing salvific acts in other persons and events. Jacquelyn Grant has no problem seeing Jesus in black women, for she disavows the centrality of the maleness of Christ and wants to discern the meaning of Jesus' suffering and salvation through the witness and ministry of black women.[17] Kelly Brown Douglas also states: "Christ can be seen in the face of a Sojourner Truth, a Harriet Tubman, or a Fannie Lou Hamer,"[18] as well as in male figures who help the entire black community to struggle for wholeness. In order to see Christ in the face of black women, Brown Douglas insists that womanist theologians must be involved in and connected with the lives of the black women in the churches and community organizations and movements.

Not all womanist theologians endorse the images of womanist Black Christ, however, for some find that still too limiting. Trying to move beyond both androcentric and anthropocentric assumptions about the Black Christ, Karen Baker-Fletcher proposes a creation-centered Christology that focuses neither on color nor on race. For her, "Jesus is fully spirit and fully dust."[19] In her womanist ecotheological project, Jesus the incarnate, embodied in dust, reminds us of God's intimate relation to creation. Consequently, she interprets the salvific work of Christ through the lens of creation: "God, embodied in Jesus, joined with the dust of the earth, reconciling the broken relationship with God and creation that we humans have involved ourselves in. Jesus realized harmony of creation and Spirit in the actions associated with his life and work."[20]

The Corn Mother

In a way similar to the black and womanist theologians, George Tinker criticizes the oppression of white Christianity, its missionary conquest, and its formulation of Jesus as Conqueror. He charges, "American Indian peoples were being co-opted into a cultural frame of reference that necessitated self-denial

17. Jacquelyn Grant, "Womanist Theology: Black Women's Experience as a Source for Doing Theology, with Special Reference to Christology," *Journal of the Interdenominational Theological Center* 13, no. 2 (Spring 1986), 195–212.

18. Brown Douglas, *The Black Christ*, 108.

19. Baker-Fletcher and Baker-Fletcher, *My Sister, My Brother*, 87.

20. Karen Baker-Fletcher, *Sisters of Dust, Sisters of Spirit: Womanist Wordings on God and Creation* (Minneapolis: Fortress Press, 1998), 19.

and assimilation to the language and social structures of the conqueror."[21] Instead of focusing on skin color, Tinker looks for symbolic and mythological structures in Indian culture to infuse new meanings into the understanding of Christ. In this regard he finds the preexistent Logos in the first chapter of the Gospel of John helpful to bridge this mental and imaginative gap. Jesus is seen as one, albeit very powerful, occurrence of the Logos in human history. Consequently, American Indian people can add to Christianity's knowledge of salvation from their own experiences of healing throughout their history. Furthermore, Tinker argues that the Logos should not be construed as male, that the American Indian understanding of bi-gender duality entertains the possibility that Christ could be female. For him, therefore, the mythic image of the Corn Mother, whose suffering and self-sacrifice offer food and sustenance for her children, prevalent in many American Indian cultures, becomes a compelling image for Christ. This image, he further argues, overcomes anthropocentrism, for in dying she becomes identified with the earth. Reading John's Gospel through Native eyes, Tinker powerfully asks: "Why should Indian people be coerced to give up God's unique self-disclosure to us? Why ought Indian people learn to identify after the fact with God's self-disclosure to some other people in a different place and time in a mythic tradition that is culturally strange and alienating?"[22]

Tinker attaches importance to the vicarious suffering of the Corn Mother on behalf of the whole people.[23] Native people have lived with the memory of the real physical sacrifice for the people as well as with the ceremonial sacrifice and suffering in Native rites such as the vision quest, the sun dance, and the purification rite sometimes called "sweat lodge." The vicarious suffering of the death of the Corn Mother provides food and sustenance for the people. Food is thus sacred and to be shared, because eating is always eating the body of the Corn Mother or First Mother. The sharing of food also reminds us of the close connection with other relatives, such as the Buffalo, the Deer, and the Fish, because they also depend on the bounty provided by the Mother. In such a way, the Corn Mother, our ancestors, and our relatives live among us not only in spirit, but are also physically present in us because we eat the produce of the earth where they have returned in one way or the other. The stories of the Corn Mother also send a stark warning against male violence,

---

21. George Tinker, "Jesus, Corn Mother, and Conquest: Christology and Colonialism," in *Native American Religious Identity: Unforgotten Gods*, ed. Jace Weaver (Maryknoll, N.Y.: Orbis Books, 1998), 139. This article appears in a revised form in Clara Sue Kidwell, Homer Noley, and George E. "Tink" Tinker, *A Native American Theology* (Maryknoll, N.Y.: Orbis Books, 2001), 62–84.

22. Tinker, "Jesus, Corn Mother, and Conquest," 152.

23. Ibid., 151–52.

because it was the male siblings who killed her. The recovery of the theological and ethical meanings of the oral texts of the Corn Mother and reading it in parallel with the first chapter of John's Gospel make it possible for the Native community "to understand the notion of Christ with much greater inclusivity and parity of power between colonizer and colonized."[24]

The theological formulation of Jesus as the Corn Mother takes into consideration two facts: that many Native Americans are converted to Christianity and find Christian symbols important in their religious life, and that a growing number of Native Americans want to reclaim and be reconnected with Native traditions and rites. However, such transposition may have the danger of obfuscating indigenous symbolic systems and spiritual traditions, which have been subjected to centuries of cultural theft and genocide. Native peoples who are not Christians may become suspicious that the Native symbols are again taken from the indigenous community, and that on them Christian categories are being superimposed. Such danger is aptly captured in the title of the book *When Jesus Came, the Corn Mothers Went Away*.[25] The pros and cons of using the Corn Mother or other Native idioms to interpret Christ will need to be continually discussed.

The Feminine Shakti

While Tinker has recovered the mythic structure of Native people in the Americas, Asian feminist theologians articulate their understanding of Christ through a dialogue between Christian faith and Asian indigenous traditions and social contexts. Chung Hyun Kyung, for example, argues that theologians should shift their focus from institutional religious traditions to people's religiosity, such as shamanism.[26] She points out that institutional dogmatic traditions are usually male-centered and authoritarian, while people's religiosity may contain liberating elements that are expressions of their faith and daily struggles. She suggests that we listen to the people, instead of turning to Scripture and dogma as our primary source and data.

A concrete example of christological reformulation comes from India, where feminist theologians are reclaiming their cultural roots to understand the life and work of Christ. They have attached great importance to the Hindu concept of Shakti, the feminine principle that is the life energy of the universe.

24. Ibid., 153.
25. Ramón A. Gutiérrez, *When Jesus Came, the Corn Mothers Went Away: Marriage, Sexuality, and Power in New Mexico, 1500–1846* (Stanford, Calif.: Stanford University Press, 1991).
26. Chung Hyun Kyung, "Asian Christologies and People's Religions," *Voices from the Third World* 19, no. 1 (1996): 214–27.

According to Aruna Gnanadason, Shakti is the source and substance of all things, pervading everything, and the creative principle of the universe.[27] The recovery of the feminine principle of Shakti has been crucial in ecological awareness in India, as evident in the writings of the noted scientist and ecologist Vandana Shiva.[28] For theologian Stella Baltazar, the transcended Christ can be imagined as the embodiment of the feminine principle, the Shakti, the energizer and vitalizer.[29] For her, it is a serious limitation to express the resurrected Christ in purely male or patriarchal terms. Using the Hindu concept of Shakti, the liberative potential of the cosmic Christ can then be expressed through the Indian cosmology of wholeness and interconnectedness.

But the use of the concept of Shakti is not without problems, given the current political situation of India, when "Hinduism" has been reconstructed to represent the national tradition of India in order to consolidate the power of the Hindu nationalist party and to suppress those who belong to other traditions. Aruna Gnanadason and other theologians are aware that the indigenization of Christianity into the cultural milieu of the Hindu tradition must not be seen as supporting a Hindu hegemony. The grafting of Christology onto the Hindu concept of Shakti needs to consider not only the philosophical and religious dimensions but also the contemporary political implications. Contrary to the case of the Native Americans, in which the appropriation of the Corn Mother might lead to the obfuscation of indigenous symbolic system, the use of Shakti in this case may be seen as supporting an elitist and overdominating tradition.

The Theological Transvestite

My fourth example comes not from Christians who want to claim christological language on their terms, but from a Jewish theologian who wants to "destabilize Christian theology and create a space for Jewish self-definition."[30] Susannah Heschel notes that the figure of Jesus stands at the boundary of Judaism and Christianity, so that the debate on the Jewishness of Jesus calls

27. Aruna Gnanadason, "Toward a Feminist Eco-Theology for India," in *Women Healing Earth: Third World Women on Ecology, Feminism, and Religion*, ed. Rosemary Radford Ruether (Maryknoll, N.Y.: Orbis Books, 1996), 75.

28. Vandana Shiva, *Staying Alive: Women, Ecology and Development* (London: Zed Books, 1989).

29. Stella Baltazar, "Domestic Violence in Indian Perspective," in *Women Resisting Violence: Spirituality for Life*, ed. Mary John Mananzan et al. (Maryknoll, N.Y.: Orbis Books, 1996), 64.

30. Susannah Heschel, "Jesus as a Theological Transvestite," in *Judaism since Gender*, ed. Miriam Peskowitz and Laura Levitt (New York: Routledge, 1997), 188–97.

into question the self-understanding of both traditions. Building on the insights of queer theory, she proposes to see Jesus as a theological transvestite. Heschel is not the only one to describe Jesus as a transvestite, for Eleanor McLaughlin has used the term to question gender essentialism and to imagine Jesus as a cross-dresser who challenged rigid boundaries of gender and tradition.[31] But for Heschel, the figure of Jesus destabilizes and questions the construction of boundary between Judaism and Christianity, as the performative activity of a transvestite disrupts the easy categorization and identifiable essence of gender. She notes that there have been various attempts on the Jewish side to emphasize the Jewishness of Jesus and to deny that Jesus initiated a new religious movement. On the other hand, the historical quest for Jesus on the Protestant side tends to present an ahistorical Jesus by focusing on his uniqueness and his superior religious consciousness. Liberal theologians downplay Jewish influences on Jesus' teachings, to safeguard the purity of Jesus as the ultimate cultural phallus for Western civilization. Heschel states: "As Jew and the first Christian, yet neither a Jew nor a Christian, Jesus is the ultimate theological transvestite" that unsettles and queers the boundaries between Judaism and Christianity.[32]

It is interesting that Heschel does not spell out whether Jesus was a man who cross-dressed as a female or a woman who cross-dressed as a male. While she questions gender binarism in our thought patterns, her focus is not on the gender difference as it may apply to the Christ figure. Her work is based on the classic study of transvestites by Marjorie Garber, who suggests that the figure of the transvestite questions binary thinking and introduces the "third"— a mode of articulation, a way of describing a space of possibility.[33] Garber notes that the transvestite figure that does not seem "to be primarily concerned with gender difference or blurred gender indicates a *category crisis elsewhere*, an irresolvable conflict or epistemological crux that destabilizes binarity, and displaces the resulting discomfort onto a figure that already inhabits, indeed incarnates, the margin."[34] Unlike Eleanor McLaughlin, who uses Jesus as the transvestite to question gender binarism in support of women's ordination, Heschel uses the transvestite figure to call into question a *category crisis elsewhere*, namely, the problematic and unsettling boundary between Judaism and Christianity.

---

31. Eleanor McLaughlin, "Feminist Christologies: Re-Dressing the Tradition," in *Reconstructing the Christ Symbol: Essays in Feminist Christology*, ed. Maryanne Stevens (New York: Paulist Press, 1993), 138–42.

32. Heschel, "Jesus as a Theological Transvestite," 194.

33. Marjorie Garber, *Vested Interests: Cross-Dressing and Cultural Anxiety* (New York: Routledge, 1992), 11.

34. Ibid., 17.

Jesus as Bi/Christ

My last example comes from *Indecent Theology*, by Marcella Althaus-Reid, who grew up among the poor in Argentina and is teaching in Scotland. With the argument that all theology is sexual, Althaus-Reid challenges theologians to come out from their sexual and theological closets. *Indecent Theology* argues that feminist theology has so far concentrated on gender and has rarely talked about sex and sexuality. While feminist and liberation theologies have emphasized the use of experience in theology, sexual stories have seldom been seen as data that could provide theological insights. Except in gay and lesbian theology, sexual theology has remained underdeveloped and marginalized, and has in fact been left in the closet of mainstream theology. Althaus-Reid counters that sexuality is not a middle-class concern, as it is often assumed to be, because the sex/gender system is integrally linked to the economic and political structures. She argues that sexual ideology pervades economic and political theories and undergirds the epistemological foundations of theology, including liberation theology. A social analysis that understands poverty in economic terms and ignores the sexual and genderized dimensions is not only incomplete, but mystifies the complex web of human relations that both constitute and sustain the social conditions that keep the people poor.

She contends that although liberation theology has shifted the theological subject to "the poor," it continues to share the masculinist and heterosexual assumptions of the dominant theology. As a result, most liberation theologians—male and female—support the sexual codification of both church and society. Likewise, Jesus is imagined to be a sexually safe celibate, and Mary assumes the role of the mother of the poor. The images of Christ and Mary that liberation theologians portray are decent and safe and will not disrupt conventional sexual norms. Jesus can be seen as a social radical, but only as an asexual or celibate figure. Althaus-Reid writes: "He has been dressed theologically as a heterosexually orientated (celibate) man. Jesus with erased genitalia; Jesus minus erotic body."[35] She offers a number of images for Christ in her book, one of which is that of a Bi/Christ. This Bi/Christ, for her, is not related to the sexual performances of Jesus, but to two important points: people's sexual identity outside heterosexualism and "a pattern of thought for a larger Christ outside binary boundaries."[36] The concept of Bi/Christ is intended to disrupt the mono-relationship, challenge dualistic submission, and subvert the "normative vision" of heterosexual difference. Instead of a Mono/Christ, the Bi/Christ has the potential to challenge religious groups, including the Basic

35. Althaus-Reid, *Indecent Theology*, 114.
36. Ibid., 117.

Christian Communities, to organize themselves based not on homophobic theology and compulsory heterosexist relationships, and to bring about social transformation based on more egalitarian principles.

Commenting on Althaus-Reid's image of the Bi/Christ, Robert Goss affirms its possibility to "destabilize the sex/gender system embedded in heteronormative christologies and used to legitimize oppressive heterosexual networks of power."[37] For Goss, while the Bi/Christ is fluid enough to include a variety of sexual configurations, it is not broad enough to include various gender constructions, including the gender conformists and gender transgressors. Using the gender performativity theory of Judith Butler, and building on the work of Eleanor McLaughlin, Goss proposes to accessorize the Bi/Christ with the modification of the Bi/Transvestite Christ. He argues that the queer postmodern representational strategies undergirding the Bi/Transvestite Christ will allow one to "reclaim the sexuality of Jesus/Christ and play with gender constructions intersected with diverse sexual attractions."[38]

CRITICAL OBSERVATIONS AND REFLECTIONS

I would like to draw some observations from these various attempts at de/reconstructing the symbol of Christ.

First, the notion of Jesus/Christ has been a very hybridized concept from the beginning, and as Christianity encounters diverse cultures the formulations of Christology continue to hybridize. There is no original or privileged understanding of Christ, whether at the beginning of the Christian movement or in the history of the church, that can be claimed as pure and foundational, not subject to the limitations of culture and history. It is a futile exercise to search for the "real" or historical Jesus in order to reconstruct a pristine Christian origin. The concept of hybridization may have advantages over the earlier notions of contextualization and indigenization, for the latter terms sometimes assume that there is a Christian essence to be transplanted, transposed, or indigenized in a foreign culture or context. Deconstructing the white and colonial constructs of Christ as hybrids allows marginalized communities to claim the authority to advance their own christological claims.

Second, there was an explosion of hybridized images of Jesus in the second half of the twentieth century because of the struggle for political independence and cultural identity of formerly colonized and oppressed peoples. Thus, the

37. Robert E. Goss, "Expanding Christ's Wardrobe of Dresses," in idem, *Queering Christ: Beyond Jesus Acted Up* (Cleveland: Pilgrim Press, 2002), 176.
38. Ibid., 181.

Black Christ emerged in the black power movement, the Corn Mother in the struggle for sovereignty on the part of Native peoples, and the feminine Shakti from the cultural and religious resources of Indian women. Each of these constructs critiques the mainstream and oppressive images of Christ, yet draws from the biblical and the theological traditions to imagine and speak about Christ in radically new ways. The identity formation of the marginalized group influences its theologians' selection of data from the tradition as well as their work on particular facets of the notion of Christ. In effect, black male theologians focus on race and ethnicity; womanists explore the intersection of race, gender, and class; Tinker pays attention to mythic and symbolic structures; Asian women are interested in interreligious dialogue and mutual transformation.

As the understanding of the identity of a group becomes more fluid and diversified, a concomitant nuanced and diverse understanding of Christ emerges. This is most evident in the development of the notion of the Black Christ. In the beginning, blackness was reappropriated and embraced by black theologians in opposition to its disavowal and denigration by the white culture. But when the notion of blackness was in danger of becoming essentialized to legitimate Afrocentrism and to exclude other viewpoints, black and womanist theologians infused the term with new meanings, and the image of the Black Christ became more nuanced and fluid. Similarly, Asian Christian women find that a rigid and stabilized differentiation between Asian wisdom traditions and Christianity often works to support colonial power, and so they suggest a much more hybridized understanding of Jesus. The process of hybridization takes place not only between two cultures, languages, and symbolic and mythic structures, but also, and increasingly, between divergent claims and identity formations within the same ethnic, religious, and cultural groupings.

Third, I suspect one of the key debates concerning Christ will be in the interpretation of his passion and suffering. In her book *The Psychic Life of Power,* Judith Butler, a Jewish feminist theorist, has raised a poignant question in a different context: How can the subjection of a person become the most defining characteristic in the subject formation process?[39] Many white feminists have criticized the language of self-sacrifice and suffering in the theories of atonement. Delores Williams has challenged the notion of the surrogate Christ and the focus on Jesus' death instead of on his life and ministry.[40] She argues that there are enough black women bearing the cross, and that for black

39. Judith Butler, *The Psychic Life of Power: Theories in Subjection* (Stanford, Calif.: Stanford University Press, 1997).

40. Delores S. Williams, "Black Women's Surrogacy Experience and the Christian Notion of Redemption," in *After Patriarchy: Feminist Transformations of the World Religions,* ed. Paula M. Cooey, William R. Eakin, and Jay B. McDaniel (Maryknoll, N.Y.: Orbis Books, 1991), 1–14.

women Jesus needs to point to healing, wholeness, survival, and quality of life. Yet, in the works of Jacquelyn Grant, Kelly Brown Douglas, and Karen Baker-Fletcher, one finds renewed interest in exploring the relation between the suffering of black women and men and the suffering of Jesus. Grant, for example, points out that the image of the "suffering servant" is problematic, given the fact that black women have been treated as the servants of all in slavery and in domestic service. Religious language when spiritualized can be used to camouflage oppressive reality and sacralize the pain of debased servanthood. Thus, black women must examine Jesus' suffering through their experience of multiple oppression and liberate Jesus from the white racist theology: "Black women/African-American women were constantly liberating Jesus as Jesus was liberating them."[41] George Tinker also speaks of the important role of vicarious self-sacrifice in Native history and ceremonies. The suffering of the Corn Mother for the life of the community is at the heart of his reconstruction of Jesus. While we should not glorify suffering and senseless sacrifice, these theologians are looking for pastoral and theological insights to address the questions of suffering and healing that they see daily in their communities.

Fourth, in constructing the symbol of Christ, we have to guard against anti-Judaism, which has shaped much of the Christian imagination. Judith Plaskow, Susannah Heschel, and Amy-Jill Levine have asserted that Judaism is often presented as monolithically patriarchal to serve as a negative foil, in order to show that Christianity is liberative for women, or that Jesus was a feminist. As I have discussed, anti-Judaism was an integral part of the ideology undergirding empire building and the colonial expansion of Europe, and was brought to the colonized world through the missionaries and theological educational institutions. Some Third World feminist theologians have used the argument that Christianity "reformed" Judaism as a precursor to the argument that Christianity would also "transform" the patriarchal elements of their own cultures, without being conscious of the fact that such a statement may reinscribe both colonialist and anti-Jewish beliefs. Susannah Heschel's Jesus as transvestite raises the question of the extent to which we need to attend to Jesus' Jewish identity when we transpose the Christ symbol into another cultural context. What are the implications of the deemphasis of Jesus' Jewishness when Jesus is transposed to another culture and is interpreted as the Corn Mother or the feminine embodiment of Shakti, or seen in the images of the black women and men?

Finally, colonialist representation and anti-Jewish ideology have much to do with gender and sexual stereotypes. In what way can an "indecent Christ"—

---

41. Jacquelyn Grant, "The Sin of Servanthood and the Deliverance of Discipleship," in *A Troubling in My Soul: Womanist Perspectives on Evil and Suffering*, ed. Emilie M. Townes (Maryknoll, N.Y.: Orbis Books, 1993), 213.

that is, a Christ who challenges conventional norms of masculinity and heteronormativity—open new avenues for our thinking about Christ and salvation? Third World feminist theology has focused on sexual exploitation such as sex tourism, sexual discrimination in the church and in the workplace, and sexual taboos such as menstruation and pollution. Seldom have we written or imagined sexual stories as sources to think about Christ, as Althaus-Reid has suggested. Indeed, how can our deepest longings, intimate desires, and fantasies be resources for our knowing about Christ? How is the love of God related to our erotic connection with others and ourselves? Instead of talking constantly about the morality of sex, how can we recover the beauty, the sublime, and the carnivalesque aspects of sex?

I would like to conclude by sharing a powerful experience I had recently in Boston's Symphony Hall as I listened to a performance of Osvaldo Golijov's *Pasión Según San Marcos* (The Passion according to St. Mark). Sung and performed in Spanish, the piece combined voice, strings, and brass, drums and percussion, and Afro-Cuban dance. Golijov is Jewish, with a Central European heritage, and he grew up in Argentina. What is most iconoclastic and nonconventional about the work is that the roles of Jesus, Pilate, Peter, and the people were sung by the soloists and the chorus without regard to numbers or to gender. Thus, Jesus was sometimes a woman, sometimes a man, sometimes a group of voices, and sometimes a dancer. I found it deeply moving to hear a Latino female vocalist sing, "Abba abba abba abba abba." The artists have ventured far ahead of us in their theological imagination. Why do we, theological faculty and students, lag so far behind and continue to find ourselves bound by the epistemological "limits" of our thinking about Christ?

8

Beyond Pluralism

Toward a Postcolonial Theology of Religious Difference

> The colonial domination of the West over "the rest" in recent centuries has caused many Western categories, ideas and paradigms to appear more universal and normative than they might otherwise have seemed. "Religion" is one such category and could be described as a key feature in the imaginative cartography of western modernity.
>
> *Richard King*[1]

On the cover of the September 2002 issue of *The Guardian*, George W. Bush was depicted as a Roman warrior with a laurel wreath around his head. The caption under the picture read: "Hail, Bush. Is America the New Rome?" In the lead article, Jonathan Freedland noted that while the enemies of the United States have shaken their fist at American imperialism for decades, what is new and surprising is that the notion of an American empire has suddenly become a lively debate within the United States after September 11, as Washington wages a global "war against terrorism."[2] It is no secret that the "new Caesar" in Washington is a "born again" Christian, who frequently alludes to the Bible and employs the religious rhetoric of the holy war, "crusade," and the apocalyptic conflict between good and evil.[3] If Christianity has served in the past as the handmaiden for European colonialism, it is pressing for schol-

---

1. Richard King, "Cartographies of the Imagination, Legacies of Colonialism: The Discourse of Religion and the Mapping of Indic Traditions," *Evam: Forum on Indian Representations* 3 (2004): 273.

2. Jonathan Freedland, "Rome, AD . . . Rome, DC?" *The Guardian* G2, September 18, 2002, 2.

3. Howard Fineman, "Bush and God," *Newsweek*, March 10, 2003, 23–30.

ars in religious studies and theologians to interrogate the ways it is being deployed and reconfigured to further the cause of the Pax Americana.

Alas, theologians in the United States are rather ill prepared for this task. For while scholars in Buddhist, Hindu, Jewish, and Islamic studies have used postcolonial theories to scrutinize how colonial interests have colored the comparative study of religion in general and their fields of study in particular, Christian theologians have seldom engaged in a parallel self-critical reflection of their discipline. The issues of colonialism and empire building have not been central concerns for American theologians, including the feminists among them. A few books on globalization and theology have been published in the last two or three years, but the subject has hardly entered into the theological mainstream.[4]

The relation between Christian theology and the academic study of religion is a complex one and has been subjected to contentious interpretations. It is well known that most of the scholars who helped establish the study of religion as an academic enterprise, such as F. Max Müller, C. P. Tiele, and Nathan Söderblom, were Christians who were keen to show that the scientific study of religion was not incompatible with Christian faith. In fact, Müller used the terms "Comparative Theology" and "Theoretical Theology" to designate the two branches of the science of religion in *Introduction to the Science of Religion* (1873), a foundational text of the discipline.[5] However, it is mainly by differentiating and dissociating from theology that the field of religious studies has gradually established itself as a distinct field. In order to maintain religious studies as an objective academic discipline, worthy of its place in the secular university, scholars have insisted that religious studies must sever its ties with any religious and theological interests and establish itself strictly within the boundaries of the ideals set up by scientific knowledge.[6] Such an argument, influenced as it is by Enlightenment beliefs in science and reason and also by positivism, is not new and has been recurrent ever since the inception of the discipline.

As one of the few theologians interested in postcolonial studies, I am more drawn to a fresher approach, which examines the relation between theology

4. See, e.g., Max Stackhouse, ed., *God and Globalization*, 3 vols. (Harrisburg, Pa.: Trinity Press International, 2000–2002); Dwight N. Hopkins, Lois Ann Lorentzen, Eduardo Mendieta, and David Batstone, eds., *Religions/Globalizations: Theories and Cases* (Durham, N.C.: Duke University Press, 2001); Heather Eaton and Lois Ann Lorentzen, eds., *Ecofeminism and Globalization: Exploring Culture, Context, and Religion* (Lanham, Md.: Rowman and Littlefield Publishers, 2003).

5. F. Max Müller, *Introduction to the Science of Religion* (New York: Arno Press, 1978), 21–22.

6. See, e.g., Donald Wiebe, *The Politics of Religious Studies* (New York: St. Martin's Press, 1999).

and the study of religion within the larger sociopolitical matrix of colonialism, out of which the academic study of religion emerged. Instead of subscribing to an "objective" and "value-neutral" modernist paradigm of religious scholarship, some scholars have used postcolonial theory to highlight the complex imbrications between power and knowledge, and the discipline's problematic production of the knowledge of the Other. Although they have not phrased it this way, they have argued that theology has *colonized* the field of religious studies, which is simply another concrete example of Christian imperialism. They surmise that under the Christian imperialistic gaze, an essentially Western religious framework was superimposed onto non-Western wisdom traditions, from determining what is and is not religion to influencing the approaches and methods of study. For example, David Chidester has pointed out that missionaries, travelers, and colonial agents who arrived in southern Africa in the early nineteenth century could not find religion in Africa at first because of their Christian assumptions. It was only after the colonial settlement that "religion" was "discovered." However, their Christian-biased reports and ethnographies had provided the kind of raw material for theory production at the metropolitan centers, making it possible for the imperial comparative study of religion to be conducted.[7]

Richard King has even argued that the concept of "religion" itself "is a Christian theological category," which is "the product of the culturally specific discursive processes of Christian theology in the West and has been forged in the crucible of interreligious conflict and interaction."[8] The Christian understanding of *religio* has cast its influence on the contemporary conceptualization of the term, he continues, such as the emphasis on faithful adherence to religious doctrines and the importance attached to sacred texts as central for the religious community and for questions of truth and falsity.[9] Furthermore, Christian assumptions about "religion" and "mysticism" helped construct "the mystic East" as Europe's Other and facilitate the fetishizing of the Veda as the authentic embodiment of Hindu religiosity. In a similar vein, S. N. Balagangadhara argues, "Christian theology is the theoretical framework within which investigations into religion have taken place."[10] This theological framework continues to exert its influence even when it has apparently been de-Christianized but remains assumed, in the comparative study of religion, and

7. David Chidester, *Savage Systems: Colonialism and Comparative Religion in Southern Africa* (Charlottesville: University Press of Virginia, 1996).

8. Richard King, *Orientalism and Religion: Postcolonial Theory, India, and "The Mythic East"* (London: Routledge, 1999), 40.

9. Ibid., 38–39.

10. S. N. Balagangadhara, *"The Heathen in His Blindness": Asia, the West, and the Dynamic of Religion* (Leiden: E. J. Brill, 1994), 267.

thus has universalized itself under a secular guise. In this way, Christianity continues to serve as the prototype of a religion, and the standard for evaluating other wisdom traditions.

These pointed observations invite serious responses and critical reflections by Christian theologians. An adequate response is to extend the postcolonial critique of the study of religion to the discipline of theology, a task that has just been begun by a few. To begin a conversation with my colleagues in religious studies, I want to outline how such a postcolonial critique can be undertaken, by focusing on: (1) a review of the interrelationships between the comparative study of religion and theology in the course of development in the nineteenth century, (2) a critique of current discussion on the "pluralistic theology of religions," and (3) a vision of a postcolonial theology of religious difference.

COMPARATIVE STUDY OF RELIGION AND THEOLOGY

Modern theology developed in a cultural space bordered by the Enlightenment on the one hand and the political expansion of Europe and ascendancy of the United States on the other. The discussion of what religion is and how to understand religious experience occupies a pivotal position in the modern theological project, from the publication of Schleiermacher's book *On Religion: Speeches to Its Cultured Despisers*[11] to the present-day theories on religious pluralism. These theological discussions influence the cultural and religious worldview of their time, contribute to Western people's understanding of the religious diversity of humankind, and have an impact on the receptivity to the new discipline called comparative religion. As Richard King argues, "religion" is a concept created in the Western imagination of modernity, which serves as a "cognitive map for surveying, classifying, and interpreting diverse cultural and historical terrains and allows a distinction to be drawn between 'secular' and 'religious' spheres of human life."[12]

Widely recognized as the founder of modern theology, Schleiermacher (1768–1834) published his first book, *On Religion*, in 1799, when he was thirty-one. Responding to the Enlightenment attack on religion, it represents the

---

11. Friedrich Schleiermacher, *On Religion: Speeches to Its Cultured Despisers*, trans. John Oman (New York: Harper Torchbooks, 1958). This is based on the third edition, originally published in 1831. Hereafter page references to this book will be cited parenthetically in the text.

12. King, "Cartographies of the Imagination," 273.

first major attempt of a Christian theologian to defend religion to people influenced by the modern worldview and to make it once again possible for theology to stake out its religious claims. Influenced by Moravian Pietism and romanticism, Schleiermacher introduced a new definition of religion and ushered in the subjective turn of theology. He emphasized the difference among religion, metaphysics, and moral philosophy, and between knowing and doing, and located religious consciousness within the experiencing subject: "Religion's essence is neither thinking or acting, but intuition and feeling. It wishes to intuit the universe, wishes devoutly to overhear the universe's own manifestations and actions."[13]

Schleiermacher's definition of religion underwent subsequent changes in the later editions of the book, when he was working on his more mature theological work, *The Christian Faith*. He had gradually dropped the word "intuition" and focused more on feeling (*Gefühl*), which was understood better as the "immediate self-consciousness."[14] Some scholars have criticized Schleiermacher for suggesting an "essence" for religion,[15] and thus contributing to the idea that religion is sui generis, separate from all other human activities. But Schleiermacher did not subscribe to a metaphysical and abstract definition of religion, as those who proposed natural religion did, for he took into consideration the historical character of religion. Others have attacked Schleiermacher's definition of religion as too individualistic, because it is rooted in self-consciousness, but Schleiermacher insisted that individuality had to be grounded in community and it was in the positive or historical religions that religion must exhibit itself.[16]

As Claude Welch has indicated, theologians at the beginning of the nineteenth century faced the daunting question of "How is theology possible?" because of the harsh critique of religion in the previous century. Schleiermacher's fresh understanding of religion, according it an integrity of its own, locating it in the immediacy of human consciousness, enables him to "develop the justification for doctrinal assertions and to restate the kind of validity and truth those assertions can have."[17] Schleiermacher states in *The Christian Faith*

13. Friedrich Schleiermacher, *On Religion: Speeches to Its Cultured Despisers*, trans. Richard Crouter (Cambridge: Cambridge University Press, 1988), 102. Translation based on the first, 1799, edition.

14. See Richard Crouter, "Introduction," ibid., 61–62.

15. Ludwig Feuerbach is most famous for his book *The Essence of Christianity*, trans. George Eliot (Buffalo, N.Y.: Prometheus Books, 1989).

16. See Francis Schüssler Fiorenza, "Religion: A Contested Site in Theology and the Study of Religion," *Harvard Theological Review* 93 (2000): 7–34.

17. Claude Welch, *Protestant Thought in the Nineteenth Century*, vol. 1, *1799–1870* (New Haven, Conn.: Yale University Press, 1972), 69.

that "Christian doctrines are accounts of the Christian religious affections set forth in speech."[18] Theology is carried out on behalf of the church and performs a hermeneutical function for the language of piety, responding to both the theologian's own conviction and the beliefs of the religious community.[19] Theology, for Schleiermacher, does not begin with revelation, but begins with an analysis of the religious consciousness of humankind. Jesus is unique and exemplary because in him we can fully witness the consciousness of the feeling of absolute dependence on God.

On Religion also opened the door for the study of religious traditions, for unlike the conservative theologians who harbored negative attitudes toward other religious traditions, Schleiermacher recognized that diverse traditions existed alongside each other and allowed room for historical interpretation and comparative study. In his fifth speech, "The Religions," he said that because human beings' intuitions are not the same, religion exists in multiple forms and must be comprehended in the sum total of all its forms (217). Contrary to the position of the Enlightenment thinkers, he held that there is no universal natural or rational religion that alone is true and that is applicable to all. He recognized that each religion has its own genesis and undergoes development of its external form, just as an individual has different stages of religious consciousness in the span of his religious life.

As the most influential Protestant theologian in the nineteenth century, Schleiermacher has been studied by generations of scholars, but few have examined his discourse on religion from a postcolonial angle. First of all, Germany was not a unified nation and did not have colonies in Schleiermacher's time. In fact, Napoleonic forces overran the city of Halle in 1806 and Schleiermacher lost his position at the University of Halle and had to move to Berlin. Moreover, postcolonial analyses of German culture, philosophy, and arts have appeared only in the 1990s, much later than comparable studies on French and English cultures. A postcolonial critique of Schleiermacher's understanding of religion must take into account nationalism, class, race, gender, and what Susanne Zantop has called colonial fantasies during this precolonial period of German history. In her study of tales, novels, scientific articles, philosophical essays, and political pamphlets, Zantop locates a colonialist subjectivity that emerged among Germans as early as in the 1770s, which became a collective obsession by the late 1800s. These colonial fantasies included the desire to "venture forth, to conquer and appropriate foreign territories, and to (re)generate the self in the process," and are particularly linked to stories of sexual

18. Friedrich Schleiermacher, *The Christian Faith*, ed. H. R. Mackintosh and J. S. Stewart (Edinburgh: T. and T. Clark, 1989), 76.
19. See Welch, *Protestant Thought*, 71.

conquest and surrender and to the encounter between Europeans and the "natives."[20]

It is important to bear this cultural and political context in mind when interpreting Schleiermacher's work. As Joerg Rieger has pointed out, Schleiermacher's thinking is best understood in the context of the rising bourgeoisie in Europe and their claim to authority in defining the world. He argues that Schleiermacher's theological project, focusing on the modern self, best served the interests of a particular social group: the upwardly mobile middle class—the educated among the cultural despisers—in the age of capitalism.[21] With the birth of political aspirations among Germans in the early nineteenth century, Schleiermacher's bourgeois self had a distinctly national character as both he and Hegel were in search of the "German spirit" that could regenerate German culture after the Napoleonic defeats. It was precisely in the religious feelings of the German people that Schleiermacher located their special national character. In contrast to the English, who he said knew only "gain and enjoyment" (9), and the French who abhorred religion more than unbridled arrogance (10), the Germans were predisposed to religion, capable of awakening to the holy and divine things (9).

Although the Germans did not rule over foreign peoples at this time, Schleiermacher displayed racial biases toward non-Europeans, a bias also found in many Enlightenment thinkers. If for Schleiermacher religion provided culture with its depth and infused it with the creative spirit, what he said about the religious traditions of other peoples was very telling. He subscribed to a developmental view of religion, considering fetishism, idol worship, and polytheism to be lower stages when compared to the higher form of monotheism.[22] Schleiermacher described the wisdom traditions of remote peoples as "rude and undeveloped," and considered Judaism a dead religion and "childlike" because of its emphasis on commandments and on retribution by a punishing and disciplining God (238–39). He also said that Judaism displayed a lingering fetishism, because of its limitation of the love of Jehovah to the race of Abraham and its frequent vacillation toward idol worship. As for Islam, Schleiermacher found its passionate character and the strong sensuous content of its ideas wanting, which suggested that Islam still displayed characteristics of polytheism.[23] Only Christianity, for him, is worthy of "adult humanity" (241) and is religion fully idealized (243). He did not change such biased views in subsequent editions of the book, and his belief in the superiority of Christianity took

20. Susanne Zantop, *Colonial Fantasies: Conquest, Family, and Nation in Precolonial Germany, 1770–1870* (Durham, N.C.: Duke University Press, 1997), 2.

21. Joerg Rieger, *God and the Excluded: Visions and Blindspots in Contemporary Theology* (Minneapolis: Fortress Press, 2001), 23.

22. Schleiermacher, *The Christian Faith*, 34–38.

23. Ibid., 37.

stronger hold when he became an established theologian. He wrote in *The Christian Faith*: "This comparison of Christianity with other similar religions is in itself a sufficient warrant for saying that Christianity is, in fact, the most perfect of the most highly developed forms of religion."[24]

Schleiermacher's definition of religion also displayed an interesting gender dimension. While the Enlightenment philosophers had constructed the "Man of Reason," Schleiermacher valorized what was traditionally regarded as the feminine: intuition, feelings, and devotion to spiritual values. His emphasis on the feeling of absolute dependence places the experiencing subject in a passive-receptive position vis-à-vis the Infinite or the Eternal. He indicates that such feeling can be found in "almost all women" (47). But as Katherine Faull points out, Schleiermacher's experiencing subject is still male; only his religious consciousness is mediated through the feminine.[25] Furthermore, Schleiermacher uses heterosexual intercourse as an important metaphor for the individual's experience of the Universe:

> I lie on the bosom of the infinite world. At this moment I am its soul, for I feel all its powers and its infinite life as my own; at this moment it is my body, for I penetrate its muscles and its limbs as my own, and its innermost nerves move according to my sense and my presentiment as my own.[26]

Faull observes that Schleiermacher endows nature and the Absolute with female physical attributes and she becomes his body as he penetrates her muscles and limbs.

Schleiermacher's gender-inflected and class- and race-conscious definition of religion exerted tremendous influence on subsequent discussions on other religious questions, such as the essence of religion, the relationship between theology and the study of religion, the public and private character of religion, the stages of development of religion, and Christianity's relation with other religions. Like Schleiermacher, F. Max Müller (1823–1900), the founder of the science of religion, grew up in the atmosphere of German idealism. Echoing Schleiermacher and learning from Kant, Müller defines religion as "the perception of the infinite under such manifestations as are able to influence the moral character of man."[27] Müller proposed a science of religion or comparative religion that is

24. Ibid., 38.
25. Katherine M. Faull, "Schleiermacher—A Feminist? or, How to Read Gender Inflected Theology," in *Schleiermacher and Feminism: Sources, Evaluations, and Responses*, ed. Iain G. Nicol (Lewiston, N.Y.: Edwin Mellen Press, 1992), 24.
26. Schleiermacher, *On Religion*, trans. Richard Crouter, 113.
27. F. Max Müller, *Natural Religion* (*Collected Works* 1, 1899), 188, quoted in Eric Sharpe, *Comparative Religion: A History*, 2nd ed. (La Salle, Ill.: Open Court, 1986), 39.

based on the comparative study of language and mythology, which in turn allows him to trace the genealogy of language, culture, and history. Many of these meticulous comparative studies of languages and cultures in the nine-teenth century were done by Germans, and scholars have attributed this to the search for identity and kinship of the German people before the formation of their nation-state. Some have rejected Edward Said's claim that "the German Orient was almost exclusively a scholarly, or at least a classical, Orient"[28] by connecting Orientalism with Germany's rising national sentiment and Ger-many's sustained political and economic interests in the Middle East.[29]

Preoccupied by the question of race, Müller traced the origin of the Aryans to India in *Comparative Mythology* (1856), and found in the Veda a rich repos-itory of the earliest thinking of the human mind. I have indicated elsewhere the deployment of the feminine in Müller's nostalgic quest for Mother India, a place he romantically referred to as the "womb of the world" and birthplace of all human cultures and religions.[30] Although Müller advocated an impartial comparative study of religion, he sometimes allowed his Christian biases to slip in.[31] He thought his comparative study would give new life to Christian-ity by providing knowledge about other religious traditions of humankind.[32] He subscribed to the developmental theory of religion, and after more than forty years of comparative study still held that "Christianity has given the best and truest expression to what the old world had tried to express in various and less perfect ways."[33]

Much has been said about how theology influenced the study of religion in its formative period; I want to stress how comparative religion in its turn influ-enced biblical studies and theology, because they worked with similar cultural presuppositions and responded to similar intellectual questions of the time.

---

28. Edward W. Said, *Orientalism* (New York: Vintage, 1994), 19.

29. Nina Berman, "Orientalism, Imperialism, and Nationalism: Karl May's *Ori-entzyklus*," in *The Imperialist Imagination: German Colonialism and Its Legacy*, ed. Sara Friedrichsmeyer, Sara Lennox, and Susanne Zantop (Ann Arbor: University of Michi-gan Press, 1998), 52.

30. Kwok Pui-lan, "Gender, Colonialism, and the Study of Religion," in *Postcolo-nialism, Feminism, and Religious Discourse*, ed. Laura E. Donaldson and Kwok Pui-lan (New York: Routledge, 2002), 14–19.

31. See Timothy Fitzgerald, *The Ideology of Religious Studies* (New York: Oxford Uni-versity Press, 2000), 34–36.

32. F. Max Müller, *Chips from a German Workshop*, vol. 1 (London: Longmans, 1867), xix.

33. Max Müller, *Anthropological Religion*, vol. 3 of *The Early Sociology of Religion*, ed. Bryan S. Turner (London: Routledge, 1997), 388. Müller's book was originally pub-lished in 1892.

The method of comparative religion and its racial bias directly impacted the search for Christian origins and the historical Jesus in the latter part of the nineteenth century. Ernest Renan, a friend of Müller who helped popularize Müller's work,[34] introduced Orientalism to the study of the New Testament. For more than forty years, both Müller and Renan worked with the racial categories of the Aryans and the Semites and believed in the superiority of the Aryan race. Renan's popular book *La Vie de Jésus*, published in 1863, not only recasts Jesus in terms of bourgeois French high culture, but also insists that Jesus had infused new spirit into the insufficiency of the Mosaic law.[35] Renan tried to show that Christianity had gotten rid of the vestiges of Judaism and was the Aryan religion par excellence. As Susannah Heschel has shown, such de-Judaization of the inception of Christianity led to the dehistoricization of Jesus, the tendency toward anti-Semitism, and the subsequent debate about whether Jesus was an Aryan because he came from Galilee.[36]

The interest in the comparative study of the Bible in its surrounding cultural and religious contexts led to the formation of the *Religionsgeschichtliche Schule*, or "the history of religion school," particularly at the University of Göttingen.[37] Otto Pfleiderer was the founder of the school, and other members in biblical studies included Hermann Gunkel, Wilhelm Bousset, and Wilhelm Heitmüller. Although these scholars identified parallels between religious, cultic, and cultural elements or motifs in the Bible and those in the ancient Near East, they also wanted to find unique elements that differentiated the biblical tradition from others.

Although the liberal theologians were not particularly interested in comparative religion as they lacked the necessary specialized knowledge, the gathering of vast amounts of data, texts, and knowledge of religious practices during the last decades of the nineteenth century intensified the discussion of Christianity's relation to culture and to other wisdom traditions. While Schleiermacher and Hegel had adopted a developmental theory of religion, the comparative study of religion, following evolutionary theory, provided a "scientific" basis for positioning "religions" in a time frame. Hence, theologians

---

34. Renan helped to popularize Müller's works by having his wife translate some of them; see Maurice Olender, *The Languages of Paradise: Race, Religion, and Philology in the Nineteenth Century* (Cambridge, Mass.: Harvard University Press, 1992), 175, n. 3.

35. Ernest Renan, *The Life of Jesus* (New York: Peter Eckler Publishing Co., 1925), 117–19.

36. Susannah Heschel, *Abraham Geiger and the Jewish Jesus* (Chicago: University of Chicago Press, 1998), 125.

37. Sharpe, *Comparative Religion*, 149–51.

interpreted Christianity as the "promise" or the "fulfillment" of other "religions," and such a position gained the official imprimatur of the first World Missionary Conference held at Edinburgh in 1910.

Ernst Troeltsch (1865–1923) was keenly aware of the challenge the comparative study of religion posed to the truth claims of theology. In his *The Absoluteness of Christianity and the History of Religions,* he upheld Christianity as the convergence point of all the developmental tendencies in religion.[38] Some twenty years later, even though he revised his view and recognized the validity of other "historical religions," he maintained the racist notion of the superiority of these "historical religions" over the animism and heathenism of the "less developed races." He said that in the encounter between the heathen races and European civilization, the morality and religion of these lower cultures disintegrated and had to be replaced with Christianity.[39]

The First World War shattered the liberal theologians' emphasis on religious experience and their optimism about progress and evolution. If Schleiermacher's liberal theology represented the rise of the bourgeoisie and its confidence in European culture and Christianity, then Karl Barth's neo-orthodoxy signals the diametric opposite. Barth has a negative view of religion and regards revelation as the abolition of all religion. For him, religion is unbelief and rebellion against God, who as the Wholly Other judges all religion, including Christianity.[40] Although Barth's neo-orthodoxy may have been prophetic during the rise of Hitler, his negative judgment of human cultures and his heavily christocentric theology could not be good news for Third World nations struggling for independence. Interestingly enough, both Schleiermacher and Barth assumed a passive and stereotypically "feminine" position vis-à-vis the Infinite and, in Barth's case, God as the Wholly Other.[41] One may ask, as both the feminist and the liberation theologians have done, if such a vulnerable and subordinating religious disposition is more appropriate for upwardly mobile bourgeois people, so that their burgeoning egos will be checked, than it is for the oppressed. What is good news for the strong may

38. Ernst Troeltsch, *The Absoluteness of Christianity and the History of Religions* (London: SCM Press, 1972). This work was based on a lecture delivered in October 1901.

39. Ernst Troeltsch, "The Place of Christianity among the World Religions," in *Attitudes toward Other Religions,* ed. Owen C. Thomas (London: SCM Press, 1969), 86–87. This was a lecture written for delivery at Oxford University in 1923, but was not delivered because of his untimely death.

40. Karl Barth, "The Revelation of God as the Abolition of Religion," in Thomas, *Attitudes toward Other Religions,* 96–112.

41. See the discussion of Barth in Sarah Coakley, *Powers and Submissions: Spirituality, Philosophy and Gender* (Oxford: Blackwell, 2002), xix–xx.

not be good news for the weak and the colonized, who have lost much confidence in themselves and in their cultures.

BEYOND A PLURALISTIC THEOLOGY
OF RELIGIONS

It was no coincidence that the problem of the relationship of Christianity to other religious traditions, the most pressing theological issue at the turn of the twentieth century, resurfaced again a century later in a different cultural and political context in the United States. Several factors contribute to American theologians' attention to other religious traditions. First, following the independence movements around the globe in the 1960s, the triumphalism of the missionary movement was challenged and with it the "fulfillment" theory. Second, church attendance in mainline denominations has been in steady decline since the 1960s, and the hegemony of the WASP came under constant scrutiny in a so-called multicultural America. Third, the arrival of new immigrants since the change of the immigration law in 1965 has significantly changed the religious landscape of the United States, as Diana Eck's Pluralism Project at Harvard has amply demonstrated. Fourth, a number of prominent theologians, such as John Cobb, Gordon Kaufman, Rosemary Radford Ruether, John Hick, and Paul Knitter, have participated in interreligious dialogue, and begun to advocate a more sympathetic attitude toward other religious traditions. Fifth, most recently the "war on terrorism" and Samuel Huntington's forecast of the clash of civilizations to replace the clash of ideology in the cold war era has put religion at the center of the political debate about homeland security.

For the liberal theologians, Christian theology needs to develop an understanding of religion that does not place Christianity as the only true religion while denigrating all others as false, because this is detrimental to peaceful coexistence among the world's peoples. For others, the issue is closer to home, namely, how to live among one's religious neighbors whose children go to the same schools as yours in an increasingly religiously pluralistic America. For advocates of interreligious dialogue, the concern is to enter into conversations with "people of other faiths" to gain a new understanding of both the religious tradition of others and of oneself. I propose, instead, to examine the discourse of theology of religions within the context of rising American imperialism and to see how religion is reconfigured to align with current political interests. Instead of focusing on the Christian right, whose conservative political agenda is quite evident, I want to look at the pluralistic theology of religions proposed by more liberal and progressive theologians.

Currently there are three major paradigms in conceptualizing Christianity's relationship with other religious traditions. The first is the exclusivist position, to which Karl Barth belongs, which believes that outside the Christian faith there is no possibility for salvation, for truth is revealed only in the Bible and its interpretation guaranteed by the church. This is also the position held by most evangelical Christians, who believe in the uniqueness of Christ and maintain that there is no other name by which humans can be saved. The second is the inclusivist position, which stresses that God's salvation is for all and affirms that other non-Christian wisdom traditions may contain some truth. Still the mediation through Jesus Christ is essential, and Karl Rahner even called those who do not explicitly acknowledge Christ "anonymous Christians." As Jeannine Hill Fletcher has noted, both the exclusivist and inclusivist positions judge other religious traditions according to sameness and difference, invariably using Christianity as the norm or standard. While the exclusivist position favors one's particular position and dismisses others' claims to truth, the inclusivist approach searches for sameness in human fulfillment though maintaining the centrality of Jesus Christ. Hill Fletcher also observes that many so-called pluralist positions follow the same logic in constructing identity and difference, though in different guises. As such, she writes: "The 'other' is not allowed to be distinctive but rather is judged by how much 'like' the Christian's his or her religious practice and achievements are."[42]

If we situate the pluralistic paradigm within the sociopolitical context out of which it emerged, we will be able to see its promise and limitation more sharply. The pluralistic approach emerged when the West was forced to face the diversity of culture and traditions in the postcolonial period of political independence. In a significant article, "Is There a Neo-Racism?" Étienne Balibar argues that the nineteenth-century associations of race with nature and biology, and a concept of race as based on bloodline, have both undergone changes since the Second World War. The former notion of biological difference has been displaced onto the cultural realm, and insurmountable cultural difference has been used as an excuse to justify racist behavior and discrimination.[43] Rey Chow identifies the tensions and contradictions of this postwar phenomenon of anthropological culturalism, especially as they manifest in the liberal academy. On the one hand, the liberals want to acknowledge the diversity and particularities of all cultures and recognize others on an equal foot-

42. Jeannine Hill Fletcher, "Shifting Identity: The Contribution of Feminist Thought to Theologies of Religious Pluralism," *Journal of Feminist Studies in Religion* 19, no. 2 (2003): 9.

43. Étienne Balibar, "Is There a Neo-Racism?" trans. Chris Turner, in *Race, Nation, Class: Ambiguous Identities*, ed. Étienne Balibar and Immanuel Wallerstein (New York: Verso, 1991), 17–28.

ing. On the other, such recognition is still operative within a cultural assumption that Western culture is the most advanced and that white people need to tolerate those who are different from them.[44]

Such ambivalence toward other cultures can be seen as undergirding some of the discussions on religious pluralism. For example, John Hick develops a Christian theology of religions that tries to honor what he calls the "rainbow of faiths" by arguing that God has many names, and underneath their divergent paths all religious traditions demonstrate similar shifts "from self-centredness to Reality-centredness."[45] Hick accords all traditions equal status because of his assumption that the religious response of humankind is basically the same, and argues for a shift from a christocentric to a theocentric approach to religion. Given that religious traditions exist in such diverse forms, his glossing over the differences that distinguish one religion from another smacks of the patronizing tendency of white liberals. Moreover, it is far too presumptuous to say that the Reality worshipped or revered by all traditions is ultimately the same, albeit with different names and guises. Though he has avoided using the term "God" and speaks of the ultimate reality instead, his approach seems to be based still too much on a Christian theistic framework.

While Hick underscores the similarities of human religious experience, George Lindbeck's cultural-linguistic approach highlights the differences that arise because each religious worldview is shaped by its language and sacred scriptures.[46] Instead of adopting an evolutionary model of "religions," Lindbeck advocates a linguistic model for comparison. Each religious person is socialized in the grammar of faith defined by one's sacred scripture, and it is difficult to be bilingual and fluent in another religious language with its own terminology and syntax. Since the religious worlds coexist and are equally valid and meaningful for their "native speakers," one's opting for a Christian worldview is ultimately the result of faith. For such an emphasis Lindbeck has been criticized as reviving "fideism" and bringing back Barth's confessionalism in a sophisticated guise.[47] But a more relevant question is the relationship between Lindbeck's postliberal theology, based on Anglo-American culture,

44. Rey Chow, *The Protestant Ethnic and the Spirit of Capitalism* (New York: Columbia University Press, 2002), 13–14, 28–29.

45. John Hick, *A Christian Theology of Religions: The Rainbow of Faiths* (Louisville, Ky.: Westminster John Knox Press, 1995), 107.

46. George Lindbeck, *The Nature of Doctrine: Religion and Theology in a Postliberal Age* (Philadelphia: Westminster Press, 1984).

47. David Tracy, "Lindbeck's New Program for Theology: A Reflection," *Thomist* 49 (1985): 465. See also William C. Placher, "Revisionist and Postliberal Theologies and the Public Character of Theology," *Thomist* 49 (1985): 392–416.

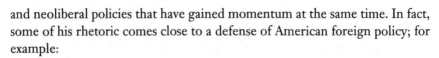

and neoliberal policies that have gained momentum at the same time. In fact, some of his rhetoric comes close to a defense of American foreign policy; for example:

> It was thus, rather than by intentional effect, that biblical religion helped produce democracy and science, as well as other values Westerners treasure; and it is in similarly unimaginable and unplanned ways, if at all, that biblical religion will help save the world (*for Western civilization is now world civilization*) from the demonic corruptions of these same values.[48]

And in the aftermath of September 11, one should also ask in what ways Lindbeck's notion of insurmountable religious differences reinforces the myth of "clash of civilizations" and fosters a narrowly constructed and tightly bound view of religious identity.

Most of the discussion about religious pluralism has taken place among men, leading Ursula King to bemoan the fact that feminism is "the missing dimension in the dialogue of religions."[49] King notes that women's voices have very little part in books on interfaith dialogue, religious pluralism, theology of religions, and global interreligious encounter. Similarly, Kate McCarthy has observed that "the effort to define a Christian theology of religions remains almost completely a Western, and masculine, academic enterprise."[50] This omission of women's voices is unwarranted, since the women's movement has brought historic changes at social, political, and economic levels, and has transformed women's consciousness as well as their reception of religious traditions. King criticizes the three paradigms of exclusivism, inclusivism, and pluralism as being "too narrow, static and insufficiently differentiated to capture the organic, fluid and dynamic reality of religion at a personal and social level."[51] She also points out that the models are thoroughly androcentric, in the sense that they are assumed to be universally applicable categories in dealing with the relationships between different religious traditions, without taking gender and other specific conditions of people into account. But apart from the feminist politics of inclusion, she provides no alternative model and admits that the challenge of feminism to interreligious dialogue has not been fully articulated.

48. Lindbeck, *The Nature of Doctrine*, 128. Emphasis mine.

49. Ursula King, "Feminism: The Missing Dimension in the Dialogue of Religions," in *Pluralism and the Religions: The Theological and Political Dimensions*, ed. John D'Arcy May (London: Cassell, 1998), 40.

50. Kate McCarthy, "Women's Experience as a Hermeneutical Key to a Christian Theology of Religions," *Studies in Interreligious Dialogue* 6, no. 2 (1996): 163.

51. King, "Feminism," 46.

Another scholar, Rita Gross, also challenges feminists to wrestle with religious pluralism and engage in dialogue to borrow a "comparative mirror" to illuminate self as well as other.[52] For her, the pluralist position is most suitable for a feminist theology of religions, because women who have been excluded by patriarchal religious traditions would not want to exclude others. She argues that openness to other religious traditions and the willingness to engage in interreligious dialogue have the potential to change the development of feminist theology and expand its horizon. If it fails to do so, Gross warns that feminist theology will be in danger of becoming a "Christian ghetto" and of falling short of a genuine inclusivity.[53] However, Gross fails to notice that Asian and African feminist theologians, such as Mercy Amba Oduyoye, Chung Hyun Kyung, and myself, have discussed the challenges of religious diversity for decades, and she includes few non-Western sources in her attempt to envision a feminist theology of religions.[54]

These different forms of pluralistic theology of religions have certainly come a long way from the nineteenth-century evolutionary theory of religion and the presumptions that Christianity is the highest of all forms of religion or the only true religion. However, because of the colonial legacy of liberal theology and the lack of self-consciousness about this legacy among Western theologians, similar stumbling blocks resurface in contemporary discussion of religious pluralism. For example, Hick is still interested in searching for some essence or commonalities in universal religious experiences, an issue that has preoccupied modern theologians and scholars of comparative religion. Constructing his "cultural-linguistic" paradigm, based on the work of Clifford Geertz and other anthropologists, Lindbeck has overlooked the critiques of Geertz's definition of religion as still based on Christianity as well as ample evidence of the collusion of anthropology with colonialism.[55] While their intention to include gender in a theology of religions is laudable, white

52. Rita M. Gross, "Feminist Theology as Theology of Religions," in *The Cambridge Companion to Feminist Theology*, ed. Susan Frank Parsons (Cambridge: Cambridge University Press, 2002), 60–78.

53. Rita M. Gross, "Feminist Theology: Religiously Diverse Neighborhood or Christian Ghetto?" *Journal of Feminist Studies in Religion* 16, no. 2 (2000): 73–78.

54. Gross cites only one book that includes non-Western authors in her article "Feminist Theology as Theology of Religions."

55. Talal Asad, ed., *Anthropology and the Colonial Encounter* (London: Ithaca Press, 1973); Sherry B. Ortner, "Theory in Anthropology since the Sixties," *Comparative Studies in Society and History* 26 (1984): 126–66. For a critique of Geertz's concept of religion as a cultural system, see Talal Asad, "The Construction of Religion as an Anthropological Category," in *Genealogies of Religion: Discipline and Reasons of Power in Christianity and Islam* (Baltimore: Johns Hopkins University Press, 1993), 27–54.

feminists speak primarily from their white context and often ignore the contributions of feminists from other parts of the world.

Before we rush to embrace a pluralistic model of theology of religion, it is important to reflect on the assumptions that make such a position possible: an uncritical use of the category of "religion" and the problematic construction of "world religions." More than forty years ago, Wilfred Cantwell Smith argued that the continued use of the terms "religion" and "religions" has blocked Western understanding of the vitality of personal faith of people from other traditions throughout the world. He has suggested to drop the term "religion" altogether, and instead use what he termed the "cumulative tradition" and "faith" to denote the outer and inner dimensions of human religiousness.[56] Recently, scholars have argued that the use of "religion" as a sui generis concept, which can be traced to Schleiermacher's notion of universal religious consciousness in human beings, leads to a distortion of the study of religion, because it assumes that religion can be separated from other social, economic, and political spheres. Timothy Fitzgerald has unequivocally said: "The construction of 'religion' and 'religions' as global, cross-cultural objects of study has been part of a wider historical process of western imperialism, colonialism, and neocolonialism. Part of this process has been to establish an ideologically loaded distinction between the realm of religion and the realm of non-religion or the secular."[57] Given such a colonial legacy, we may need to radically reappraise the current interests in interreligious dialogue and religious pluralism within a much larger ideological framework.

Raimundo Panikkar, a religious thinker who is comfortable in both the Hindu and Christian traditions, has summarized the self-understanding of Christians in relation to other religious traditions in different epochs of Christian history. He points out that while conversion, crusade, and mission have been the dominant modes of interaction for centuries, it was only when the colonial empires declined in power, and the colonized peoples tried to reembrace their own cultures, that dialogue became a catchword.[58] In most interreligious dialogues conducted in Western ecumenical or academic settings, a handful of Third World elites, usually all males, are invited to speak as representatives of their traditions to a largely white Christian audience. The themes and subject matters to be discussed are mostly determined by the interests of

56. Wilfred Cantwell Smith, *The Meaning and End of Religion: A Revolutionary Approach to the Great Religious Traditions* (1963; reprint, New York: Harper and Row, 1978), 50–51.

57. Fitzgerald, *The Ideology of Religious Studies*, 8.

58. Raimundo Panikkar, "The Jordan, the Tiber, and the Ganges," in *The Myth of Christian Uniqueness: Toward a Pluralistic Theology of Religions*, ed. John Hick and Paul F. Knitter (Maryknoll, N.Y.: Orbis Books, 1987), 93–95.

Christianity.[59] The different "world religions" are reified as if they were distinct and insoluble entities, represented primarily by male elitist traditions, while intrareligious differences are ignored and women's voices neglected. To the organizers, that one person or two have been invited to speak on behalf of "Buddhism" or "Hinduism" does not seem to be awkward or inadequate. Instead of promoting genuine understanding, such a kind of interreligious dialogue can be a device used by the metropolitan centers to manage religious differences and to co-opt Third World elites in a postcolonial world. Ecumenical theology, with its good intentions to overcome Christian exclusiveness, has promoted dialogue and a pluralistic theology of religions. But it has its drawbacks, as Timothy Fitzgerald astutely observes:

> Ecumenical theology is designed to build bridges of what it calls interfaith dialogue between the world religions, but it also articulates a relationship between imperialist western politics and their colonized native elites, or between the dominant culture of a western nation and its ethnic minorities. In the postcolonial world these relations of dominance and subordination have been transposed into a new form, that of the inequality that exists between the West and the third world, and the way that the analysis of this inequality is mystified by shifting the realm of equality to the transcendent.[60]

Thus, if we are not vigilant about the ideological framework within which such an ecumenical theology is embedded, it can be used to preserve the status quo and camouflage the real differences between Western dominant powers and Third World societies.

TOWARD A POSTCOLONIAL THEOLOGY OF RELIGIOUS DIFFERENCE

Do we still need a theology of religions, or has the project run its course? Given how Christian theology has contributed to Western constructions of the Other through its strategic use of the category of religion, a critical theological reflection on the subject is important. Instead of grounding our thinking in the liberal paradigm of religious pluralism, we must begin to envision a postcolonial theology of religious difference. Theologians can learn from scholars of religious studies how they have questioned the concept of religion and the methodological assumptions of their own discipline. For example,

---

59. See, e.g., Donald G. Dawe and John B. Carman, eds., *Christian Faith in a Religiously Plural World* (Maryknoll, N.Y.: Orbis Books, 1978).
60. Fitzgerald, *The Ideology of Religious Studies*, 23.

should we perpetuate the use of the terms "religion" and "religions" in the postcolonial era? If "religion" as a concept has been so much shaped by Christian theism, will continued use of the term reinforce Christian imperialism? Timothy Fitzgerald proposes that we get rid of the term "religion" altogether, for the term suggests that religion is something over and above and in addition to society and culture.[61] Richard King, on the other hand, points out it is difficult to abandon the term altogether, given how it has shaped Western social imagination and everyday discourse. He proposes to use the term strategically, noting how it has been used in the Western cartographical imagination, such as in the demarcation of the "religious" from the "secular," and in the mapping of diverse cultures, traditions, practices, and communities.[62] I would agree with King on this point.

Both Richard King and Timothy Fitzgerald advocate the interface between religious studies and cultural studies,[63] and I think a postcolonial theology of religious difference should follow the same course. In fact, Paula M. Cooey, writing in another context, has argued that academic theology is a species of cultural studies, because its task is not just to evaluate and construct central religious symbols, but also to analyze and challenge "religious and, more specifically, theological regulation of gender, class, ethnicity, and political power."[64] A postcolonial theology of religious difference goes beyond asking the usual questions, such as: Is there only one transcendental reality? Do human beings have common, universal religious experience? Do different religions have the same ultimate goal, or are there different salvations?[65] These questions, though important to some scholars in religion and theologians, are contingent on one's epistemological and theological viewpoints. They may not be the kind of questions that would broaden our conversations with colleagues in cultural studies, transnational studies, and postcolonial studies, because these questions often assume that religion can be separated from other cultural and social relations.

What, then, should a postcolonial theology of religious difference be concerned about? In the past, theologies of religions were concerned with the truth claims of religion, given the Christian belief that there is only one God and one true religion, that is, Christianity. With the shift toward religious pluralism, the dilemma of Christian theologies of pluralism has been: "How do

---

61. Ibid., 222.

62. King, "Cartographies of the Imagination," 283–85.

63. King, *Orientalism and Religion*, 57; Fitzgerald, *The Ideology of Religious Studies*, 10.

64. Paula M. Cooey, "Fiddling While Rome Burns: The Place of Academic Theology in the Study of Religion," *Harvard Theological Review* 93 (2000): 47.

65. See, e.g., S. Mark Heim, *Salvations: Truth and Difference in Religions* (Maryknoll, N.Y.: Orbis Books, 1995).

we move toward a de-absolutized, pluralism-endorsing understanding of Christianity's relation with non-Christian traditions without losing the distinctiveness of Christian identity and the solid foundation on which to base committed Christian praxis?"[66] Christian theologians have spent a lot of time trying to revisit the teachings of the church to provide plausible answers. Paul Knitter, in his many writings, helpfully elucidates the different approaches Christian theologians have taken in response to this dilemma, such as the fulfillment model, the mutuality model, and the acceptance model.[67]

I would argue that a postcolonial theology of religious difference begin with the question: How do we deal with the fact that Western Christian theological discourse about religious difference is constructed in such a way as to justify a hierarchal ordering of religious traditions, which always puts Christianity on the top? Instead of subscribing to a reification of "religions" as if they are bounded cultural systems—such that one is fulfilling another, entering into dialogue with another, or accepting each other—I find David Chidester's definition of religion as "intrareligious and interreligious networks of cultural relations"[68] helpful. To take into consideration religion's role in multiple and contested border zones, he says, "the study of religion can resituate itself as a human science of contact."[69] Such contacts have been imbued with power, inequality, and domination, and the study of religion can examine "the production of meaning and the contestation of power in situations of cultural contact and exchange."[70] Theologies of religion have far too often treated religion as if it exists in a vacuum, separated from all other networks of social relations. A postcolonial theology of religious difference needs to examine how Christianity constructs difference in various historical epochs, taking into consideration the contestation of meaning, the shaping of the imagination, and the changing power relations. The issue before us is not religious diversity, but religious difference as it is constituted and produced in concrete situations, often with significant power differentials.

A related area to which a postcolonial theology of religious difference should pay attention is the relationship between religion and civil society. As Richard King has noted, the separation of the "religious" from the "secular" is a key feature of the imagination of Western modernity. Within such a construct, modern Western countries organize their societies according to secular reason, with

66. McCarthy, "Women's Experience as a Hermeneutical Key," 163.
67. See, e.g., Paul F. Knitter, *Introducing Theologies of Religions* (Maryknoll, N.Y.: Orbis Books, 2002).
68. David Chidester, "Anchoring Religion in the World: A Southern African History of Comparative Religion," *Religion* 26 (1996): 155.
69. Ibid.
70. Ibid.

the supposed separation of religion from politics, while "underdeveloped" countries remain steeped in their traditions, with religion impinging on every sphere of social life. After September 11, however, renewed Orientalist constructions of difference and misrepresentation of the Muslims permeated the media and popular culture. The Muslim nations were portrayed as if they were all theocratic societies, governed and ruled by people like the Taliban. Women wearing the burka flashed across the TV screens to reinforce the view of the "backwardness" of Muslim culture with its burdensome and irrational restrictions placed on women. While this was going on, George W. Bush used biblical and Christian language to mount his attack against the terrorists, telling religious broadcasters that "the terrorists hate the fact that . . . we can worship Almighty God the way we see fit," and that the United States was called to bring God's gift of liberty to "every human being in the world."[71] The White House and the Christian right have strategically deployed religious difference to promote their war against terrorism and to stir American people's patriotism. So instead of a secular West clashing with a theocratic Orient, we have Bush using Christian rhetoric to legitimate the United States' drive to global dominance. Rosemary Radford Ruether has called theologians to challenge this deeply disturbing American messianic nationalism, which she defines as "an ideology rooted in the belief that the United States of America is uniquely an elect nation chosen by God to impose its way of life on the rest of the world by coercive economic means, and even by military force, if it deems necessary."[72]

A postcolonial theology of religious difference will also attend to the transformation of religious symbols and institutions in migration, exile, diaspora, and transnationalism. As people of religious faith migrate to other cultures, they often form hybridized religious identities in the new contexts, which cannot be pinned down by fixed and reified notions of "religion." This critical inquiry would require a creative dialogue among theology, religious studies, and ethnic studies, a conversation that has hardly begun. Part of the reason is that the field of religion has been perceived as having such a narrow focus (on religion per se), and is oblivious to the cutting-edge scholarship in ethnic studies and cultural studies. Another reason is that scholars in ethnic studies tend to harbor biases against religion, either as the opium of the people or as postcolonial association of Western missionary activities.[73] Recent research on the

71. Fineman, "Bush and God," 24.

72. Rosemary Radford Ruether, "Christians Must Challenge American Messianic Nationalism: A Call to the Churches," Pacific School of Religion, http://www.psr.edu/page.cfm/1=62&id=1802.

73. Pyong Gap Min, "Introduction," in *Religions in Asian America: Building Faith Communities*, ed. Pyong Gap Min and Jung Ha Kim (Walnut Creek, Calif.: Altamira, 2002), 6.

gender

religious experience of immigrant populations has yielded new and interesting information on the roles religion plays in preserving ethnic culture and identity, building fellowship in the ethnic group, and providing services and support in face of racism in mainstream culture.[74] Jung Ha Kim and Ai Ra Kim have done research on the adaptation of Christianity in the cultural passage from Korea to America, including the preservation of patriarchal values and practices in Korean immigrant churches.[75]

Feminist scholars can contribute to a postcolonial theology of religious difference not simply by adding gender to the categories of analysis, but by placing gender within the wider intrareligious and interreligious network of cultural and religious relations. For example, we cannot just stop at asking how the gender-inflected theological understanding of religion, religious consciousness, the universe, and the Absolute has affected the position of women in the church and religious communities. We must continue to ask how such an understanding has helped construct the identity of Christians and signify racial, cultural, and religious difference in the relations between Christianity and other wisdom traditions. The concern of a postcolonial feminist theology of religious difference is not to compare and contrast in order to find which religion is most patriarchal, as has been done by some feminists, because such comparison tends to be ahistorical, too generalized, and relies on debatable evidence.[76] The focus should be on how patriarchal relations in the religious arena intersect with and are transformed by colonial and other unequal relations.

In the age of globalization, how religion intersects with gender, race, and transnationalism should concern theologians and religious scholars. Religion has been called the "original globalizer," as it has been "a natural accompaniment of conquest and colonization."[77] Roman Catholicism, for example, created a religious identity, culture, and institution across cultural and political frontiers, while reinventing, removing, or sometimes violently destroying indigenous cultures. In our contemporary world, the fundamentalist forms of religious globalization have proven to be very successful in adapting to local

74. Min and Kim, *Religions in Asian America*; Jane Naomi Iwamura and Paul Spickard, eds., *Revealing the Sacred in Asian and Pacific America* (New York: Routledge, 2003).

75. Ai Ra Kim, *Women Struggling for a New Life: The Role of Religion in the Cultural Passage from Korea to America* (Albany: State University of New York Press, 1996); Jung Ha Kim, *Bridge-Makers and Cross-Bearers: Korean American Women and the Church* (Atlanta: Scholars Press, 1997).

76. Kwok, "Gender, Colonialism, and the Study of Religion," 26.

77. David Lehman, "Religion and Globalization," in *Religions in the Modern World: Traditions and Transformations*, ed. Linda Woodhead et al. (London: Routledge, 2002), 302.

cultures and incorporating them into their ritual and religious practices. In the fundamentalist movements in Judaism, Christianity, and Islam, a dualistic and hierarchical relation exists between God and the world, and between men and women. Yet, we find not only that women participate in these movements, but that some have even converted to them. In the Third World, Pentecostal and charismatic Christianity, which respects traditional authority and the authority of men, draws a large number of female adherents. According to Linda Woodhead, these movements attract men and women because they reassert the values of traditional family and reaffirm some elements of traditional patriarchal religion and culture undermined by the secularizing forces of modernization.[78]

In a world torn by competing ideologies, ethnic strife, and economic disparity, women of faith have also come together to work for peace across racial division and religious differences. Israeli Jewish feminists, such as the group Women in Black, have worked in solidarity with Palestinian women for a peaceful solution to the crisis in the Middle East. Groups of Sri Lankan women of different religious traditions have also formed alliances with one another. A postcolonial feminist theology of religious difference lifts up these as beacons of hope and seeks to understand the social conditions that make women stand up for themselves and work with one another across religious boundaries. In her lecture when she received the Nobel Peace Prize in December of 2003, Shirin Ebadi of Iran said that her selection will be "an inspiration to the masses of women who are striving to realize their rights" not only in Iran, but in other parts of the world.[79]

Let us hope with her that "patriarchal culture and the discrimination against women . . . cannot continue forever."[80] For if it does, then as Christian theologians we have failed to take up the challenge of seeing "religion" as an integral part of culture and society, which cannot be construed as concerned only with the sacred and not with the mundane. And we have failed to challenge intrareligious and interreligious networks of power relations that seek to maintain control over women. Christian feminist theologians have the responsibility to network and build coalition with women of many different religious and cultural traditions to make Ebadi's dream come true.

78. Linda Woodhead, "Women and Religion," in Woodhead, *Religions in the Modern World*, 350.

79. Shirin Ebadi, "Nobel Lecture," Oslo, Sweden, December 10, 2003, Nobel e-Museum, http://www.nobel.se/peace/laureates/2003/ebadi-lecture-e.html.

80. Ibid.

9

Mending of Creation

Women, Nature, and Hope

Turning back to ancient times, the Four Pillars were shattered and the Nine Provinces dislocated. The sky did not cover [the earth] completely; nor did the earth uphold [all of the sky]. Fire roared with inextinguishable flames, and waters gushed forth in powerful and incessant waves. Ferocious animals devoured the good people, and birds of prey snatched away the old and weak. Thereupon, Nu Kua fused together stones of the five colours with which she patched up the azure sky. She cut off the feet of the turtle with which she set the Four Pillars. She slaughtered the black dragon in order to save the Land of Chi. She piled up reed ashes with which to check the flooding waters.

When the azure sky was patched up, the Four Pillars set up straight, the flooding waters dried up, the Land of Chi made orderly and the cunning wild animals exterminated, the good people thrived.

Milton M. Chiu[1]

In a popular Chinese creation story, the female mythological figure Nu Kua uses precious stones to mend the sky, thereby stopping the deluge and restoring order from chaos. Nu Kua also creates human beings from yellow earth. Although there are other Chinese creation myths associated with a male figure, it is significant that the saving of human beings and other forms of life from disaster is attributed to a female figure in this story.

---

1. Milton M. Chiu, *The Tao of Chinese Religion* (Lanham, Md.: University Press of America, 1984), 158–60, quoted in Archie C. C. Lee, "The Chinese Creation Myth of Nu Kua and the Biblical Narrative in Genesis 1–11," *Biblical Interpretation* 2 (1994): 313–14.

In her publications and lectures, Letty Russell often uses the metaphor "mending of creation" to describe the responsibility of women to fight injustice and to restore wholeness in our society. Many years ago, Russell heard Krister Stendahl quoting from a rabbinic saying that theology is worrying about what God is worrying about when God gets up in the morning. Reflecting on this saying, Russell wrote:

> It would seem according to Stendahl that God is worrying about the mending of creation, trying to straighten up the mess so that all of groaning creation will be set free. In order to do this, God has to be worrying about those who have dropped through the "safety net" of society, about those who are victims of injustice and war, and about the destruction of their bodies, their lives, and the environment in which they live.[2]

Today, we need desperately many new Nu Kuas, as mending the creation is so critical for the survival and flourishing of the whole planet. In the past several years, floods in the basin of the Yangtze River have plagued China, this time not because of holes in the sky, but because of massive uncontrolled development, land reclamation, and degraded environment. The controversial construction of the Three Gorges Dam led to the relocation of 1.2 million people and the submerging of towns and scenic and historical sites. China is the world's second largest emitter of greenhouse gases, though it has tried to curb its carbon dioxide emission in the late 1990s by using more efficient energy. At the global level, the United States has refused to sign the Kyoto Protocol to reduce its carbon dioxide emissions, though many industrialized countries have agreed to it. The United States accounts for approximately 6 percent of the global population, but consumes about 30 percent of the world's resources. About a quarter of the global population live in developed countries and consume about 80 percent of the total energy. This consumption pattern invariably leads to the depletion of valuable resources and the extinction of species. For example, in 2003 more than nine thousand square miles of Amazon rain forest were lost, one of the highest Amazon deforestation figures in history.[3] Since 1990 one species a day is disappearing, and at this rate in 2000 one species per hour would have disappeared.[4]

Facing such alarming environmental crises, I examine in this closing chapter some aspects of the debate regarding women, nature, and hope, lifting up

2. Letty M. Russell, *Church in the Round: Feminist Interpretation of the Church* (Louisville, Ky.: Westminster John Knox Press, 1993), 196.

3. According to news release on the World Wildlife Fund Web site, http://www.worldwildlife.org/news/headline.cfm?newsid=645.

4. Leonardo Boff, *Cry of the Earth, Cry of the Poor*, trans. Philip Berryman (Maryknoll, N.Y.: Orbis Books, 1997), 1.

the contributions of indigenous and Third World women theologians. The construction of women's hope for themselves and for nature is largely dependent on their social location and historical background. The questions "Who are the women?" "Whose nature?" and "Whose hope?" must be constantly kept in mind. I begin with an analysis of Third World women and nature, under the three waves of globalization: colonialism, development, and green imperialism. Such an analysis provides a vantage point from which to assess the discussion of the relation between women and nature in feminist religious discourse. In the last part, I examine the voices of women who have experienced conquest, slavery, and colonization to explore their articulation of body, nature, and hope.

COLONIALISM, DEVELOPMENT, AND GREEN IMPERIALISM

There have been several waves of globalization, and colonization—with conquest, commerce, and Christianity—is the first great wave.[5] Race, gender, and class intersected in the Western colonial project because it involved the subjugation of the dark-skinned people, the transmission of white, male power through the control of colonized women, and the imperial command of natural resources and the accumulation of capital. It is well known that Columbus imagined the land he "discovered" to be a female waiting to be explored, a fecund woman who would provide nourishment to regenerate an Old Europe. The New World and the tropical islands had a strong attraction for European men, for they had projected onto these distant lands the images of the lost Garden of Eden or the much-sought-after Paradise to ease the social and psychic ills of Europe. Shakespeare's *The Tempest* and Daniel Defoe's *Robinson Crusoe* both had such an island in mind as their dramatic context.[6]

As Alfred Crosby has shown, colonization was both a historical and biological process. The colonizers brought permanent changes to the flora and fauna and natural habitation of the New World by introducing their plants,

5. Larry Rasmussen identifies three waves of globalization: colonization, development, and post-1989 free-trade capitalism. See idem, "'Give Us Word of the Humankind We Left to Thee': Globalization and Its Wake," *EDS Occasional Papers* 4 (August 1999): 3–15. I have changed the last wave to take into consideration the impact of green imperialism on women.

6. Richard H. Grove, *Green Imperialism: Colonial Expansion, Tropical Island Edens and the Origins of Environmentalism, 1600–1860* (Cambridge: Cambridge University Press, 1995), 16–72.

animals, and cultures in a "self-replicating and world-altering avalanche."[7] In Crosby's vivid description:

> The seams of Pangaea were closing, drawn together by the sailmaker's needle. Chickens met kiwis, cattle met kangaroos, Irish met potatoes, Comanches met horses, Incas met smallpox—all for the first time. The countdown to the extinction of the passenger pigeon and the native peoples of the Greater Antilles and of Tasmania had begun.[8]

The colonizers looked down on the cultures of the indigenous people, and treated them as "savages" or "primitives" to be taken by brute force. In addition, white settlers brought in germs and diseases unknown to the New World, such as smallpox, measles, diphtheria, malaria, typhoid fever, and influenza, which infected and exterminated many indigenous people, who lacked immunity to such new diseases.[9]

In this drastic altering of the natural environment, colonized women's relation to nature changed, as did their social status. Prior to colonization, these women could gather and grow their food and bring it to market, and their economic roles in the family were valued and important. With colonialism and the introduction of industries, women's productivity was controlled by the colonial economy, which was not geared toward serving local needs but toward the colonial markets. The colonizers also introduced their marriage system and gender arrangements, resulting often in the curtailment of the power of colonized women. Paula Gunn Allen saw the subjugating of Native American women as crucial in subjugating Native societies as a whole: "The assault on the system of woman power requires the replacing of a peaceful, nonpunitive, nonauthoritarian social system wherein women wield power by making social life easy and gentle with one based on child terrorization, male dominance and submission of women to male authority."[10]

The control of colonized women's sexuality and reproductive labor was key to the colonial enterprise. In order to make up for the depleted population because of genocide and diseases, the white masters colonized the bodies of Native women, resulting in the production in some places of a whole mixed race—the mestizo. While the colonizers benefited from the reproductive labor of Native women, these women were often blamed in a blatant reversal as lustful, beastly, and loose. In addition, the colonizers brought in slaves from Africa, who were kidnapped from their own land or paid for by the lucrative New

---

7. Alfred W. Crosby, *Ecological Imperialism: The Biological Expansion of Europe, 900–1900*, 2nd ed. (Cambridge: Cambridge University Press, 2004), 194.

8. Ibid., 131.

9. Ibid., 195–216.

10. Paula Gunn Allen, *The Sacred Hoop* (Boston: Beacon Press, 1986), 40.

World trade. These slaves were treated as property and "cattle," and slave women were coerced as "breeders" through rape, beating, and other forms of violence and torture. Although living in such dehumanized situations, slave women were not just passive victims, as they had risen again and again against such brutality. For example, as acts of resistance to the slave system, slave women in the Caribbean initiated a birth strike in the nineteenth century, since they did not want to see their children sold into slavery to add to the riches of their masters.[11]

The exploitation of the colonies sustained the economic growth of the metropolis and created an ever-expanding middle class. Luxurious commodities that used to be affordable only for the higher classes became more readily accessible, and served as symbols of refined taste and pleasure. European women, who had increasingly stayed at home as housewives after the industrial revolution, emerged as a new class of consumers in the capitalist market economy. Sugar, coffee, cacao, and tea were once luxuries, but in the eighteenth and nineteenth centuries they became affordable for the "cultured" taste of European households. Whereas colonized women had to sell their labor and sometimes their bodies in prostitution as a means of survival, white women in the metropolis could rise to the status of "ladies." This irony is not lost on Maria Mies, who observes: "The colonial process, as it advanced, brought the women of the colonized people progressively down from a former high position of relative power and independence to that of 'beastly' and degraded 'nature.' This 'naturalization' of colonized women is the counterpart of the 'civilizing' of the European women."[12]

The second wave of globalization was development, initiated after the Second World War to help poorer countries with economic growth and production. Although development had many aspects, it meant primarily capitalist democracy, economic progress, and advanced science and technology, modeled after the West. In the 1950s, many countries in the Third World embraced the development model as a panacea to get out of poverty and increase their level of productivity. But as Gustavo Gutiérrez has noted, these countries soon became disillusioned as development did not address the root causes that made some countries dependent on others, and as they gradually realized that the process was controlled by international organizations linked to the groups and governments that dominated the world economy.[13] The ideology

11. Maria Mies, *Patriarchy and Accumulation on a World Scale: Women in the International Division of Labor* (London: Zed Books, 1986), 91.

12. Ibid., 95.

13. Gustavo Gutiérrez, *A Theology of Liberation: History, Politics, and Salvation*, 15th ann. ed. (Maryknoll, N.Y.: Orbis Books, 1988), 16–17.

of development was linked to Third World women in two fundamental ways: the relation of population growth to development, and the integration of women into development.

Many developmentalists and environmentalists have attributed the poverty of the poor countries to the high fertility rates and population growth of these countries. Some have rehashed Malthus's hypothesis that the production of food could not catch up with the growth of population in these societies. Yet, these theorists have conveniently forgotten that Malthus was the bourgeoisie's spokesperson, who supported neither helping the poor nor women's use of contraceptives, because he believed that the poor should curb their sexual instincts.[14] Many measures that coerce Third World women into having fewer offspring—such as forced sterilization, testing of new contraceptive products on their bodies, forced abortion, and China's one-child policy—curtail women's rights to choose and maintain their bodily integrity. In the name of national development or survival of the planet, women's fundamental rights were often compromised, denied, or delayed.

The debate on population is a heated and contentious one, because many have argued that it is not the poor people in the Third World who use up the world's natural resources, but the insatiable consumers in the First World. For instance, the city of Chicago, at 2.9 million people, consumes as much as the country of Bangladesh with 97 million people.[15] Moreover, as Nobel laureate Amartya Sen has demonstrated, there is no significant crisis in food production at this time, as many regions of the world have shown steady increases in food production over the last two decades. By means of empirical data, Sen also shows that the reduction of fertility rate is better achieved by empowering women's agency through education and job opportunities rather than by coercive measures.[16]

In the early 1970s, development studies and policies began to see women as producers and economic actors, and not just as housewives and mothers relegated to the domestic sphere. Programs such as Women in Development aimed to increase women's productivity in agriculture and commodity production in the Third World as a crucial means to achieve the success promised by development. The basic premise was that integrating women into the work-

---

14. John Bellamy Foster, "Malthus's Essay on Population at Age 200," in idem, *Ecology against Capitalism* (New York: Monthly Review Press, 2002), 137–54.

15. Larry Rasmussen, *Earth Community, Earth Ethics* (Maryknoll, N.Y.: Orbis Books, 1996), 39.

16. Amartya Sen, *Development as Freedom* (New York: Anchor Books, 1999), 204–26. See also Gita Sen, "Women, Poverty and Population: Issues for the Concerned Environmentalist," in *Feminist Perspectives on Sustainable Development*, ed. Wendy Harcourt (London: Zed Books, 1994), 215–25.

force and production sectors was key to economic growth and modernization.[17] Instead of growing food for the family, Third World women engage in the production of large-scale cash crops, such as rice, vegetables, flowers, and fruits for export. In the economic takeoff of Asian countries on the Pacific Rim, women provide the unskilled and semiskilled expandable labor for the computer, textile, toy, and other industries, often working long hours in unacceptable conditions without adequate compensation. The combination of neo-Confucianism, capitalist development, and patriarchy has created the so-called Asian miracle, often hailed as a successful model for other poor countries to emulate.[18]

In *Staying Alive*, Indian physicist and ecologist Vandana Shiva argues that Western-styled development is in fact maldevelopment that is a continuation of the process of colonization and creates new forms of affluence for the rich and new forms of deprivation for the weak.[19] She chastises development as a "new project of western patriarchy," because it reproduces the structures and patterns of Western capitalist patriarchy on a global scale. It is based on the exploitation and degradation of nature, the exclusion and exploitation of women, and the erosion of other cultures. She documents women's significant roles in the food chain and their critical contributions as sylviculturalists, agriculturalists, and traditional natural scientists. She writes: "The new insight provided by rural women in the Third World is that women and nature are associated, *not in passivity but in creativity and in the maintenance of life*."[20] The introduction of large-scale development projects and the green revolution has led to the disastrous results of hunger, malnutrition, and loss of economic control for women and their families.

The third wave of globalization is green imperialism, an integral part of the free-trade capitalism developed in the post–cold war era. While colonization has always involved the exploitation of natural resources, this new form of green imperialism seeks to control and privatize basic necessities of life as well as to patent and monopolize life forms. Water wars over the control of vital water resources have erupted in Punjab, India, and in Palestine, as well as in many other countries, threatening the collective livelihood of communities. Water wars are global wars, pitting local communities struggling to gain access

17. For a discussion of Women in Development and other projects, see Noël Sturgeon, *Ecofeminist Natures: Race, Gender, Feminist Theory, and Political Action* (New York: Routledge, 1997), 140–46.

18. Kwok Pui-lan, "Business Ethics in the Economic Development of Asia: A Feminist Analysis," *Asia Journal of Theology* 9, no. 1 (1995): 133–45.

19. Vandana Shiva, *Staying Alive: Women, Ecology and Development* (London: Zed Books, 1989), 5.

20. Ibid., 47. Emphasis hers.

to a basic ecological necessity against the corporate culture of greed, privatization, and enclosure of water commons.[21] Corporate greed also undergirds the competition for monopoly of life-forms through patents, licenses, genetic engineering, and other biotechnological devices. Vandana Shiva has called this "biopiracy," which entails the insidious commercialization of science and technology and the commodification of nature: "Biopiracy is the Columbian 'discovery' 500 years after Columbus. . . . The land, forests, the rivers, the oceans, and the atmosphere have all been colonized, eroded, and polluted."[22] The control of basic resources such as water disproportionately affects women and their families, because women traditionally are water resource managers in many poor and subsistence economies. In addition, genetic engineering, the Human Genome Project, cloning, and fertility technologies have far-reaching implications for women's reproductive functions and control of their eggs, cells, and bodies.

Another form of green imperialism expresses itself in the global management, by the World Bank and other international agencies, of environmental problems such as biodiversity and the reduction of greenhouse gas emissions. These agencies formulate their policies without adequate representation of local interests and grassroots participation. The "global" today reflects a modern version of the global reach, a continuation and expansion of colonial plunder and looting on a grand scale. Wolfgang Sachs writes: "It is inevitable that the claims of global management are in conflict with the aspirations for cultural rights, democracy and self-determination. Indeed, it is easy for an ecocracy which acts in the name of 'one earth' to become a threat to local communities and their life-styles."[23] In the Chipko movement, Indian women have resisted profitable logging by outside contractors by hugging onto their trees to protect them. Such successful mobilization of grassroots women will be harder to accomplish in the age of global reach, when national governments and local businesses are under the whims of transnational capital and international financial agencies. Joseph E. Stiglitz, a former economist of the World Bank, has detailed in a sobering account the increased control of the International Monetary Fund and other institutions over the restructure of national economy and management of recession from East Asia to Russia and on to Latin America.[24]

21. Vandana Shiva, *Water Wars: Privatization, Pollution, and Profit* (Cambridge, Mass.: South End Press, 2002).

22. Vandana Shiva, *Biopiracy: The Plunder of Nature and Knowledge* (Boston, Mass.: South End Press, 1997), 5.

23. Wolfgang Sachs, "Global Ecology and the Shadow of 'Development,'" in *Global Ecology: A New Arena of Political Conflict*, ed. Wolfgang Sachs (London: Zed Books, 1993), 19.

24. Joseph E. Stiglitz, *Globalization and Its Discontents* (New York: W. W. Norton, 2003).

WOMEN, NATURE, AND FEMINIST
RELIGIOUS DISCOURSE

Given my analysis of the three waves of globalization and their devastating effects on women's lives, I proceed to evaluate the discussion of the relation between women and nature in feminist religious discourse. In the early 1970s, feminists in the United States were concerned to find grand theoretical explanation for the subordination of women and the reproduction of a hierarchical ordering of gender. Based on Western tradition, white feminists noticed that women have been perceived to be closer to nature than men, and since nature was considered lower than the mind, women were deemed inferior and subordinate to men. Such an analysis resulted in two contrasting feminist positions: one was to challenge the connection between women and nature and any forms of biological determinism that contribute to women's subordination. The other was to celebrate the identification of women and nature and to reclaim women's embodiment, the natural cycles of the body, and women's closeness to earth.[25]

Sherry B. Ortner published an important essay, "Is Female to Male as Nature Is to Culture?" in 1974.[26] Arguing that female subordination is a universal phenomenon, she discovers what she believes to be a common structure upheld in all human cultures: culture is valued more than nature, and women are seen as being closer to nature than men. Ortner's definition of culture is Eurocentric, influenced by Enlightenment thought and Western technological advance. She writes: "We may thus broadly equate culture with the notion of human consciousness, or with the products of human consciousness (i.e., systems of thought and technology), by means of which humanity attempts to assert control over nature."[27] Her argument that women are seen as closer to nature is based on Simone de Beauvoir's similar observations, on Lévi-Strauss's work on structural anthropology, and on Nancy Chodorow's study of the female psyche and the pattern of mothering. Her essay relies primarily on an analysis of middle-class white society, devoting little space to the discussion of

25. For a discussion of various positions of ecofeminists on the relation between women and nature, see Karen J. Warren, *Ecofeminist Philosophy: A Western Perspective on What It Is and Why It Matters* (Lanham, Md.: Rowman and Littlefield Publishers, 2000), 21–41; Ynestra King, "Healing the Wounds: Feminism, Ecology, and the Nature/Culture Dualism," in *Reweaving the World: The Emergence of Ecofeminism*, ed. Irene Diamond and Gloria Feman Orenstein (San Francisco: Sierra Club Books, 1990), 106–21.

26. Sherry B. Ortner, "Is Female to Male as Nature Is to Culture?" in *Women, Culture, and Society*, ed. Michelle Zimbalist Rosaldo and Louise Lamphere (Stanford, Calif.: Stanford University Press, 1974), 67–87.

27. Ibid., 72.

other cultures. Although she acknowledges in the beginning that it is difficult to generalize the position of women within a single country, China,[28] she finds no problem in generalizing their position in all cultures. Writing in the early 1970s, Ortner overlooked differences among women, glossed over the specificity of culture, and provided no nuanced understanding of nature. In short, her essay essentializes "women," "culture," and "nature," in a way that is similar to the works of other early feminists.[29]

Ortner's theory has been quite influential in feminist theological thinking on the subject. Rosemary Radford Ruether, for example, cites Ortner's work in *Sexism and God-Talk* and agrees basically with her argument. Ruether at the same time points out that nature can be seen both as dominated by human beings and as the matrix of life, and that male culture symbolizes control over nature in ambivalent ways.[30] Ortner provides her with a "universal" context, and a framework to examine the pattern in Hebrew and Christian tradition as well as in Greek thought. Ruether notes that the Hebrew Bible does not equate creation or the material realm with evil and that there is no spirit/nature split. But the priestly story in the first chapter of Genesis speaks of human beings as charged to have dominion over the earth, and the Hebrew Bible assumes that women, children, and slaves are to be dominated in patriarchal families by men. Ruether faults the Greek philosophers for creating a more radical dualism between mind and body, wherein women are seen as analogous to matter or body. As an heir to both apocalyptic Judaism and Platonic thought, Christianity perpetuates the pattern of dualistic thinking, reinforced by the misogyny of some church fathers.[31]

To correct the biases against women and nature in these traditions that have shaped Western civilization, some white feminist religious thinkers project their hope through a reclaiming of the body, a revaluation of nature, and an emphasis on women's connection with nature in various ways. Early on in her work, Rosemary Radford Ruether offers the metaphor "new Woman, new Earth" and links closely the liberation of women from sexism with the renewal of creation.[32] Eschatological hope, for her, lies not in the "salvation of the soul" in some traditional sense, but in *metanoia*, or conversion of each person to the

28. Ibid., 68.

29. Anthropologist Peggy Sanday, after studying 150 tribal societies, argues that women's subordination is neither universal nor always associated with an inferior nature, see Peggy Sanday, *Female Power and Male Dominance: On the Origins of Sexual Inequality* (New York: Cambridge University Press, 1981).

30. Rosemary Radford Ruether, *Sexism and God-Talk: Toward a Feminist Theology* (Boston: Beacon Press, 1983), 72, 75–76.

31. Ibid., 75–79; and also her *New Woman, New Earth: Sexist Ideologies and Human Liberation* (New York: Seabury, 1975), 187–90.

32. See Ruether, *New Woman, New Earth*, 186–211.

earth and to one another.[33] In her later work *Gaia and God*, she is more specific that she is speaking from Western Christian tradition, and does not claim to speak for women in general.[34] She continues to think that women's subordination is due to the fact that they have been tied historically to nature, and advocates for the empowerment of women as moral agents.[35] For Ruether, the prophetic tradition is central to the Christian tradition. The prophets emphasize God as the God of history, not only the God of creation. Within history, human beings have a power of agency to change society and the environment—to work, therefore, for justice.

Not all Christian white feminists subscribe to the notion that women are closely linked to nature in an undifferentiated manner. For example, having learned from the writings of black women, Susan Brooks Thistlethwaite argues that in the racist culture in the United States, the black woman is consigned to signify body and sexuality, while the white woman is the "angel of the home," the soul, and spirituality. She claims that "white women in the United States are culture, not nature."[36] Since the "natural" roles of many white women, such as mothering and housekeeping, have historically relied on the exploited labor of black women, white women seek to reunite with nature and see nature as a source of strength. Thistlethwaite argues that white and black women, separated by race and class, have different experiences of nature; furthermore, the connection between women and nature has been bad for black women. She cautions against a simplified and intuitive understanding of nature without recourse to social and economic analysis.[37] Thistlethwaite's analyses echo Maria Mies's observation mentioned above, that the "naturalization" of colonized women is a corollary of the "civilizing" of white women.

Ruether has also written more explicitly of the complex and multilayered relationship between women and nature in her introduction to *Women Healing Earth*, an anthology of Third World women's writings she has collected. She notes that: "Among Northern ecofeminists the connection between domination of women and domination of nature is generally made first on the cultural-symbolic level."[38] She cautions that Northern ecofeminists are myopic if they

33. Ruether, *Sexism and God-Talk*, 254–56.

34. Rosemary Radford Ruether, *Gaia and God: An Ecofeminist Theology of Earth Healing* (San Francisco: HarperCollins, 1992), 11.

35. Ibid., 264–65.

36. Susan Brooks Thistlethwaite, *Sex, Race, and God: Christian Feminism in Black and White* (New York: Crossroad, 1989), 42.

37. Ibid., 58–59.

38. Rosemary Radford Ruether, "Introduction," in *Women Healing Earth: Third World Women on Ecology, Feminism, and Religion*, ed. Rosemary Radford Ruether (Maryknoll, N.Y.: Orbis Books, 1996), 2.

do not take into consideration simultaneously the socioeconomic system that colonizes women's bodies and their labor for the profit of the rich in the world. Women in the Third World, she notes, are much more likely to make the socioeconomic connection between the domination of nature and the impoverishment of their people. She calls on women in the North to come out from cultural escapism, illusions, and irresponsibility in order to form concrete alliances with women in the South for justice and social change.

Other white feminists find their hope in reclaiming the close relationship between women and nature. This is especially true in some forms of feminist spirituality, and in the radical feminist philosophy of white women who have come to stand outside the Christian tradition. Many have turned to the Goddess tradition for self-empowerment and spiritual sustenance, as Charlene Spretnak has described:

> In the mid-1970s, many radical/cultural feminists experienced the exhilarating discovery, through historical and archaeological sources, of a religion that honored the female and seemed to have as its "good book" nature itself. . . . What was intriguing was the sacred link between the Goddess in her many guises and totemic animals and plants, sacred groves, and womblike caves, in the moon-rhythm blood of menses, the ecstatic dance—the experience of *knowing* Gaia, her voluptuous contours and fertile plains, her flowing waters that give life, her animal teachers.[39]

For some Western women who have grown up in a religious environment with dominant androcentric Christian symbols, the discovery of the Goddess tradition was a relief and exhilarating. Some have argued that there existed an ancient, prepatriarchal period when women were food gatherers and human beings lived in harmonious relationship with each other and with nature. It was later that war, violence, and male domination came with the patriarchal images of God as king and warrior replacing the Goddess.

Whether such a prepatriarchal period was historical reality or a modern myth has been vigorously debated. But there is no denying that the Goddess tradition provides rich resources to meet the psychological and spiritual needs of some women. In her book *Rebirth of the Goddess*, Carol P. Christ suggests we overcome the mind/body and culture/nature split by practicing "embodied thinking" and by reminding ourselves constantly that we are part of nature. She writes: "The image of the Goddess also evokes the sacredness of nature. This confirms a deep intuition that has been denied in our culture: that we are nature and that nature is body."[40] Starhawk, a post-Jewish peace activist,

---

39. Charlene Spretnak, "Ecofeminism: Our Roots and Flowering," in Diamond and Orenstein, *Reweaving the World*, 5.

40. Carol P. Christ, *Rebirth of the Goddess: Finding Meaning in Feminist Spirituality* (Reading, Mass.: Addison-Wesley Publishing Co., 1997), 8.

reclaims the Old Religion of Witchcraft and uses magical formulas and earth-based rituals to evoke the power of the Goddess and the power-from-within.[41] The radical feminist writer Mary Daly uses the term "biophilia" to describe women's inclination toward nature. She speaks of radical self-identifying women as bonding "biophilically with each other, and with the sun and the moon, the tides, and all of the elements."[42]

Some have criticized that these cultural feminists who espouse the close connection between women and nature are essentialists, because they tend to generalize women's experiences. It is true that their writings stress the cultural and symbolic dimensions, and do not focus on socioeconomic aspects as social-ist feminists do. Furthermore, the emphasis on female bonding, based on women's closeness to nature, may also camouflage unequal relationships between women in a world polarized between the haves and the have-nots. But a close reading of these feminist writings suggests that some do pay some attention to the differences among women. For example, Carol P. Christ chal-lenges the assumption that those who are educated in the Western intellectual tradition are more self-reflective and therefore more human than others, while women and ethnic, cultural, and racial groups are deemed closer to nature, as barbarians, savages, peasants, and slaves.[43] In her many writings on green pol-itics and women's spirituality, Spretnak clearly challenges women in the richer countries to pay attention to the living conditions of poor women in the world.

Even the portrayal of women and nature in Hinduism by Vandana Shiva has been criticized as essentialized. Critiquing modern science as a patriarchal project, based on reductionism and hierarchal domination of nature, Shiva lifts up nature as a feminine principle (Shakti) in Hindu cosmology. She writes: "Women in India are an intimate part of nature, both in imagination and prac-tice. At one level nature is symbolised as the embodiment of the feminine prin-ciple, and at another, she is nurtured by the feminine to produce life and provide sustenance."[44] Like the feminists in the Goddess tradition, Shiva wants to reclaim the woman-nature connection in Hinduism as creative and positive, and as a spiritual resource for women's involvement in protecting the earth and for social transformation. But given the mobilization of Hinduism as a nationalist ideology, one may wonder whether Shiva's uncritical stance toward Hinduism may display a caste bias and open her to misunderstanding. Also, Shiva has been challenged as generalizing the relationship of Third

41. Starhawk, *Dreaming the Dark: Magic, Sex, and Politics* (Boston: Beacon Press, 1982).

42. Mary Daly, *Pure Lust: Elemental Feminist Philosophy* (Boston: Beacon Press, 1984), 311.

43. Carol P. Christ, "Rethinking Theology and Nature," in Diamond and Oren-stein, *Reweaving the World*, 67.

44. Shiva, *Staying Alive*, 38.

World rural women and the environment based on examples drawn primarily from women in northwest India.[45]

The above discussion shows that both the binary split and the claims of harmony among women, nature, and body, on the one hand, and men, culture, and mind, on the other, must be subjected to closer scrutiny from cross-cultural perspectives. At least four problems can be identified, each of which follows from the others.

First, Ortner's notion that all human societies devalue nature is far from being true. In the Native traditions of the Americas, in the Buddhist, Taoist, Confucian, Shinto, and Hindu traditions, and in African traditions, nature has not been seen as belonging to the lower realm, to be controlled and dominated by human beings. The Western notion of the split between culture and nature must be seen as culturally specific and not generalizable to all cultures. Many Native people feel a very close connection to their land and regard the four-legged animals as their relatives. Chinese landscape painting and poetry have a long tradition of glorifying the beauty and awe of nature, and living harmoniously with nature is a Taoist ideal. But women in these traditions cannot simply recover the spirituality of their traditions without paying attention to how they have been transformed by the colonial experience and have been presently redeployed to serve globalization.

The second problem emerges from the first because, in the Western imagination of the "primitive" and the "modern," qualities such as "magic, ritualism, closeness to nature, mythic or cosmological aims" are usually associated with the "primitive."[46] White women's new attempts to valorize these so-called primitive qualities can be a way of appropriating the values of other cultures simply to compensate for a lack in one's own. The construction of "indigenous" women as the "ultimate ecofeminists" displays a kind of racial essentialism, because it tends to see native cultures as unchanging, while failing to note that nature and the environment are culturally and socially constructed. Some feminists have argued that the dominant construction of "nature" in American culture is not only gendered, or dualistic, but raced as well. The fascination with the "indigenous" and the "primitive" can be a continuation of the colonial legacy of seeing nature, the Native Americans, and African American slaves as resources for "civilization."[47]

---

45. Celia Nyamweru, "Women and the Sacred Groves in Coastal Kenya: A Contribution to the Ecofeminist Debate," in *Ecofeminism and Globalization: Exploring Culture, Context, and Religion,* ed. Heather Eaton and Lois Ann Lorentzen (Lanham, Md.: Rowman and Littlefield Publishers, 2003), 42.

46. James Clifford, *The Predicament of Culture: Twentieth-Century Ethnography, Literature, and Art* (Cambridge, Mass.: Harvard University Press, 1988), 201.

47. Sturgeon, *Ecofeminist Natures,* 132.

That is why, third, Thistlethwaite is right to argue that an abstract and romanticized notion of nature may not be helpful for continued dialogue and solidarity among women. During the colonial days, white men saw land, rivers, and mountains simply as nature, to be possessed without the recognition of national boundaries and respect for people's relationship with their land. White women's limitless reunification with a boundless and abstract nature may fall prey to similar colonial impulses. Instead of seeing nature as "natural," it may be more productive to remember nature is always "political," because we have to talk about distribution of resources, ownership of the land, and the extraction of natural resources for profit.

Finally, women in the ecofeminist movement and Goddess spirituality have devised rituals and liturgies to honor women's bodies and the cycles of the moon and nature, participated in mostly by white women. Though these periodical rituals may be important ways to value both women and nature and have spiritual and psychological benefits, they are not radical enough without concomitant concrete social action. While Starhawk and other healers have conducted rituals in front of nuclear plants and during political demonstrations, others have conducted such rituals in a more commercialized form of New Age spirituality in order to ease psychic pain and to search for individual wholeness, and not for the sake of mobilizing communal resources for social change.

WOMEN, NATURE, CONQUEST, SLAVERY, AND COLONIZATION

To theorize about women and nature with those who are on the underside of history, we cannot begin by deconstructing Aristotle's philosophy, nor by adopting generalized notions of "women," "nature," and "culture." Instead, we must start with the actual bodies of women who have experienced conquest, slavery, and colonization in the past and who continue to be subjected to neocolonialism, militarism, and economic exploitation in the global market. The colored female body is simultaneously "a site of attraction, repulsion, symbolic appropriation."[48] This body has been consigned to signify nature in demeaning and ambiguous ways.

The brown, black, and yellow bodies of women have been treated as inferior to the white bodies in the Western history of domination of the world. During the conquest of the Americas, the Spaniards colonized Native women's sexuality and vented their masculine libido through the subjugation of Native women's bodies. Enrique Dussel has called this colonization of Native

48. Clifford, *The Predicament of Culture*, 5.

women's bodies "erotic violence."[49] During slavery, as Delores Williams has pointed out, black women were indeed treated as animals and their bodies as a "lower order of nature."[50] In what she has called *colorism*, black women's bodies were regarded as less adorable and beautiful than light-skinned women's bodies. Black women were systematically raped to increase the number of slaves for the slave owners, yet they were accused of being temptresses and lustful. Many yellow women are reduced to sex machines in the sex industry, which turns Southeast Asia into the "brothel of the world." Because of the AIDS epidemic, girls as young as two and three are abused to satisfy the sexual cravings of customers.[51]

The bodies of women of color have been and still are subject to severe control and surveillance, often through violent means. In *Remembering Conquest*, the Asian, black, and Native American authors share a view of

> the interconnection and intersection of patriarchy, colonialism, imperialism, racism, classism, capitalism and militarism which simultaneously and multi-facetedly contribute to violence against women. Regrettably, as pointed out by the authors, religions of the lands through their teaching and treatment of women have historically been a collaborating force of institutionalized exploitation and subordination of women. This results in the inferiority of woman and the use of her body at the will of an imperialistic, colonialistic, racist and patriarchal power.[52]

Genocide and forced sterilization of Native women, as well as their relegation to missionary schools for education and discipline, were violent crimes committed against humanity. Branding by fire, forced breeding, and merciless whipping were meant to instill fear and submission in black slave women, so that the body could remember the lesson. If such cruelty is regarded as belonging to a bygone era, we need only look at what happens in the twentieth century. During the Second World War, as many as two hundred thousand Korean, Chinese, and other Southeast Asian women were drafted or kidnapped for sexual servicing of Japanese soldiers throughout the Asian Pacific region. Beatings and torture were routinely used to subdue the unwilling,

---

49. Enrique Dussel, *The Invention of the Americas: Eclipse of "the Other" and the Myth of Modernity* (New York: Continuum, 1995), 46.

50. Delores S. Williams, "Sin, Nature, and Black Women's Bodies," in *Ecofeminism and the Sacred*, ed. Carol J. Adams (New York: Continuum, 1993), 24.

51. See Rita Nakashima Brock and Susan Brooks Thistlethwaite, *Casting Stones: Prostitution and Liberation in Asia and the United States* (Minneapolis: Fortress, 1996).

52. Nantawan Boonprasat Lewis and Marie M. Fortune, "Introduction," in *Remembering Conquest: Feminist/Womanist Perspectives on Religion, Colonization, and Sexual Violence* (New York: Haworth Pastoral Press, 1999), 2.

while the women were given little food and forced to live in crowded and unsanitary conditions.[53] What is ironic is that having celebrated their independence from the colonizers, Third World countries are now eager to welcome them back in the form of foreign investors and owners of multinational corporations. An international division of labor characterizes our contemporary world economy, with women in Third World countries providing the cheapest unskilled labor. Multinational corporations use "modern" management techniques and technological surveillance to "manage" laborers, to increase their productivity.

To remember the atrocities committed against the bodies of women of color is not to generalize all women of color as victims, because some women of color benefit from the status quo and some even collaborate with the oppressors. But the painful and dangerous memories should never be forgotten; we must learn from history to prevent such suffering from happening again. Multiply oppressed women have their history inscribed on their bodies, as Chandra Talpade Mohanty notes: "It is especially on the bodies and lives of women and girls from the Third World/South—the Two-Thirds World—that global capitalism writes its script."[54] Thus, Elsa Tamez has asserted, the woman's body is a text to be read.

> Women's bodies, then, can manifest themselves as sacred text setting out their stories to be read and re-read and to generate liberating actions and attitudes. Women's lives enshrine a deep grammar, whose morphology and syntax need to be learned for the sake of better human interrelationships.[55]

If we theorize about women and nature from the broken bodies of women of color, we can see the relationship between women and nature is much more complex, ambiguous, and multidimensional than is often assumed. For the sake of clarity, we need to distinguish symbolic and social levels of meaning, although the two are interconnected. In many indigenous traditions and in Asian and African myths and legends, the female symbolizes the earth or the land. Ancient Chinese people worshiped Timu (earth mother); the Philippine people venerate Ina; Indians have the feminine principle Shakti; and Native

53. Chung Hyun Kyung, "Your Comfort vs. My Death," in *Women Resisting Violence: Spirituality for Life*, ed. Mary John Mananzan et al. (Maryknoll, N.Y.: Orbis Books, 1996), 129–40.

54. Chandra Talpade Mohanty, *Feminism without Borders: Decolonizing Theory, Practicing Solidarity* (Durham, N.C.: Duke University Press, 2003), 235.

55. Elsa Tamez, "Women's Lives as Sacred Text," in *Women's Sacred Scriptures*, ed. Kwok Pui-lan and Elisabeth Schüssler Fiorenza, Concilium 1998, no. 3 (Maryknoll, N.Y.: Orbis, 1998), 63.

Americans respect Mother Earth. Although these traditions in general hold nature in high regard, the female symbolization of nature has not been translated into a higher position for women in society. Because I have not found many efforts to explain this, I can only tentatively suggest some reasons.

The symbolic order of any given society may or may not be symmetrical with the social order. The female symbolism of nature is often restricted to the reproductive roles of women, such as fertility and nurturance; this, in turn, reinforces the domesticity of women. Thus the female symbols of the goddess or the earth mother may have been appropriated into a male symbolic structure, so that the symbolization of the feminine in connection with nature serves to justify women's subordination. For example, the Goddess of Mercy in popular Buddhism is worshipped because of her alleged capacity to bestow sons on women, all the while losing sight of the fact that in the Chinese legend she is a strong woman who defies her father's will.

Even though women's status was lower than men's in precolonial societies, there is evidence that women still enjoyed relatively more freedom and privilege than in colonial times. During the colonial era, an element was added in the association of women with nature. Here the very ideology of colonization included the symbolization of foreign land as a female body to be possessed and conquered. For example, Edward Said argues that Orientalism is a praxis of male gender dominance or patriarchy, which defines the Orient routinely as feminine, "its riches as fertile, its main symbols the sensual woman, the harem, and the despotic—but curiously attractive—ruler."[56] Such imagery is connected to "the configurations of sexual, racial and political asymmetry underlying mainstream modern western culture."[57]

Catherine Keller's careful reading of Christopher Columbus's descriptions of the Americas shows that he imagined the mysterious land as like the lost Eden, having the shape of a pear, culminating at something like the nipple of a woman's breast. The serious measuring and mapping of the nipple of paradise, for Keller, was not just cartography but carto-pornography.[58] She continues: "The continent looms as forbidden fruit, the virgin body ripe for plucking, the mother breast ready to suckle a death-ridden, depressed Europe into its rebirth."[59] The fertile continent was thus imagined to be a dark and wild virgin, lying before the adventurers, waiting to be possessed to give birth to a new people.

56. Edward W. Said, "Orientalism Reconsidered," in *Reflections on Exile and Other Essays* (Cambridge, Mass.: Harvard University Press, 2000), 212.
57. Ibid.
58. Catherine Keller, *Apocalypse Now and Then* (Boston: Beacon Press, 1996), 156–57.
59. Ibid., 157.

Subjugated women were not used only to symbolize the land figuratively, they were literally treated as part of nature—as beasts and cattle. Although white women have been regarded symbolically and philosophically as close to nature, in modern times they have never been thought to be other than human. This is one of the reasons that anthropological analysis takes a new point of departure in theologies by enslaved and colonized women. Whereas white women differ from white men because of their gender, the black and Native women were regarded as belonging to a different species, occupying a lower rung in the evolutionary ladder. Many black and formerly colonized women observe the white women's rush to reclaim the close connection with nature as full of historical irony.

When we turn to consider the relationship in the Third World between women and nature on the social level, we can also discern ambiguities and uneasy phenomena. Many impoverished women do not have the luxury to seek harmony with nature. Gabriele Dietrich, a feminist theologian who has worked for a long time in India, describes the poverty-stricken Indian communities in this way:

> Ecology then does not come in as a striving force after reconciliation with the earth, honoring cosmic forces and non-human forces of life. It comes in more with a focus on setting ourselves in relationship with one another in the day-to-day survival struggles for water, a piece of land to dwell on, a patch of beach to dry the fish on, the sea as a source of bounty.[60]

Dire poverty and the struggle for survival impose heavy burdens on many women in the Third World, who are responsible for putting food on the table and fetching clean water for the family. Ironically, while some poor women are creative managers of the environment, others have been forced to abuse the environment for the sake of their own survival and that of their children. In a balanced analysis of women's role in the ecological crisis, Indian theologian Aruna Gnanadason reports: "While women are the worst afflicted by resource depletion, it is also true that because of forces they can scarcely understand, still less control, they are often the agents of their own resource depletion."[61] Although we should not blame the victims of our global economy who have to struggle to obtain even basic necessities, we also should not close our eyes to poor women's capacity to destroy nature.

Given the ambiguity of women of color's relation with nature, what are their hopes and aspirations for the future? Let me highlight several salient

60. Gabriele Dietrich, "The World as the Body of God: Feminist Perspectives on Ecology and Social Justice," in Ruether, *Women Healing Earth*, 82.

61. Aruna Gnanadason, "Toward a Feminist Eco-Theology for India," in Ruether, *Women Healing Earth*, 76.

aspects of their eschatological hope. First, many Third World and indigenous women believe that their own traditions, where the natural is not separated from the cultural and the spiritual, can offer enormous contributions to saving ourselves and our planet. Victoria Tauli-Corpuz, who comes from the tribal community of the Igorots in northern Luzon, the Philippines, describes her heritage in this way:

> Nature to the indigenous women and men is thought of in spiritual terms. In spite of the aggressive Christianization drive among the Igorots, the majority are still animist in orientation and practice. Nature spirits are revered, respected and feared. Rituals are done to thank or appease nature spirits and ancestors.[62]

While westernization and modernization are considered irresistible forces of history, indigenous women have persistently pointed us to another alternative. Nobel prizewinner Rigoberta Menchú noted during the Earth Summit in Rio de Janeiro that the conquerors killed the Mayan people and put their artifacts in the museum, telling the world that the Mayan culture was long gone. But she pointed out her people are still alive and still struggling.[63]

Second, women of color's eschatological hope is grounded in their continual struggle and resistance, creating new resources for survival. A reconnection with one's cultural and spiritual traditions does not mean romanticizing the past, nor overlooking the fact that one's culture has been transformed and appropriated in the political and spiritual conquest by the West. Rather, what is under way is a lifelong process of searching for cultural and spiritual resources to live by in a world dominated by white supremacy, capitalist greed, and patriarchy. This is an effort to create a way out of no way. It is to live under the power of the myth of modernity but refuse to give up resistance. It is to construct cultural hybrids out of fragments that still exist in our collective memory. It is to live to honor our ancestors and to consume as if the next seven generations count.

Third, indigenous women and women of color still hope to work in solidarity with white people, although the latter have exploited them and even stolen their religious symbols. Andrea Smith observes that many white women are attracted to Native spirituality, especially through the New Age movement. She warns against the "wanting to become Indian" syndrome, in which

62. Victoria Tauli-Corpuz, "Reclaiming Earth-Based Spirituality: Indigenous Women in the Cordillera," in Ruether, *Women Healing Earth*, 100.
63. Rigoberta Menchú, in a speech delivered at the World Council of Churches conference "Searching for the New Heavens and the New Earth," Earth Summit, Rio de Janeiro, Brazil, May 1992.

people want to learn Native secrets and ceremonies without accountability and responsibility for white racism: "Of course, white 'feminists' want to become only partly Indian. They do not want to be part of our struggles for survival against genocide, and they do not want to fight for treaty rights or an end to substance abuse or sterilization abuse."[64] But Smith and other indigenous leaders look to the day when white people will genuinely respect their cultures and express their solidarity concretely through joining their struggles for land rights, employment, and health care. Smith expresses her vision:

> Respecting the integrity of Native people and their spirituality does not mean that there can never be cross-cultural sharing. However, such sharing should take place in a way that is respectful to Indian people. The way to be respectful is for non-Indians to become involved in our political struggles and to develop an ongoing relation with Indian *communities* based on trust and mutual respect. When this happens, Indian people may invite a non-Indian to take part in a ceremony, but it will be on Indian terms.[65]

Finally, even in desperate and exhaustive situations, women of color believe they do not struggle alone, because the tender web of life still holds. Alice Walker, in her meditation on life, spirit, art, and her work, discusses her inner spiritual reserve which can be drawn on to face meanness of spirit, racism, sexism, homophobia, hypocrisy, and craziness. The spiritual lessons she has learned include: life is grand, no matter what; that suffering has a use; and that she and all that she loves are inseparable. Moreover, the universe responds and takes care of us, no matter which god we believe in: Goddess, Nature, Spirit, Mother Earth, the universe, or God of the ancestors.[66] When we work intimately with the universe and follow its rhythm, Walker believes, we become most creative. She has a memorable description of her late mother, a woman with modest means, working ecstatically in her garden:

> I notice that it is only when my mother is working in her flowers that she is radiant, almost to the point of being invisible—except as Creator: hand and eye. She is involved in work her soul must have. Ordering the universe in the image of her personal conception of Beauty.[67]

64. Andrea Smith, "For Those Who Were Indian in a Former Life," in Carol J. Adams, *Ecofeminism and the Sacred*, 169.

65. Ibid., 171.

66. Alice Walker, *The Same River Twice: Honoring the Difficult* (New York: Scribner, 1996), 284–87.

67. Alice Walker, *In Search of Our Mothers' Gardens* (San Diego: Harcourt Brace Jovanovich, 1983), 241.

Inspired by Walker's work, Letty Russell, Katie Geneva Cannon, Ada María Isasi-Díaz, and I coedited a volume, *Inheriting Our Mothers' Gardens: Feminist Theology in Third World Perspective*.[68] Working on our book, we soon recognized that as women of different colors, our inheritances are vastly different, because our mothers' gardens are not the same. Katie spoke of the awesome task of "surviving the blight," and Ada María had to transplant delicately a "Hispanic garden in a foreign land." My mother had no garden, and I grew up in a land colonized by the British. Letty, by contrast, had her father's victory garden and her grandmother's rose garden as part of her middle-class American inheritance. Letty found it was not easy for her to write about inheriting our mothers' gardens, for she recognized her privileges from her long work promoting global solidarity and network among women:

> I find myself having to confess that as a white middle-class North American woman I have inherited benefits that accrue to me disproportionately because of the social structures of racism, classism, and imperialism.[69]

She said courageously that white women like her sometimes have to reject their mothers' gardens in the struggle for justice. Women of all colors need to search for the liberating fragments in our inheritance so that we can mend the creation for our daughters and their daughters.

68. Letty M. Russell, Ada María Isasi-Díaz, Kwok Pui-lan, and Katie Geneva Cannon, eds., *Inheriting Our Mothers' Gardens: Feminist Theology in Third World Perspective* (Philadelphia: Westminster Press, 1988).
69. Ibid., 143.

Index

CPSIA information can be obtained
at www.ICGtesting.com
Printed in the USA
LVHW081445151118
597256LV00031B/656/P

9 780664 228835